ACTORS AND

Actors & Audience

A STUDY OF ASIDES
AND RELATED CONVENTIONS
IN GREEK DRAMA

DAVID BAIN

OXFORD UNIVERSITY PRESS

Oxford University Press, Walton Street, Oxford OX2 6DP

Oxford New York Toronto
Delhi Bombay Calcutta Madras Karachi
Petaling Jaya Singapore Hong Kong Tokyo
Nairobi Dar es Salaam Cape Town
Melbourne Auckland

and associated companies in
Beirut Berlin Ibadan Nicosia

Oxford is a trade mark of Oxford University Press

Published in the United States
by Oxford University Press, New York

British Library Cataloguing in Publication Data

Bain, David, 1945–
Actors & audience: a study of asides and
related conventions in Greek drama.—
(Oxford classical & philosophical
monographs)
1. Greek drama—History and criticism
2. Asides (Drama)
I. Title
882'.01   PA3131
ISBN 0–19–814724–4

Printed in Great Britain
at the University Printing House, Oxford
by David Stanford
Printer to the University

PREFACE

IT is the task of reviewers to decide whether the connections I have seen between asides and other conventions are real ones and whether my work forms a unity rather than a two-part collection of essays on various aspects of Greek dramatic technique. To assist them, however, I would point out that in both parts of the work, that dealing with tragedy as well as the one concerned with comedy, I have tried to keep in mind two related themes. One is the nature of convention in drama, the extent to which the poet expects his audience to accept a stage-event simply because it is a regular feature of the kind of drama he writes and the extent to which the poet feels obliged to make concessions to realism or to apologise in some way for the unnatural and contrived action he may be presenting to his audience. The second is the wider question of the relationship of the audience to the play, the degree to which spectators 'participate' in the stage action, and the extent to which they are aware that they are watching a play and not real life.

With some misgivings I have acceded to a request that all the Greek passages in the text should be translated or paraphrased. The translations are there solely to enable the Greek-less reader to follow without interruption the thread of the argument and are quite devoid of literary pretensions.

Works published after February, 1975 became known to me too late, I am afraid, for more than partial consideration or mention, a fact I particularly regret when re-reading the second part of the book.* Whatever one writes about New Comedy tends towards obsolescence even before the ink has dried upon the paper.

When I was innocent of book-writing I often used to find

---

*However, in the paperback edition a few references to later work have been added within square brackets.

those sections of prefaces of scholarly works which acknowledged the author's debts to others embarrassingly fulsome and prone to a degree of name dropping that would not have disgraced a William Hickey. With experience I realise that such acknowledgements tend in fact to understatement and that in most cases the author is ruthlessly selective in apportioning thanks. Such is the case with me and I hope I will be forgiven for referring here only to the most pressing of my obligations.

If only because the literature on the subject of asides is so small, I would have to mention the large dissertation by L. Barbieri. Although in what follows it might appear that I refer to this work only to criticise it, I would by no means wish it to be assumed that I have derived no benefit from it. Often Barbieri made me reconsider what I had written or consider for inclusion a passage which I had originally passed over.

I am most grateful to Mr. J. Blundell for allowing me to consult and make use of his excellent unpublished thesis on monologues in Menander. I must thank Mr. P. G. McC. Brown not only for introducing me to this thesis but also for reading and commenting on part of my own work in typescript and then for assisting with incredible selflessness in the proof correction of the whole work. Dr. Colin Austin and Mr. T. C. W. Stinton read and criticised an earlier version, saving me from many errors and suggesting new avenues for me to explore.

Any research student who is supervised by Professor Hugh Lloyd-Jones is extremely fortunate and not just because of the great store of learning that becomes available for consultation or for the acute criticism that is dispensed. In thanking him I am conscious that but for his encouragement this work might never have been completed. When its completion even as a thesis seemed a remote prospect, he did wonders for my morale by constantly referring to my wretched type-written notes as 'your book'. Now that by some miracle a book has emerged, I hope he will not find too much to disapprove of in it.

DAVID BAIN

University of Manchester
October, 1976

CONTENTS

ABBREVIATIONS, ETC.

Barbieri   L. Barbieri, *Das Beiseitesprechen im antiken Drama*, Disser-
                 tation, Innsbruck, 1966.

Blundell *   J. Blundell, 'Observations on Menander's Monologues',
                 unpublished B.Phil. thesis, Oxford, 1974.

Bradbrook   M. C. Bradbrook, *Themes and Conventions of Elizabethan
                 Tragedy*, Cambridge, 1935.

CGF   *Comicorum Graecorum Fragmenta in papyris reperta*, ed. Colinus
                 Austin, Berlin and New York, 1973.

Denniston   J. D. Denniston, *The Greek Particles*², Oxford, 1954.

Dover *AC*   K. J. Dover, *Aristophanic Comedy*, London, 1972.

Fraenkel *QS*   Ed. Fraenkel, *De media et nova comoedia quaestiones selectae*,
                 Dissertation, Göttingen, 1912.

Fraenkel *EP*   Ed. Fraenkel, *Elementi plautini in Plauto*, Florence,
                 1960.

GLP   D. L. Page, *Greek Literary Papyri*, vol. i, London and
                 Cambridge, 1942 (repr. as *Select Papyri*, vol. iii).

K–G   R. Kühner, *Ausführliche Grammatik der griechischen Sprache*,
                 2. Teil (Satzlehre), 3. Aufl., besorgt von B. Gerth, Hanover
                 etc., 1898–1904.

Legrand   Ph. E. Legrand, *Daos: Tableau de la comédie grecque pendant la
                 période dite nouvelle*, Lyons, 1912.

Leo   F. Leo, *Der Monolog im Drama* (Abhandlungen Gött.
                 Gesellschaft der Wissenschaft, Phil.-hist. Klasse, N.F. x. 5),
                 Berlin, 1908.

Leo *PF*   F. Leo, *Plautinische Forschungen*², Berlin, 1912.

LSJ   H. G. Liddell and R. Scott, *A Greek–English Lexicon*, 9th
                 edition revised by Sir H. Stuart Jones, Oxford, 1940.

Meineke   A. Meineke, *Historia Critica Comicorum Graecorum* (being vol.
                 1 of *Fragmenta Comicorum Graecorum*), Berlin, 1839.

Ménandre   *Entretiens sur l'antiquité classique publiés par Olivier Reverdin*,
                 Tome xvi, *Ménandre*, Vandoeuvres–Genève, 1970.

Nestle   Walter Nestle, *Die Struktur des Eingangs in der attischen
                 Tragödie* (Tübingen Beitr. zur Altertumswissenschaft, Heft
                 x), Stuttgart, 1930.

*[J. Blundell, *Menander and the Monologue*, Hypomnemata 59, Göttingen, 1980.]

RE	*Paulys Realencyclopädie der classischen Altertumswissenschaft*, neue Bearbeitungen von G. Wissowa (etc.), Stuttgart, 1893– .
Schadewaldt	W. Schadewaldt, *Monolog und Selbstgespräch* (Neue philol. Untersuchungen herausgegeben von W. Jaeger, Heft 2), Berlin, 1926.
Schäfer	A. Schäfer, *Menanders Dyskolos — Untersuchungen zur dramatischen Technik* (Beiträge zur klassischen Philologie, Heft 14), Meisenheim am Glan, 1965.
Schaffner	O. Schaffner, *De aversum loquendi ratione in comoedia*, Dissertation, Giessen, 1911.
Schmid	W. Schmid und O. Stählin, *Geschichte der griechischen Literatur*, 1. Teil: Die klassische Periode, von W. Schmid, Munich, 1928–48 (cited as Schmid I 1 p. 1, etc.)
Schwinge	E.-R. Schwinge, *Die Verwendung der Stichomythie in den Dramen des Euripides*, Heidelberg, 1968.
Schwyzer	E. Schwyzer, *Griechische Grammatik*, Munich, 1939–53.
Spitzbarth	A. Spitzbarth, *Untersuchungen zur Spieltechnik der griechischen Tragödie*, Winterthur, 1945.
Sprague	A. C. Sprague, *Shakespeare and the Audience*, New York, 1935.
Webster *SLGC*	T. B. L. Webster, *Studies in Later Greek Comedy*[2], Manchester, 1970.
Tycho von Wilamowitz	T. von Wilamowitz-Moellendorff, *Die dramatische Technik des Sophokles* (Philol. Untersuchungen herausgegeben von A. Kiessling und U. von Wilamowitz-Moellendorff, Bd. 22), Berlin, 1917.
Zwierlein	O. Zwierlein, *Die Rezitationsdramen Senecas mit einem kritisch-exegetischen Anhang* (Beiträge zur klassischen Philologie, Heft 20), Meisenheim am Glan, 1966.

The lines of Menander's plays are enumerated as in the edition of F. H. Sandbach (*OCT* 1972) with the exception of *Epitrepontes* and *Periciromene* for which I adhere to the enumeration found in the third edition of Koerte. Comic fragments other than those of Menander are cited either from *CGF* or from Kock. Periodicals are cited following the usage of *L'Année philologique*.

Note that

(1) 'on stage' means 'in view of the audience' and is not intended to imply an opinion about the existence of a raised acting area in the fifth-century theatre.

(2) 'Eur. *Hel.* 133a' means part of l. 133 of Euripides' *Helen* considered from its beginning; 'Eur. *Hel.* 139b' part of l. 139 considered from its end.

1. Convention and Illusion

i

THIS work is concerned centrally with a particular convention of the Greek theatre, the aside, and peripherally with various conventional effects related to the aside. It is necessary to say at the outset what is meant here by the word 'convention' and to indicate at least some of the problems that arise when the word is used in a theatrical connection and when other terms which inevitably enter any discussion of dramatic convention are employed. The primary object of this initial discussion is to prevent misunderstanding in later chapters when words like 'conventional', 'natural', 'realistic', and 'illusion-breaking' are used to describe particular passages in Greek drama. Without such a discussion there would be a danger that by using such terms I might be taken to be implying more than I mean to imply. I hope too, however, that, by commenting on such terms and clarifying my own attitude towards them, I may manage to say something about the general character of Greek drama or, at the least, since lack of space forbids too deep a plunge into these murky waters, to suggest some points of approach towards a discussion of that topic.

When defining theatrical convention, it is natural to think in terms of an agreement.[1] One envisages a kind of compact between playwright and audience which entails the audience accepting without qualm or question some technical device used by the dramatist. I imply a belief in such a compact when later I use expressions like 'these lines are by convention aside' or

---

[1] 'A convention may be defined as an agreement between writers and readers, whereby the artist is allowed to limit and simplify his material in order to secure greater concentration through a control of the distribution of emphasis' Bradbrook, p. 4. Sprague, p. 61, describes the aside-convention as a kind of 'tacit agreement' between actors and audience.

when I question whether an audience would *accept* and understand a particular effect or when I speak of certain effects as
straining an audience's powers of belief. It seems to me hard not
to use such terminology when treating a topic like the one under
discussion. It would be possible, however, to make out a case that
such terminology is merely a *façon de parler* and that little reality
underlies it. It might be argued that, when applying to ancient
drama and particularly to our earliest examples of ancient
drama, the tragedies and comedies which were first performed in
the fifth century, such a definition of theatrical convention as the
one suggested above, we are speaking with benefit of hindsight.
Is the matter as rational as the definition would suggest? If a
society has only *one* idea of what a play is like, why should there
be any suggestion that the individual of that society is *putting up
with* or *accepting* what is set before him when he goes to see a play?[1]
He knows of nothing else.

There is a risk, then, that 'theatrical convention' is a descriptive
term applied retrospectively to ancient drama by people familiar
with numerous kinds of drama and as a consequence capable of
selecting, and highlighting as characteristic, aspects of each kind
of drama so as to classify them as conventions of each genre,
forgetting that few, if any, of the people who first saw plays of
each genre were able to make a comparison of this kind with
other genres. There are, however, two ways of considering the
conventions of any particular dramatic genre. The way we have
just mentioned, whereby the conventions are isolated by comparison with those of other genres, will obviously tell us little
concerning the way the original audiences felt about the character of the drama they saw performed, but we may find a more
promising approach to the attitudes, feelings, and standards of
the original audiences, if we make a comparison not with other
plays but with *life*. Plays, or at any rate most plays, purport to
enact real events, and the actors generally play people. Modern
playgoers and readers tend to regard as conventional anything

---

[1] Dover, *PCPhS* n.s. 12 (1966), 3: 'The question "What does this play need?"
is answerable only with reference to the standards and expectations of the audience
before which it is performed.'

on stage that diverges greatly from what would happen in real life. We must ask, without perhaps much hope of obtaining an answer, how far the Greeks applied this standard to the plays they went to see.[1] If they were even dimly conscious of it, we should, I think, be entitled to speak of them accepting certain conventions and to feel free of anachronism in so speaking.

Before we say anything further on this question, we must confront a Hydra. Whenever one mentions real life or reality or uses the word 'natural' in connection with drama, there springs forth to meet one that monstrous term 'the dramatic illusion'.[2] With regard to ancient drama one meets the term most often in connection with Old Comedy. Scholars commonly refer to those parts of the drama where the characters address or refer to the audience or make allusion to theatrical conditions as 'ruptures of the illusion'.[3] That is to say they apply the term to those parts of the play that interrupt the dramatic action and appear to destroy the pretended reality, such as it is, of the play. Such interruptions are of course extremely common in this genre. Recently, however, it has been suggested that it is misleading and mistaken to regard Old Comedy as consisting of action *interrupted* by extra-dramatic elements. Sifakis[4] has launched a brief but vigorous attack on the notion that there was such a thing as 'the illusion' in Greek drama. He has pointed to modern theatrical practice and particularly to the theories of Bertolt Brecht in order to show that it is quite possible to have drama without the dramatic illusion. Sketching the character of modern 'realistic' and 'illusionist'

---

[1] Of course we should expect different answers in the case of different genres. An audience watching Old Comedy is asked to accept complete fantasy. The same sort of demand is not made of the audience of New Comedy.

[2] For discussion of whether the ancients had a kindred term see Pohlenz, *NGG* 1920, 159 f. (= *Kl. Schr.* II. 453 f.) where the treatment of Ar. *Ran.* 909 is mistaken (see Pfeiffer, *A History of Classical Scholarship*, Oxford, 1968, p. 47), E. Rechenberg, *Beobachtungen über das Verhältnis der alten attischen Komödie zu ihrem Publikum* (Berlin, 1966), p. 196, n. 322, and W. Görler, *Antike und Abendland* 18 (1973), 42, n. 5.

[3] See Schmid I 4 p. 43, R. Crahay–M. Delcourt, 'Les Ruptures d'illusion dans les comédies antiques', *Annuaire de l'Inst. de Phil. et d'Hist. Orient. de l'Univ. Libre de Bruxelles* 12 (1952) (= *Mélanges Grégoire* IV), 83–92, H. L. Stow, *The Violation of the Dramatic Illusion in the Comedies of Aristophanes*. Philol. Diss., Chicago, 1936.

[4] *Parabasis and Animal Choruses* (London, 1971), Ch. 1.

drama in order to contrast it with ancient drama, he finds that the elements in the former which conspire to create the illusion are without exception absent from the latter. 'The notion of dramatic make-believe and illusion is unknown to the Greek comedian' is his somewhat startling conclusion.

It seems to me that Sifakis's approach blurs an important distinction.[1] One may admit that there is much in Greek drama that appears to us unreal and strange, much indeed that might seem to foreshadow Brecht's celebrated *V-Effekt*:[2] the masks worn by the actors, the presence of a chorus, the formal dialogue of tragedy manifested especially in stichomythia. It is easy to seize on such phenomena and to use them to illustrate the lack of naturalism of Greek drama. There is surely a distinction to be drawn, however, between the outward appearance of Greek drama and its essentially dramatic character. Greek drama portrays actions and its actors play at being people involved in real situations. They identify themselves with the characters they are playing and speak in the person of those characters. There is a world of difference between an actor saying 'I am Achilles' and a rhapsode singing *about* Achilles. This difference, obvious enough to Aristotle and determining his approach to drama and epic in the *Poetics*, is too often obscured, particularly by those who write about the origins of drama. Brecht, however, was well aware of it. Part of the novelty of 'epic theatre' is the conscious attempt made in it to mix the genres 'epic' (in the sense of narrative) and 'drama'. Brecht's actor was not to attempt to feel his role, to feel that he *was* a particular character, a Hamlet

---

[1] For similar criticism of Sifakis's position see H.-J. Newiger in *Museum Africum* 1 (1972), 82–4 (a reference I owe to Dr. Austin). Newiger quotes with approval Dover, *AC*, p. 56 who defends the use of the term 'provided that by "illusion" we do not mean visual ingenuities of production ... but simply the uninterrupted concentration of the fictitious personages of the play on their fictitious situation'. A further weakness of Sifakis's case is his failure to take account of the difference between tragedy and comedy as regards audience address and reference to theatrical conditions (on this see my article 'Audience address in Greek Tragedy', *CQ* n.s. 25 (1975)). If there was no such concept of the illusion in ancient drama why do we never find such phenomena in tragedy?

[2] See the interesting introductory chapter of K. von Fritz's *Antike und moderne Tragödie* (Berlin, 1962), and most recently H. Flashar, 'Aristoteles und Brecht', *Poetica* 6 (1974), 17–37.

or an Othello: he was to *demonstrate* the character to the audience.[1] He would do this by means of the *V-Effekt*. The actor might speak about the part he was playing, referring to the person he was playing in the third person. He might speak of what is supposed to be happening on the stage in the past tense. He might insert comments on the play. Something similar to the first and third devices does occur in Greek drama. Comments on the play are confined to comedy and when in Greek drama a character speaks of himself in the third person and perhaps mentions his own name the effect is not to distance himself from his role: either the speaker enhances his own dignity or the effect is to create pathos.[2]

On many people's definition of drama, what Brecht was aiming at was scarcely drama at all. However that may be, there are many occasions even in Brecht's own plays where the actor speaks in the person of the character he is playing, where he does play a role. What name do we give such passages? The device of the *V-Effekt* is designed to prevent an audience from taking them as illusionistic. There would be no need for such a device were it not that audiences are always liable to sympathize with the characters and to become willing victims of the illusion.[3] Just as in the anti-illusionistic theatre of Brecht there are many such apparently illusionistic scenes,[4] so in the form of drama that Sifakis alleges knew nothing of the illusion, Old Comedy, there are extended passages where no overt account is taken of the audience and where the actors are clearly maintaining the pretence of being people involved in an action (it does not

[1] 'Der Schauspieler lässt es auf der Bühne nicht zur restlose Verwandlung in die darzustellende Person kommen. Er ist nicht Lear, Harpagon, Schwejk, er *zeigt* [my italics] diese Leute', Brecht, *Schriften zum Theater*, p. 109.

[2] e.g. the effect of Soph. *Ai.* 864 is pathetic, that of Trag. Anon. *GLP* 33. 6 indignant. Görler, *Antike und Abendland* 18 (1973), 50, notes that the position of the ancient audience is not coincident with the position required by Brecht for his audience. They are not always aware that the actors are actors.

[3] Brecht was well aware of this: 'Kurz, es wurde nicht angestrebt, das Publikum in Trance zu versetzen und ihm die Illusion zu geben, es wohne einem natürlichen uneinstudierten Vorgang bei. Wie man sehen wird, muss *die Neigung des Publikums*, sich in eine solche Illusion zu werfen, durch bestimmte Kunstmittel neutralisiert werden', op. cit., p. 106.

[4] At least this is my experience in watching Brecht in performance. It would only be fair to add that these plays were produced in a manner which would almost certainly have been unacceptable to Brecht.

matter that often the action is a totally fantastic one—the actor is still for the moment Trygaeus and not the unknown Athenian who played him).[1] For such passages it is surely necessary to keep the term 'illusion' so that one may speak of the illusion being preserved.

Nevertheless the term is far from satisfactory. It suggests that the audience is in some way deceived by what goes on on stage and confuses play-acting and reality. It may be foolhardy to generalize about audiences of any age—even of one's own—but I should have thought that only the most unsophisticated audiences would have such an experience when watching a play.[2] It is perfectly possible for the audience of an 'illusionist' play to be at the same time emotionally involved in the action and in possession of its critical faculties. One may be charmed, bewitched, or subject to whatever one cares to call the effect of 'stage magic', and still be able to comprehend the finer details of the play and assess the qualities of the production. Here I tend to agree with the characteristically robust judgements of Dr. Johnson: 'It is false, that any representation is mistaken for reality: that any dramatic fable in its materiality was ever credible, or, for a single moment, was ever credited.... The truth is that the spectators are always in their senses and know, from the first act to the last, that the stage is only a stage, and that the players are only players.... It will be asked how the drama moves if it is not credited. It is credited with all the credit due to a drama.'[3] It would have been more satisfactory if, instead of speaking of illusion, dramatic critics had used the word *pretence*.[4] Actors pretend to be the people they play and the audience

[1] See below, pp. 90 ff.

[2] No doubt there were *some* people in the Athenian audience who reacted towards the plays they attended similarly to the heroine of the film *Never on Sunday*, whose distress at the murder of Medea's children was alleviated at the end of a performance when she saw that they were after all alive and able to take a curtain call along with their mother.

[3] These quotations are taken from his 1765 *Preface to Shakespeare* (pp. 70–1 in *Dr. Johnson on Shakespeare*, ed. W. K. Wimsatt). Dr. Johnson did live in an age of exceptionally artificial and unrealistic acting (see B. L. Joseph, *The Tragic Actor* (London, 1959), pp. 241–2).

[4] Görler, op. cit., p. 50, n. 34, dislikes the notion of deceit underlying the term 'illusion' and would prefer to substitute the idea of 'play'.

accepts that pretence. That is all that I mean to imply when henceforward I use the term 'dramatic illusion'.

ii

Obviously it is vain to hope to enter the psyche of a fifth- or fourth-century spectator, but anyone writing about Greek drama must at least make the attempt. The only approach towards an understanding of the presuppositions and attitudes of the audiences of the plays is through the plays themselves. It would be useful to have reliable ancient information about the way the plays were acted, the kind of contemporary anecdote so valuable for the student of the history of Elizabethan and Jacobean drama. Unfortunately most anecdotes that we possess about actors and acting in the early Greek theatre are either of doubtful authenticity or of little relevance to the kind of inquiry here undertaken.[1] Nor is there any ancient critical literature dealing with the topics under discussion.[2] The text of the plays then must be our guide when we try to determine what sort of demands were made on the audience.

An extreme sceptic might deny that Greek drama in the fifth century could be described as representational in anything like the sense in which we use the word.[3] He might seek to argue that

[1] For collections of anecdotes about acting and actors see Spitzbarth, pp. 57 f., and Page, *Actors' Interpolations in Greek Tragedy* (Oxford, 1934), pp. 15–20. There is some fifth-century evidence—e.g. the tragic actor Mynniscus (a competitor at the Dionysia of 422) called his younger contemporary, Callippides (winner of the Lenaea prize in 418) 'ape' (Aristotle, *Poetics*, 1461b, 29 ff.). Presumably he did so because he felt that the latter's acting was excessively mimetic. This may be evidence for the emergence of a more natural and realistic style of acting in the latter part of the fifth century. However, what appears natural to one type of audience may often look formal to another (see Bradbrook, p. 25). Wilamowitz connects the anecdote with the demands that would be made on the actor who played the modern, 'unheroic' Euripidean characters (*Hermes* 59 (1924), 262 = *Kl. Schr.* IV. 355). Another anecdote, which concerns Sophocles playing the part of Nausicaa, although it becomes confused in the retelling (see Athenaeus 20 f, Eustath. *Il.* 381, 10, *Od.* 1553), does appear to provide evidence for a considerable amount of movement on stage in fifth-century acting.

[2] Leo, p. 44, notes the absence of ancient critical literature on monologues.

[3] For a refutation of this view see W. Steidle, *Studien zum antiken Drama* (Munich, 1968), pp. 11 f. On the relationship between the words of the text and what the audience sees see T. von Wilamowitz, pp. 140 ff. and J. Dingel in *Bauformen der*

stage movement indicated in the text of the plays need not necessarily have been carried out on stage (to do so he would have to
discount the anecdote about Sophocles playing Nausicaa).[1]
Scenes like Soph. *O.C.* 821 ff. which, on the face of it, contains a
considerable amount of movement and some physical violence,
would not necessarily have been performed realistically. The
physical contact and movement implied by the words of the text
need not have been translated into action. Instead we should
have a totally statuesque and non-representational scene where
it was often the case that the lack of movement of the actors was
in conflict with their utterances.

Such scepticism, which might be extended to a disbelief in the
existence of objects and stage effects mentioned by the actors,[2] is
by no means absurd. What militates against more than partial
acceptance of it is this. If the sceptical view were true, the dramatist would be almost completely free in what he might let his
characters say: they would be able to describe themselves as under-
taking actions that were well-nigh impossible to stage or in some
cases contrary to the laws of nature. I believe that the tragedians
would have composed rather differently if they were under no
obligation to make their characters' actions square with their
words. One has only to consider a type of drama where such an
obligation was not felt, to realize how comparatively restrained
fifth-century tragedians were in the demands they made of their
audience's imagination. Zwierlein provides evidence to demonstrate that the tragedies of Seneca were not originally intended
for performance on stage. Using the conventions and recurring
situations of Greek drama as his standards, he totally discredits

---

griechischen Tragödie herausgegeben von W. Jens (Munich, 1971), p. 356. On scenes
where the text implies physical contact between actors in tragedy (these are much
more common than one would gather from reading general books about Greek
drama) see, as well as Spitzbarth, O. Zwierlein, *GGA* 1970, 214.

[1] See above, p. 7 n. 1. Demetrius, *Eloc.* 195 is not parallel. It is not evidence for
fifth-century acting but mere inference from the text of Eur. *Ion* 184 ff.

[2] With regard to comedy, however, there is evidence with which to refute the
sceptic. Sometimes comic characters refer to, without naming, objects, and use
deictic pronouns when doing so (see Ar. *Ach.* 346 and Dover on Ar. *Nub.* 1146).
That this phenomenon is not confined to neuter pronouns is clinching. This would
obviously make no sense unless the audience could see the objects in question.

Seneca's scenic imagination. In Seneca there are scenes which could be performed realistically only with the aid of the tricks of modern cinematic technology. If his plays had been performed in antiquity, they could only have been performed in a non-representational manner.[1] What the characters said would not have measured up to what the audience saw them doing. One cannot, for example, entertain the idea of Manto conducting a real extispicy on stage. That is clearly what is supposed to be happening in Sen. *Oed.* 303–85.[2]

There is nothing like this in Greek tragedy. There are indeed a few scenes that would make considerable demands on the producer if they were to be done realistically, but the problems of production they impose tend to be external to the actors—for example, the cataclysm at the end of Aesch. *P.V.* and the 'palace miracle' in Eur. *Bacch.* Apart from the hammering scene at the beginning of the *P.V.*, it is hard to think of any passage in Greek tragedy where an actor describes gestures (his own or those of other people on stage) that could not actually be performed or at least mimed realistically enough to suggest that they were being performed.[3]

Such considerations make it easier to speak a little more confidently about conventions when discussing Greek drama. There is in tragedy, at any rate, a kind of minimal realism, enough to allow us to assume that when an actor says he is leaving the

---

[1] I agree with B. Walker when she says in her review of Zwierlein (*CPh* 64 (1969), 183–7): 'there is nothing which can be termed unstageable *tout court*' (cf. E. Lefèvre, *Gnomon* 40 (1968), 783 f. and the quotation from Dover cited above, p. 2 n. 1). Nevertheless it is not sufficient as a refutation of Zwierlein's case. To confute him one would have to establish that there existed in the ancient world a stage tradition into which the plays of Seneca could be accommodated.

[2] On this scene see Zwierlein, pp. 24 f. Note that the animal is ostensibly slaughtered *on stage* and from 372 Manto is grubbing around among its intestines: 'scrutemur [scrutetur *A* cannot be right: a subject would be required] unde tantus hic extis rigor'.

[3] See Spitzbarth, pp. 38 f. I assume that, in Sophocles' *Aias*, Ajax commits suicide off stage (in Hellenistic times a special device was used for enacting the scene on stage—see Polemo, fr. 95—but that tells us nothing about the way the scene was originally played). In cases where change of facial expression is reported actions could not square with words when the actors were masked. Only a minority of the audience, however, could be expected to see in detail the face of the actor on stage.

stage, he does so and does not remain seated in full view of the audience. The Athenian spectator had at least some expectations of realism when he went to see a play.

There are two kinds of dramatic convention. One kind may be said to be natural or to originate in life. It is merely its recurrence that makes us call it a convention. One example of such a device makes a virtue out of a necessity. The action of a Greek play must needs take place in the open air. The opening of Sophocles' *Antigone* is a secret conclave[1] between Antigone and Ismene. In it we are told that Antigone has summoned Ismene out of the house to talk with her. This action, though at first sight having the appearance of a mere technical contrivance to bring the sisters on stage, would not have seemed surprising or unnatural to a Greek audience.[2] Greeks in a house or an enclosed space who wanted to converse privately were always liable to be overheard by their slaves (note the implications of Ar. *Ran.* 750–7): privacy might more easily be obtained in an unconfined space, in the street or in a forecourt of the house. We need not believe that audiences felt that scenes like Soph. *Ant.* 1 ff. or Eur. *I.A.* 1–48[3] were conventional in the sense that they conflicted with the kind of behaviour to be expected in real life. Even so, conventions that have their origins in real life, like this type of secret conclave or like the monologue,[4] are liable to harden into mannerisms. If an

---

[1] N.B. 18 f. ἤδη καλῶς, καί ς᾽ ἐκτὸς αὐλείων πυλῶν
τοῦδ᾽ οὔνεκ᾽ ἐξέπεμπον, ὡς μόνη κλύοις.
Antigone's attitude towards the end of the scene might seem to contradict this statement. We are concerned, however, only with the reaction of the audience when the two are first seen entering. The change in Antigone's attitude, her new inclination to throw caution to the winds, is provoked by her anger at Ismene's pusillanimous reaction to what she has just told her.

[2] On this see W. M. Calder III, *GRBS* 9 (1968), 392, n. 18, arguing against Kaibel's remarks in his *Electra* commentary, p. 65. Modern audiences familiar with the techniques of modern spies and U.S. presidents should not find it too strange that people who want not to be overheard go out of doors.

[3] It seems to me certain that whoever wrote the anapaests at the beginning of this play intended them to begin the play and to serve as exposition in exactly the same way as the opening of Soph. *Ant.* [See *CQ* n.s. 27 (1977), 10 ff.]

[4] Leo and others (cf. Wilamowitz, *Menanders Schiedsgericht*, p. 149) lay great stress on the habit of Mediterranean peoples (as distinct from Northerners) of expressing their thoughts aloud. Leo remarks on the way soliloquies in Homer are introduced by verbs of speaking: 'Dafür gibt es nur eine Erklärung. Der Grieche sprach, wenn er lebhaft empfand oder nachdachte, auch mit sich selber . . . Der

effect is repeated over and over again, an audience ceases to think about its realistic origins and begins to regard it simply as a regular feature of drama, that is to say as a convention. In the case of plotting scenes in New Comedy (e.g. Plaut. *Mil.* 596 ff.) where characters come out on stage, look around for eaves-droppers, and, seeing none, begin plotting, it seems unlikely that audiences felt that what was going on on stage approximated to the conditions of real life.

The second type of convention on the other hand is almost totally contrived and has only a tenuous connection with life. A prime example in Greek tragedy is the *ekkyklema*[1] whose existence is due to the necessity of revealing interior scenes. An audience must simply accept that, when Phaedra is rolled out in the *Hippolytus*, the scene is now the interior of Theseus' palace. The spectator will do best not to meditate too deeply on this or he will soon realize the essential absurdity of the device (something which comedy was glad to exploit).[2]

The aside hovers between the two kinds of conventions—it

Monolog war ihm, wenigstens dem jonischen Griechen, etwas Natürliches, aus dem Leben ihn her Geläufiges' (pp. 3–4). There is no doubt a certain amount of truth in this, but Homeric soliloquies are surely conventional, just like soliloquies and monologues in drama (cf. the sensible remarks of Legrand, p. 415). Leo himself points out that in drama, particularly New Comedy, monologues hardened into a convention (pp. 44 ff.) and comes near to admitting that the same was true of Homeric soliloquies (p. 72). There is a world of difference between speech, or thought expressed in speech, in literature and speech or thought, expressed aloud or not, in life. Leo's remarks may hold good for exclamations, but it is hard to believe that the ancient Greeks talked to themselves as the Homeric heroes do, any more than would the modern English or German. Verbalizing mental de-liberation is a prerequisite for any communicable literature.

[1] *Ekkyklema*, the name of an object in Pollux, is generally the name of an action in dramatic scholia. The scenes of parody in Ar. *Ach.* 408 ff. and *Thesm.* 96, 265 are sufficient to prove that this action was common on the tragic stage and that there was some sort of machinery for effecting it.

[2] In *Acharnians* Euripides is 'in' and has not the time to come 'out'. Instead he is rolled 'out'. Despite this he behaves as if he is still 'in' his house. Where is 'outside' or 'inside' when someone is rolled out on to the stage? It would be disastrous for the spectator to ask such a question of a tragic scene like Soph. *Ai.* 346 ff. There Tecmessa opens the door of the stage building and the scene of carnage within is revealed with Ajax sitting amid the carnage he has created. We are thus notionally inside and this is confirmed when Ajax in trying to dismiss Tecmessa says (369) οὐκ ἐκτός;. But this remark would make little sense to any audience if taken at face value. Tecmessa is not inside any building she can leave by going out. The same sort of problems arise with Soph. *El.* 1465.

has a certain realistic basis in that people do sometimes speak *sotto voce*—but it has more in common with the second than with the first type. It is essentially unrealistic,[1] particularly when it is treated as silent thought or when the person in whose presence an aside has been delivered shows no sign of having heard a sound from the speaker.[2]

[1] See below, pp. 15, 84.
[2] See below, p. 156, and cf. Barbieri, p. 38.

2. Asides in Euripides

i

THE second epeisodion of Euripides' *Hecuba* contains one of the most striking pieces of stage action to be found in Greek tragedy. The Trojan queen lies on the shore in front of the Greek tents, before her the body of her son Polydorus lately brought there by her attendant. During the scene of lyric lamentation that has just ended Hecuba has guessed the identity of her son's murderer. Now the chorus commiserates with her (722–3) and announces a new arrival, Agamemnon (724–5). Agamemnon comes on stage and addresses Hecuba. He is surprised, he says, that she is late in attending the funeral of her daughter, Polyxena (726–32). Only after saying this does Agamemnon observe that something is untoward on stage, that in front of Hecuba there lies a corpse. After an initial cry of surprise (ἔα), he speculates on who it might be, guessing from the clothing that it is a Trojan. Hecuba does nothing to relieve his uncertainty. She says nothing to him, either in reply to his earlier complaint or his present question, but addresses herself:

> 736 δύcτην', ἐμαυτὴν γὰρ λέγω λέγουcα cέ,
>   'Εκάβη, τί δράcω; πότερα προcπέcω γόνυ
>   Ἀγαμέμνονοc τοῦδ' ἢ φέρω cιγῆι κακά;

You poor wretch—I mean myself when I say 'you'—Hecuba, what am I to do? Am I to fall at the knees of Agamemnon here or should I bear my troubles in silence?

These lines are followed by a distich[1] from Agamemnon:

---

[1] On the pattern of the dialogue in this scene see A. Gross, *Die Stichomythie in der griechischen Tragödie und Komödie. Ihre Anwendung und ihr Ursprung* (Berlin, 1905), p. 17, n. 4.

739   τί μοι προσώπωι νῶτον ἐγκλίνασα còν
      δύρηι, τὸ πραχθὲν¹ δ’ οὐ λέγεις; τίς ἔcθ’ ὅδε;

Why do you turn your back on me and lament? Why don't you tell
me what has happened? Who is this?

Hecuba does not reply to these questions either. She continues
her reflections, taking up (N.B. ἀλλά in 741) where she left off
in 738. This time she speaks two lines. These are followed by
a second distich from Agamemnon who says he cannot divine
what she is deliberating about without hearing her (μὴ κλύων).
Hecuba, however, still ignores him and continues her reflections
in another distich. Once more Agamemnon addresses her. Now,
he says, he does not care whether he hears her or not, the implication being that he is about to leave. In the next three lines
Hecuba comes to a decision and steels herself for action. She opts
for the first of the alternatives mooted in 736 ff., that of asking
Agamemnon for help. At 752 she addresses Agamemnon for the
first time, preventing his departure by detaining him physically.

There is no difficulty in visualizing the scene just described.
It is quite clear from the text what happens in 736 ff. and since
antiquity the action has been correctly interpreted. The scholia
(MB) on 736 rightly state that 'she turns away and speaks to
herself. It is clear from what Agamemnon says to her "Why do
you turn your back on me?".'² The obvious way to describe

---

¹ κρανθέν was an ancient variant here (see K. Matthiessen, *GRBS* 10 (1969), 302
and the apparatus in Daitz's Teubner edition of this play). Matthiessen and Daitz
are wrong, however, to prefer it to the better attested πραχθέν. κραίνω carries with
it the notion 'ratify' and is applied particularly to gods and to mortals in positions
of authority (see Fraenkel on Aesch. *Ag.* 369). Of the two occasions when τὸ κρανθέν
occurs in Euripides, at Eur. *Ion* 77 the reference is to something Apollo has decided will happen and at Eur. *Hipp.* 868 the text is incurably corrupt (see Barrett
ad loc.), although before the occurrence of the word there is mention of the *god*
bringing on the trouble. The neutral τὸ πραχθέν is what we want in the *Hecuba*
passage: cf. Theseus' request in similar circumstances at Eur. *Hipp.* 842 εἴποι
τις ἂν τὸ πραχθέν;

² πρὸς ἑαυτὴν ἀποστραφεῖca λέγει. δῆλον δὲ ἐξ ὧν ὁ Ἀγαμέμνων πρὸς αὐτὴν λέγει 'τί
μοι προσώπωι . . .;'. The scholion continues with a report of the view of Didymus
that l. 736 is addressed to the corpse of Polydorus, ἐμαυτὴν γὰρ λέγω δύστηνον
ἀποκαλοῦcά cε. This is quite mistaken. Two vocatives, δύστην᾽, Ἑκάβη, addressed to
different people but separated only by a γάρ clause would be very difficult to
follow. The arguments adduced by Hermann ad loc. show that he shared Didymus'
misapprehension. According to him Ἑκάβη must be nominative since, if it were
vocative, it would have to be followed not by τί δράcω but by τί δράcεις.

Hecuba's utterances at 736–8, 741–2, 745–6, and 749–51 is to call them 'asides' and most scholars agree in using the term here. Admittedly Hecuba's remarks do not constitute what might be considered the purest form of aside. Agamemnon is supposed to hear something of what Hecuba is saying, but not to be able properly to make out its meaning. In 740 he asks her why she is lamenting (δύρηι) and this might be thought to take up 'wretched ... Hecuba' (δύcτην' ... 'Εκάβη).[1] His other interruptions (743–4 and 747–8) mention or imply his inability *properly* to hear Hecuba.[2] The reason for this inability is explained in the 'stage-directional' question he puts to her at 739 'Why do you turn your back?'. All this is different from the type of aside where the other character is quite unaware that the aside-speaker is speaking at all.[3] Still we are dealing with a convention, a demand on the audience. Hecuba's utterances cannot have been delivered in such a way as to be heard and understood by the audience in the theatre and yet have been partially inaudible to the actor playing Agamemnon.

The employment of such a convention in a tragedy produced

Admittedly this would be a more normal form of self-apostrophe (cf. Eur. *Med.* 401 ff.), but it is precisely the abnormality of this way of speaking that the γάρ clause is meant to explain, an extension of the Euripidean mannerism whereby a speaker addresses someone and immediately explains why he has chosen a particular form of address (on this see Kannicht on Eur. *Hel.* 1194). On Hermann's interpretation, l. 736 would have to mean something like 'when I call you δύcτηνος, I call myself δύcτηνος'. λέγουcα cέ, however, is not the same as καλοῦcά cέ τι. When correctly interpreted the line presents no problems, λέγω meaning 'I mean' and λέγουcα cέ, 'saying you'. Kannicht finds a parallel for the form of Eur. *Hec.* 736–7 in Eur. *Hel.* 164–6, but ἐγώ there is not usually regarded as vocative (K–G 1. 46).

[1] δύρηι, however, need not necessarily imply that Agamemnon has heard anything. Cf. ἀλγῶ πάλαι δὴ τἀπὶ coὶ cτένων κακά (Soph. *Phil.* 806) where cτένων must refer to inward groaning since Neoptolemus has made no utterance since 781 and Philoctetes has just drawn attention to his silence.

[2] I am not certain whether we are meant to take cῶν ὁδὸν βουλευμάτων 744 as implying that Agamemnon can hear but cannot make out clearly Hecuba's deliberations or simply that he has deduced from her refusal to reply that she is trying to make up her mind about something. The clearest indication that Hecuba is deliberating comes from πότερα ... ἤ in 737 f., but this is the utterance of Hecuba that Agamemnon characterized or most probably characterized (see previous note) as lamentation.

[3] Schadewaldt presumably means this when he says of Hecuba's speech 'sie ist kein rein technisches Beiseite' (p. 30).

some time in the early 420s[1] suggests many questions. Is there
anything like it elsewhere in Greek tragedy? Are we confronted
here with a developed convention or with one which the playwright is only tentatively introducing? Is there a connection
between the asides so frequently to be found in comedy and the
type of aside we have found here? Answers of a sort have been
put forward for each of these questions, but mostly in passing and
without much thought or thorough investigation of the evidence.
There is no real agreement about the number of asides in tragedy
except perhaps that it is very small and that this *Hecuba* passage
provides the most striking and possibly the first example.[2] The
standard history of Greek literature devotes a footnote to the
compilation of an almost wholly unsatisfactory list of tragic
asides.[3]

Disagreement on the number of asides in tragedy is due in no
small part to differing views of what exactly constitutes an aside.

---

[1] ll. 171 ff. are parodied in Arist. *Nub.* 1165 (and possibly 159 ff. in *Nub.* 718:
see Dover ad loc.). This makes it likely, but not certain (since *Nub.* as we have it is
a revised version of the play first produced without success at the city Dionysia of
423), that the play was produced some time before 423. Such a date squares with
the metrical statistics that have been compiled to show a progressive increase in
resolution in Euripides' trimeters. See T. Zieliński, *Tragodumenon libri tres* (Cracow,
1925), pp. 153–63, E. B. Ceadel, *CQ* 35 (1941), 70 f., and T. B. L. Webster, *The
Tragedies of Euripides* (London, 1967), pp. 2–5.

[2] J. P. Mahaffy, *A History of Classical Greek Literature* (London, 1880), i. 345;
A. E. Haigh, *The Tragic Drama of the Greeks* (Oxford, 1896), p. 349; R. C.
Flickinger, *The Greek Theater and its Drama*[4] (Chicago, 1936), p. 312; P. W. Harsh,
A Handbook of Classical Drama (Stanford, 1944), p. 22; A. Lesky, *Geschichte der
griechischen Literatur*[3] (Bern, 1971), p. 741, n. 1. Barbieri in his dissertation finds
many more asides than people have up to now. This is because of the wideness of
his definition of an aside and because of a reluctance to consider the dramatic
context (see below, p. 17 n. 3, and p. 20).

[3] Schmid I 2 p. 83, n. 1. Only one of the passages he mentions (apart from Eur.
Hec. 736 ff.) is worth considering as an aside (Eur. *Or.* 671, on which see below,
p. 44). Few would call Soph. *Ai.* 1266–71 an aside; the scholion on Soph. *Ant.* 327
is mistaken (see below, p. 71); and Soph. *Phil.* 934, although not addressed to
Neoptolemus, is scarcely meant to be concealed from him. In general Schmid's
attempt to find asides by cataloguing comments in the scholia is unprofitable (see
below, p. 18): the comment on Eur. *Med.* 764 is idiotic, at Eur. *Hec.* 414 and 426
(misprinted as 420 in Schmid), the scholia merely tell us that Polyxena ignores
Hecuba's words and continues as though there had been no interruption, but this
on its own does not constitute an aside: the explanation offered as an alternative
(ἄλλως) on Eur. *Phoen.* 520 (misprinted as 526 in Schmid), τοῦτο κατ' ἰδίαν . . .
μεθ' ὑποκρίσεως, is quite misconceived. I do not know what warrant Schmid has for
saying that the scholia describe Soph. *Ant.* 572 and Soph. *Phil.* 934 as asides.

It is necessary to state at the outset what, for the purposes of this inquiry, an aside is taken to be.

When X and Y are on stage together, an aside is any utterance by either speaker not intended to be heard by the other and not in fact heard or properly heard[1] by him. A modern example would be Othello's 'O, hardness to dissemble!' (*Othello* III. iv. 34), where he turns aside after greeting Desdemona, a remark clearly not meant for her ears and clearly not heard by her since she makes no comment upon it. This is the simplest form of aside and there are many possible variations on the basic pattern. When X, Y, and Z are on stage together, any remark made by, say, X to Z which is not meant to be heard by, and is not heard or heard properly by, Y is obviously to be called an aside.

The definition of an aside adopted here is a narrow one, but one, I believe, which accords with present-day theatrical usage. To detect an aside one must first consider the intention behind a remark and then examine its effect. If it is taken up by the next speaker in such a way as to suggest that he has heard it properly, it is not an aside whatever the intention behind it. The audience are not being asked to accept a convention.[2] If on the other hand it is not taken up, it may well be an aside, particularly if the dramatic situation makes it incredible[3] that a remark of its kind should go without comment.

---

[1] This covers a case like the one we have been discussing where Agamemnon is supposed most probably to be aware that the aside speaker is making sounds. It is not applicable to cases where the actor hears what the other party says but does not take it in. See below on Eur. *Hipp.* 1060 ff., p. 30.

[2] This is where Barbieri and I differ. He defines asides with reference only to the intention behind the remark: 'Beiseite sind alle jene Worte eines Sprechers, die er, sei es zu sich selbst, sei es zu den Zuschauern hin spricht, in der Absicht, bei seinem Partner ungehört zu bleiben' (p. 47). Consequently he discusses many passages where remarks have obviously been overheard by the other person present (in many of these it seems to me extremely unlikely that the first speaker is supposed to be trying to speak apart; there are no grounds for considering Soph. *Ant.* 243, since γάρ makes it clear that the guard is replying to Creon), Soph. *Ant.* 1105 f., *Tr.* 1230 f., 1243, *O.T.* 738, 744, 1061b, *Phil.* 779 ff., 969 f., Eur. *Ion* 752, 754, 756, 758, 760, *Tro.* 717, *Phoen.* 1335.

[3] Many of the passages Barbieri discusses where remarks are not taken up by other persons on stage do not meet this requirement (Soph. *Ai.* 88b which is also regarded by Kamerbeek as 'undoubtedly an aside', 587a, *O.T.* 747, 754, 1068, *El.* 1112 f., *Phil.* 1074 f., 1231, Eur. *Alc.* 551a, *Hipp.* 342, *Hcld.* 737b, 739b, *Tro.* 713b, *I.T.* 548b, 568, *Hel.* 622 ff., *Or.* 1610). See below, p. 20.

Two further points should be made before we proceed to a search for asides in Euripides.

Ancient commentators and readers were aware that certain lines in drama might be delivered aside and we often encounter in scholia comments which say that such and such a line is an aside, as for example in the scholion quoted above on Eur. *Hec.* 736. Such comments, do not, however, depend upon a transmitted set of stage directions: they are based simply upon inference from the text. Thus ancient commentators demand no more and no less respect here than do modern. In some cases they are demonstrably wrong (for example on Soph. *Ant.* 327, on which see below, p. 71).[1] I have accordingly made no systematic collection of such comments, mentioning them only where they seemed relevant.[2] Where commentators do not simply say 'he/she speaks to him/herself' (*Σ* Eur. *Hec.* 736), they speak of *sotto voce* delivery, using the adverbs ἡcυχῆι (e.g. the Venetus scholion on Ar. *Ran.* 606) or ἠρέμα (e.g. *Σ* Eur. *Med.* 899), sometimes combining the two ways of expressing the idea of aside by saying 'quietly and to himself' (e.g. *Σ* Eur. *Or.* 671, *Σ* Eur. *Med.* 899).[3]

Secondly, since it is clear from the definition of an aside given above that dramatic context is all-important in determining whether or not a particular line is an aside, it must be stated that the evidence of the fragments of Greek drama is of doubtful value and must be used with great caution. Passages quoted out of context may give the formal appearance of asides, but how can we be sure that they fulfilled the second requirement of the definition, that they went by without comment from other characters (or indeed that they were not delivered on an empty

---

[1] Another inappropriate scholion is to be found at Aesch. *Cho.* 46: δεῖ νοεῖν ὅτι τὸ δύcθεος γυνά ἠρέμα πωc ἐφθέγξατο· διό φηcι, φοβοῦμαι γὰρ ἔποc τόδ' ἐκβάλλειν.

[2] There is a random collection of such scholia (culled for the most part from the *Codex Ravennas* of Aristophanes) in W. G. Rutherford, *A Chapter in the history of Annotation (Scholia Aristophanica* III) (London, 1905), 111. See also J. Andrieu, *Le Dialogue antique; structure et présentation* (Paris, 1954), p. 186. On ἡcυχῆι in the Bodmer papyrus of Menander see below, p. 132. One meets *secum* in the margin of Plautine manuscripts (see Andrieu, p. 149 and *Ménandre*, p. 219). Schaffner collects comments on asides in Terence from Donatus and Eugraphius and this list is supplemented by Barbieri (pp. 1 ff.) who surprisingly ignores Greek scholia, missing for example *Σ* Soph. *Ant.* 328.

[3] Also λεληθότωc (*Σ* Ar. *Ach.* 778 where it is inappropriate).

stage)? A case in point is a fragment of Sophocles which Leo suggested was an aside (fr. 690N = 757P):

> ὦ γλῶcca, cιγήcαcα τὸν πολὺν χρόνον,
> πῶc δῆτα τλήcηι πρᾶγμ᾽ ἐπεξελθεῖν τόδε;
> ἢ τῆc ἀνάγκηc οὐδὲν ἐμβριθέcτερον
> ὑφ᾽ ἧc τὸ κρυφθὲν ἐκφανεῖc ἀνακτόρων.

O tongue, silent for so long, how then will you bring yourself to explain this matter? To be sure nothing is stronger than compulsion. This is what will force you to reveal the secret of the palace.

It is possible that these lines constituted an aside, but without their context we are at a loss. The speaker may be alone on stage or alone with the chorus. Or, if it is the case that the speaker is about to reveal something to someone else on stage, that does not force us to assume that such a preparatory remark as this (cf. Eur. *Ion* 859 ff.) was concealed from the person the speaker was about to address. The lines may well have provoked some sort of response from whoever happened to be present at the time.

ii

It is now time to examine the rest of Euripides, applying the definition set out above to such passages as look to contain asides. Though the chronology of Euripides' plays is by no means settled, it seems less artificial to treat the plays in some sort of chronological order rather than in alphabetic sequence. Hence the order of plays treated below is in accordance with my own chronological assumptions. No statements or conclusions will depend on these assumptions. It goes without saying that the order adopted depends on no unshakeable conviction.

Alcestis

There are no asides in this play.[1] It would be mistaken on the strength of the deictic pronoun τοῦδε (749) to assume that the servant's speech (747–72) was delivered in the presence of

---

[1] The suggestion of J. P. Mahaffy (*Euripides* (London, 1879), p. 124) that the exit-speeches of Death and Apollo are asides is misconceived. When Apollo exits at 71, he is obviously addressing death: Death's speech is addressed to Apollo's 'retreating back' (on this see below, p. 34).

Hercules and apart from him. When he uses the pronoun, the man is pointing to, or, at any rate, making reference to the house just as he does in the following line ἐc τήνδ' ἑcτίαν ἐδεξάμην 'I received into this hearth'. Even though the servant does not provide a formal introduction, it is clear that Hercules enters with the words:

773   οὗτοc, τί cεμνὸν καὶ πεφροντικὸc βλέπειc;[1]

You there, why so serious and gloomy?

Medea

(a) In the dialogue at the beginning of the play between paedagogus and nurse, something the paedagogus has said about Medea troubles the nurse and she asks for clarification:

63   Τρ. τί δ' ἔcτιν, ὦ γεραιέ; μὴ φθόνει φράcαι.
     Πα. οὐδέν· μετέγνων καὶ τὰ πρόcθ' εἰρημένα.

'What is it, old man? Please tell me.'
'Nothing—I'm sorry I said as much as I have already said.'

Barbieri (p. 97) believes that part of the old man's reply is meant to be aside. He considers it possible that the nurse hears part of the line but does not understand it. 'In erster Linie aber hat sie nur das οὐδέν gehört.' Here is another case where Barbieri has failed to ask the question 'is it really surprising that the second speaker fails to take up a remark of the first?'.[2] The nurse is not interested in the old man's regrets: she pursues her inquiry, begging him not to conceal anything from her. It is also mis-conceived in a case like this to regard the speaker as trying to speak aside.[3] The words μετέγνων . . . εἰρημένα are surely not a considered judgement, orienting the audience's opinion of the old man's behaviour. They are rather an involuntary exclamation. We shall meet many such cases where exclamations and emotional outbursts are mistakenly described as asides.[4] Such a de-scription is warranted only in cases where it is obvious that the

---

[1] For οὗτοc in the mouth of a newly entered character, cf. Aesch. *Suppl.* 911.
[2] See above, p. 17 n. 2.
[3] Cf. above, p. 17.
[4] See below, pp. 32, 37.

dialogue could not proceed as it does if the second speaker had heard the exclamation.[1]

(b) When Creon enters for the first time and tells Medea that she is to leave Corinth forthwith, Medea's immediate response is as follows:

> 277 αἰαῖ· πανώλης ἡ τάλαιν' ἀπόλλυμαι.
> ἐχθροὶ γὰρ ἐξιᾶσι πάντα δὴ κάλων,
> κοὐκ ἔστιν ἄτης εὐπρόσοιστος ἔκβασις·
> ἐρήςομαι δὲ καὶ κακῶς πάςχους' ὅμως·
> τίνος μ' ἕκατι γῆς ἀποστέλλεις, Κρέον;

Ah! I am quite undone, for my enemies are letting out every brailing rope and there is no anchorage available against shipwreck. Even so I shall ask the question: why do you banish me from this land, Creon?

As far as I know, no one has suggested that 277–80 or any part of them are meant to be delivered aside, but the dramatic situation enables one to make out a case that they were. The lines constitute Medea's (perfectly genuine) emotional reaction to Creon's announcement. By 281 she has brought her emotions under control and is able to confront Creon directly with a question. Once he has explained why he fears her, she defends herself in a speech of great subtlety (292 ff.) and manages to extract some concessions from him. Her behaviour throughout is apologetic and conciliatory and she goes out of her way to stress that she is no enemy of Creon: it is her husband whom she hates and regards as responsible for her present situation (308 ff.). Once Creon has gone, however, she explains to the chorus that she has been playing a game with him and that her conciliatory attitude towards him was merely a pose adopted so as to win concessions (368 f.). As to her true attitude towards the king of Corinth:

> 370 οὐδ' ἂν προςεῖπον οὐδ' ἂν ἠψάμην χεροῖν.

I would not have addressed him or touched his hands.

---

[1] See above, p. 17.

Can Creon be supposed to have heard Medea's first reaction towards his proclamation? What deters one from classifying 277–9 as simply an uncontrolled emotional outburst without any hint of convention is the word 'enemies' in 278. The use of the word chimes in well with Medea's description of her attitude towards Creon when he has left the stage and she is alone with a friendly chorus. Is it possible for Creon to hear the word and still accept Medea's defence (292 ff.), a defence designed to show that she feels no hostility towards him? If 277–9 are not heard by Creon, his capitulation to Medea's entreaties seems less foolish than it would be if he heard the lines. If the lines are not aside, we should probably assume that 'enemies' is taken by him to refer to Jason alone and that the audience will understand the ambiguity and see that Medea includes Creon and his daughter in this category.[1]

Decision as to whether the lines are an aside depends on consideration of the dramatic situation just outlined and upon whether we believe that 'enemies' is ambiguous. If we decide that the lines are an aside then the formal pattern of 277–81 fits in well with our decision, an exclamation followed first by a decision to speak out (280) and then by a question addressed directly to Creon. Formal patterns in Greek tragedy, however, are often misleading. Characters are wont to announce their intentions even when there is no suggestion that they are soliloquizing[2] and in this case ἐρήϲομαι is ambiguous: it is open to

---

[1] For ἐχθροί referring to Jason alone, cf. Aesch. *Cho.* 615 and the similarly ambiguous φίλοιϲ of Eur. *Hipp.* 524. On 'allusive plurals of relationship' see E. Bruhn (*Sophokles*, erklärt von F. W. Schneidewin und A. Nauck, 8. Bändchen, *Anhang von E. Bruhn*, Berlin, 1899, 2–3), H. L. Jones, *The Poetic Plural of Greek Tragedy* (*Cornell Studies in Classical Philology*, XXIX, Ithaca, 1910), p. 157, n. 4, and Schwyzer, II. 45.

[2] Mr. M. D. Reeve draws my attention to Eur. *Hypsipyle* 1. iv. 15–25 where Amphiaraus slips from monologue (essentially an 'Auftrittsmonolog' of the type described by Leo, p. 30) into an address of Hypsipyle:

> 20   ἄϲμενος δ' εἶδον δόμους
> τούϲδ' ἐν Διὸς λειμῶνι Νεμεάδος χθονὸς
> καί ϲ' εἴτε δούλη τοῖϲδ' ἐφέϲτηκας δόμοιϲ
> εἴτ' οὐχὶ δοῦλον ϲῶμ' ἔχειϲ, ἐρήϲομαι.

Cf. too Oedipus' ἀλλ' ἐρῶ at Soph. *O.C.* 218 which Barbieri considers might be an aside.

understand either 'you' or 'him' as object. If we understand the former, we might still regard 277–9 as an aside, but δέ in 280 would make that difficult.[1]

(c) While giving instructions to her children to embrace their father, Medea breaks off and utters the following exclamation:

899   οἴμοι κακῶν
ὡς ἐννοοῦμαι δή τι τῶν κεκρυμμένων.

Alas! How I recall the hidden troubles!

The scholia state that these words are spoken aside since she is thinking of the cruel murder of the children she projects.[2] Clearly this is what Medea is referring to. The audience and chorus have earlier been informed of Medea's grisly design (764 ff.). If the lines are not an aside, there must be some overt meaning that allows Jason to hear them without interrupting and asking what Medea is speaking of. Commentators from the scholia onwards suggest that Jason is to understand Medea to be referring to the general sorts of trouble that may beset the children at various stages of their lives: 'the common troubles of mankind' (scholia), 'the uncertainty of fate' (Verrall), or 'the uncertainty of his children's life and health' (Paley). This fits in well with what follows. After Medea, as Jason thinks, has mentioned the illnesses and disasters that might befall the children and remove them prematurely from life, she asks them whether they will make (or be able to make) the same gesture (holding their father's right hand) as they are making now, towards their father, at his funeral. This would give Jason the impression that first Medea was expressing a mother's fear for her children and then the fervent hope that they may live long.

Probably 899b–900 is not an aside. Nevertheless the view that it is has some attractions for, if the sentiment it contains squares with what follows, it comes perilously close to being

---

[1] Cf. what is said below (p. 50) on Eur. *I.A.* 655.

[2] τοῦτο (since the lemma is λάβεσθε χειρὸς δεξιᾶς we should probably assume a lacuna before τοῦτο) ἠρέμα καὶ καθ' ἑαυτήν, ὡς ἐννοοῦσα τὴν ἀπήνειαν τοῦ φόνου κατὰ τῶν παίδων. Alternatively κακῶν τῶν κεκρυμμένων is to be regarded as ambiguous.

incomprehensible to Jason when introduced here without qualification.[1] This is not the only occasion in this play when Euripides seems to be flirting with strained double meaning.[2]

(d) Medea's second monologue (1021 ff.), the great speech in which she takes leave of her children and hardens her resolve to kill them and revenge herself on her husband, contains many problems of interpretation. It is not my purpose here to review the controversy over 1056–80 and in any case there is little that could be added to the article of M. D. Reeve[3] which contains a complete survey of the problem and reaches a conclusion that seems inescapable, that 1056–80 cannot have been written by Euripides. The passage is mentioned here only because it has sometimes been assumed that the children do not hear part of what Medea says (see Reeve, loc. cit., p. 60, n. 2).

There is only one point in the part of the speech ending at 1055—the part which Reeve and Müller argue is the genuine Euripidean speech and which has in contrast with 1056–80 aroused no suspicion—where this possibility arises. This is 1046–7:

τί δεῖ με πατέρα τῶνδε τοῖc τούτων κακοῖc
λυποῦcαν αὐτὴν δὶc τόcα κτᾶcθαι κακά;

Why must I by grieving their father by means of their sufferings win twice as much grief for myself?

'Their sufferings' can only be a reference to the murder of the children and that is how the chorus and the audience will take it. What about the children? Reeve suggests either that the audience would not have expected the lines to give away their impending fate to the children or that the lines were delivered

---

[1] I have some sympathy with Wecklein's comment: 'Es sind nicht Worte, die Jason nicht hören darf, sondern Worte, die für Jason unverständlich sind'. Wecklein, like Weil and Barbieri, assumes that we have an aside here. Verrall tries to have his cake and eat it: 'τὰ κεκρυμμένα signifies to Jason's ear the uncertainty of fate . . . the exclamation is involuntary and forced from Medea by the painful thought of her purpose. The others *do not understand it* and she *covers* it by an ordinary explanation' (my italics).

[2] Cf. 1046–7 where τοῖc τούτων κακοῖc can make sense only to someone in the know.

[3] 'Euripides, *Medea* 1021–80', *CQ* n.s. 22 (1972), 51–61.

aside. The former alternative is preferable. To the children the words must sound threatening but all the same obscure. It may be in this instance that an audience would find less difficulty in a speaker all but giving away his intentions within earshot of people from whom his intentions should be concealed when these people are children rather than adults. But this is to postulate a convention from only one instance: the other scenes in tragedy with children present do not contain anything similar.[1]

In 1056–80 there are at least seven lines which contain in varying degrees admissions that Medea intends killing the children. Of these 1073–4 are addressed to the children, but, as Reeve has shown, they are inconsistent with 1021–39 and thus part of the evidence against the authenticity of the whole section. With 1057, 1062–3, and 1067–8, it is uncertain whether the children are supposed to be present. Medea apparently dismissed them at 1053 f., but, if they did depart, how do they know to come out and be embraced at 1067 ff.? The beginning of 1069 is the first indication that Medea wishes to see them again, yet by the end of the line it is obvious that they are present for Medea to request them to embrace her.[2] If we suppose, however, that the children have not at any point left the stage, the effect is odd and unparalleled. If that is the case, they would not only ignore an explicit command from their mother, but also remain on stage without commenting while Medea utters unambiguous threats against their lives. Either the children are present or they are not, but, whichever is the case, the dramatic technique is without parallel in the fifth century and this uncertainty and awkwardness of the staging is one of the strongest arguments against the authenticity of 1056–80.

It would be possible to argue that the person who wrote 1056–80 was not writing for the stage at all and did not feel any compulsion or perhaps showed no capacity to visualize stage

[1] It is unsafe to argue as does H.-D. Voigtländer (*Philologus* 101 (1957), 230) that because the children's death cries are not childish (1272), we may infer that the children are old enough to be able to perceive that something is amiss with their mother at 1052. One cannot make inferences about the age of a child in tragedy from its diction. See Miss Dale on Eur. *Alc.* 393–415.

[2] Dodds's emendation of the manuscripts' δότ' to δεῦτ' in 1069 is in itself hazardous and does not really solve the problem. See Reeve, loc. cit., p. 56, n. 6.

action. More probably, however, since at least part of the speech was composed before Chrysippus, we are dealing with a speech composed for a fourth-century production of the play. Hence it is legitimate to speculate on the method of production of the scene.

If the children are to remain at 1053 ff. (and surely they must, since there is no legitimate way of bringing them back if they depart), they must communicate to the audience some reason for their failure to obey their mother's command. Those who argue that they remain do indeed assume that there is something about their mother's behaviour which makes them stop. Diller[1] suggests that it is their mother's cry at 1056 that stops them in their tracks. He may be on the right lines. Medea begins at 1053 telling the children to leave, but there is no real difficulty in assuming that they are still on stage when Medea cries out at 1056 ἆ ἆ.[2] Is there anything about this cry that might cause the children to stop or rather that might cause the audience to expect them to stop? Perhaps a scene in the *Bacchae* is relevant: in *Bacch.* 809, Pentheus gives instructions to his attendants ἐκφέρετέ μοι δεῦρ' ὅπλα 'carry out my weapons here', turns to Dionysus σὺ δὲ παῦσαι λέγων 'and you stop talking', and obtains from him the reply:

βούληι cφ' ἐν ὄρεci cυγκαθημέναc ἰδεῖν;

Do you want to see them (sc. the maenads) sitting together on the mountains?

This question is prefaced by the interjection ἆ on which Dodds notes: 'Pentheus has broken off negotiations and turned to leave the stage when the Stranger (Dionysus) recalls him with ἆ. This can hardly be a gasp of astonishment or a groan of pain: but often it expresses an urgent protest "Stop!" cf. *Her.* 1051, *Or.* 1598, *Hel.* 445, *Phil.* 1300.'[3] If one adds to these examples ἆ ἆ in *Med.* 1056, perhaps one has an explanation for the children

---

[1] *Hermes* 94 (1966), 269.

[2] According to Wecklein they are still walking at 1069: 'die Kinder nähern, immer noch nach der Mutter zurückblickend, dem Hause'. They must have been moving *spississimo gradu*.

[3] To Dodds's examples one may add Eur. *Hipp.* 503 where Nauck's conjecture is certain (see Barrett) and Ar. *Thesm.* 689. At Ter. *Phorm.* 809, Chremes' single exclamation 'Ah!' is enough to halt Demipho.

remaining on stage. Medea cries something that corresponds to 'Stop!' and the children, believing themselves to be addressed and that the previous order to depart has been countermanded, naturally stop and wait. In fact it is her heart that Medea is addressing, begging it to desist.

This somewhat melodramatic stage effect might be thought to conform to the known taste of fourth-century actors and audiences. It violates or comes close to violating an 'unwritten law' of Greek dramatic technique: 'one thing at a time':[1] ἆ ἆ must do double duty, misleading the audience and at the same time prefacing Medea's address to her heart.

Heraclidae

When Iolaos apostrophizes Hope in the presence of Demophon (433 ff.) and goes on to speak of Demophon in the third person (τὰ τοῦδ' 435), we ought not to be misled by formal considerations into thinking in terms of an aside. Nor need we think of Iolaos and 'Macaria'[2] as conversing 'apart from', in the sense of out of earshot of, Demophon, in 478–566. There is nothing in their conversation that needs to be concealed from him. The Athenian king stands by politely and allows the exiled Argives to reach their own decisions. As a consequence he is not the centre of the audience's attention and no one will ask what he is supposed to be doing during the course of the long conversation between the two other actors. In fact the subsequent action shows (and dramatic economy demands) that he has heard the conversation, since he interrupts at 567 anticipating the request Iolaos is about to make on Macaria's behalf.

Hippolytus

(a) There are several occasions during the first scene between Phaedra and her nurse where the nurse speaks of Phaedra in the third person. None of these should be called asides. After 249 Phaedra has sunk back on her couch and is, as Barrett says, 'dead to the world'. It is thus easy for the nurse and chorus to converse

[1] See Fraenkel, EP, p. 419.
[2] She is not named during the course of the play.

about her without the audience feeling it odd that she does not take up their remarks. The situation is similar to that found in Soph. *Tr.* 983 ff. There, although the old man and Hyllus converse apart from the newly awakened Hercules who takes no note of their conversation (987–92—formally these resemble eavesdropping asides), their talk can hardly be described as an aside. Conversations in the presence of people who are mad or otherwise distracted or incapacitated by pain need not appeal to convention.[1]

At 288 the nurse makes a renewed attempt to capture Phaedra's attention and continues unsuccessfully down to 300 when she breaks off and talks with the chorus for four lines. This is hardly likely to be an aside. The complaint she makes that she is making no progress is probably meant for Phaedra's ears.

At the end of the scene, however, there is a passage which merits serious consideration as an aside. The nurse, having promised Phaedra that she will bring a potion which will cure her passion, is about to leave the stage. Her exit lines begin as a reassurance to Phaedra that she will reveal nothing to Hippolytus. They end as a prayer to Aphrodite whose statue is on stage:

> 522   μόνον cύ μοι, δέcποινα ποντία Κύπρι,
> cυνεργὸc εἴηc· τἄλλα δ' οἳ ἐγὼ φρονῶ
> τοῖc ἔνδον ἥμιν ἀρκέcει λέξαι φίλοιc.

Only may you be my helper, Aphrodite queen of the sea. The rest of my plans it will suffice to tell my friends inside.

These are, as Barrett says, 'veiled words' and are most likely to suggest to an audience that there is some sinister project in the nurse's mind. If Phaedra hears them, she must accept the invocation of Aphrodite as relevant to the *cure* for love that the nurse has promised her (when one calls on Aphrodite to help in an affair of the heart, it is generally to advance rather than to stop the affair and the audience is probably meant to suspect that this is what the nurse means by her invocation) and the reference to

---

[1] e.g. it would be wrong to speak of the chorus at Aesch. *Ag.* 1078–9 speaking aside.

'friends' as referring to some 'crony' or 'cronies' who are to help effect this cure (Barrett). The audience will probably guess that the reference is in fact to Hippolytus. This may be, then, another of those cases where Euripides is exploiting ambiguous language to heighten the tension,[1] but it is easy to see why some have taken 522–4 and particularly 523b–4 as an aside.[2] Is it conceivable that Phaedra hears the lines without suspecting some sinister implication? On any realistic considerations they ought to awaken the misgivings the nurse has tried to quiet in the line preceding them: even the suggestion that Phaedra's secret is to be shared by the nurse's friends—for that is surely the implication of 523b–4 (so Barrett and Barbieri)—ought to cause Phaedra disquiet. Of course realistic considerations are not always apposite in a discussion of tragic dialogue, and formal considerations may be more to the point here.[3] If the scene had continued with dialogue, the chorus conversing with Phaedra for example, and no mention had been made in it of the nurse's remarks, the lack of realism would have been much more striking. As it is, the lines end the scene and almost before we have time to work out fully their implications and the effect they might have on Phaedra, the chorus is singing the great ode about Eros.

Perhaps the exit lines of the nurse go halfway to being an aside and are in a way not unlike a phenomenon we shall presently discuss, 'the address to a retreating back'[4] (they would be a kind of obverse of this convention). The nurse has moved away from Phaedra towards the door of the palace where stands Aphrodite's statue[5] and it may be that she is far enough away from Phaedra to be imagined as being out of earshot.

(*b*) During the scene where Theseus confronts and accuses his son, Hippolytus turns away and speaks as follows:

---

[1] See above, p. 24.
[2] Murray in his translation has a stage direction describing the nurse's utterance as 'a prayer apart'. Donner in his translation marks the passage 'für sich'. Barbieri assumes that we have an aside (p. 100).
[3] Cf. below, p. 75.   [4] See below, p. 34.
[5] It is clear that this statue is in the actor's line of vision just as he is about to enter the stage building. Note the old attendant's prayer (114 ff.) just before he exits.

1060 ὦ θεοί, τί δῆτα τοὐμὸν οὐ λύω στόμα,
      ὅστις γ' ὑφ' ὑμῶν, οὓς σέβω, διόλλυμαι;
      οὐ δῆτα· πάντως οὐ πίθοιμ' ἂν οὕς με δεῖ,
      μάτην δ' ἂν ὅρκους συγχέαιμ' οὓς ὤμοσα.

O gods, why then don't I break my silence since I am being de-
stroyed by you whom I reverence? No, I shall not. In any case
I would not convince those whom I must and I would in vain break
the oath I swore.

Theseus reacts as follows:

1064 οἴμοι· τὸ σεμνὸν ὥς μ' ἀποκτενεῖ τὸ σόν.
      οὐκ εἶ πατρώιας ἐκτὸς ὡς τάχιστα γῆς;

Alas! How your arrogance will kill me! Get out of this land with
all haste!

Several critics have assumed without question that 1060–3 is an
aside.[1] Only Paley states his reasons. Commenting on 1033, he
says 'by οὐ θέμις Theseus is to understand merely that he [Hippo-
lytus] does not mean to inquire into what may concern husband
and wife. For Theseus does not know he has taken any oath of
secrecy. Hence in v. 1063 the words are addressed to the gods
only and are not supposed to be heard by Theseus.' The lines
may or may not have been supposed to have been heard by
Theseus, but his reply surely indicates that he has heard them.[2]
It was open to Euripides to make it clear that Hippolytus' outburst was not heard by Theseus. If Theseus had not taken up the
lines, but proceeded directly to his command to Hippolytus to
leave Trozen, we would be justified in describing the lines as an
aside. As it is, Theseus clearly takes up Hippolytus' σέβω when he
says τὸ σεμνόν. He has heard what his son has said, but has not
really been listening.[3] Hippolytus has all but let slip the truth,

    [1] Of commentators, in addition to Paley, Mahaffy and Bury, and Harry (J. E.
Harry, *Euripides, Hippolytos*, (Boston, 1904)) take it in this way. They are followed
by Flickinger, *The Greek Theater and its Drama*, p. 312.
    [2] Barbieri (p. 101) points this out.
    [3] 'Theseus is blind to the implications of what Hippolytos has said' (Barrett on
1064). See also Schwinge, pp. 44 f. Paley's comment on 1064 is curious: 'τὸ σεμνόν:
he means the invocation of the gods, but . . . it is not intended that Theseus should
hear that any oath has been taken of secrecy. For this would at once have afforded
a very specious evidence of his son's guilt.' This would imply that Theseus hears
1060–1, but not 1062–3.

but it is characteristic of Theseus in this scene that he will not listen to him: lines 1034–5, riddling though they may be, are another hint that Hippolytus is keeping something back. To regard 1060–3 as an aside obscures a fine touch by the poet. It is easy to see why the lines should have been taken thus: the form suggests it.[1] The aside convention might well have grown out of a turning away such as this one.

Hecuba

(a) When Hecuba asks her attendant why she has returned carrying (as Hecuba thinks) Polyxena's corpse, the woman exclaims:

> ἥδ' οὐδὲν οἶδεν, ἀλλά μοι Πολυξένην
> 675 θρηνεῖ, νέων δὲ πημάτων οὐχ ἅπτεται.

This woman knows nothing: she laments over Polyxena to me and does not touch upon her new woes.

Hecuba then says:

> οἲ 'γὼ τάλαινα· μῶν τὸ βακχεῖον κάρα
> 677 τῆς θεσπιῳδοῦ δεῦρο Κασσάνδρας φέρεις;

Wretched me! Surely you are not bringing me the frenzied seer Cassandra?

There are two questions to be decided here. Whom is the woman addressing in 674–5? Does Hecuba hear what she says? Since the attendant earlier conversed with the chorus (657–60, 663–4), it is tempting to assume here that she breaks off her conversation with Hecuba and resumes her talk with the chorus. It is possible, however, and perhaps indeed more probable that the lines do not presuppose any particular auditor. They simply express an uncontrolled emotional reaction. Of this, more below.[2]

---

[1] Cf. below, p. 79. The suggestion that a secret is about to be revealed helps people to think of the lines in this way. Cf. Leo's approach to the Sophocles fragment quoted above (p. 19).

[2] See below, p. 72. Aesch. *Ag.* 1078–9 is a good parallel since there the chorus is alone with Cassandra.

Since the lines, whoever they are addressed to, are clearly not directed at Hecuba, they have often been taken as an aside.[1] This is possible, but there is another way of imagining the production here. With the lines as an aside, Hecuba, on hearing no reply to her question, interprets the attendant's silence as portending something sinister and *guesses* that the body is that of another of her children, one whom she had believed alive. If, however, the emotional reaction of the attendant in 674–5 is overt (and is there any cogent dramatic reason for assuming that the woman is concealing her feelings?), then Hecuba's emotional reaction and query about Cassandra are motivated by what she has just heard νέων δὲ πημάτων 'new woes'. This point is made by Hadley ad loc. He notes: 'this couplet 674–5 is spoken half-aside, but Hecuba hears enough to learn that the body is that of some fresh victim.' I do not see that the qualification 'enough' is necessary. Hecuba's response does just as well if she has heard the whole of the attendant's speech. This and the term 'half-aside' which often crops up in commentaries betray a confusion of approach towards asides. Hadley appears to be assuming that some sort of dramatic convention is operating, yet his own explanation makes this assumption unnecessary. Again a 'turning away' has been mistaken for an aside.[2]

(*b*) At 812, Hecuba sees Agamemnon making as if to depart (ποῖ μ' ὑπεξάγεις πόδα;) and for the moment gives up her attempt to persuade him to give her aid. Instead she makes some general reflections on the personified abstraction Πειθώ, 'Persuasion', and the insufficient attention given to that deity. Only at 824 does she resume her plea with a new argument. Tierney[3]

---

[1] Meridier places 'à part' beside them without further comment. M. Tierney (*Euripides Hecuba* (Dublin, 1946)) too takes them as an aside. Paley accepting without question that the lines are an aside wants to read ἡ δ' in 674, 'for this distich is said aside, the less direct reference to Hecuba seems more appropriate'. I do not understand this reasoning or see what the point of δέ would then be. Nor do I understand why Barbieri (p. 102) describes the lines as an unsuccessful aside in counter-distinction to many other similar passages where a remark overheard is taken without qualification as an aside.

[2] See above, p. 31.

[3] Op. cit., p. 91.

describes 812–23 as 'virtually a soliloquy, if not actually an aside'. Mention of an aside in this connection is misleading. What we have here is one of many instances in Greek drama where some pressure from without or within causes a character to turn away from the person he has been addressing to reflect generally or to express his emotions.[1] Such a quasi-soliloquy is conventional in the sense that it is unrealistic for conversations to be interrupted at length and for the interlocutor to stand idly by, waiting for his partner to end his reflections. The aside, however, is a convention which makes the further demand that the audience assume the interlocutor incapable of hearing his partner. A passage like this is not an aside because nothing in it is obviously meant to be concealed from the interlocutor and there is nothing remarkable about his failure to refer to it later. The fact that a character turns away is not on its own evidence that he is speaking aside.[2]

Electra

(a) On first entering (54), Electra does not observe her husband. He addresses her at 64 with a question that we believe she has already answered in her entrance speech (57 ff.).[3] This, however, does not necessarily mean that the man has not heard what she said there, that the audience are to assume that some sort of convention was operating whereby Electra's remarks went unheard.[4] The question the *autourgos* puts to her at 64 is scarcely a demand for information. Its tone is one of wry resignation at his wife's behaviour: he has told her before not to carry out tasks like

---

[1] See the index to Schadewaldt, s.v. Selbstäusserung; he discusses this passage on pp. 129 f.
[2] See above, p. 32, and below, p. 57.
[3] The text of 57 ff. is uncertain. I do not think either Murray's or Denniston's acceptable and believe with Kirchhoff and Morel (*Bursian* 238 (1933), 241) that 59 should be deleted (perhaps officiously interpolated by someone thinking ahead to 125 ff.). I do not share their belief that 57 and 58 should go as well. J. Diggle (*PCPhS* n.s. 15 (1969), 52) would read the lines in the order 56, 59, 57.
[4] Even if they were, they ought not to be described as an aside. See below, p. 61.

the one she has just performed.[1] His question is in fact a kind of gentle rebuke.[2]

(b) ll. 1142–6, although addressed to Clytaemnestra, cannot be heard by her since they explicitly forecast her death (the line preceding them θύϲειϲ γὰρ οἷα χρή ϲε δαίμοϲιν θύῃ 'for you will make the kind of sacrifice to the gods that you must', though sinister, is still ambiguous).[3] Presumably Clytaemnestra starts to move towards Electra's house at 1139. If she has not gone in by 1142, we must assume that she is out of earshot and that a kind of convention similar to that of the aside is operating. But Murray is probably right to insert a space between 1141 and 1142 to indicate that between the delivery of the two lines Clytaemnestra has left the stage.

There are many occasions in Greek drama where a character pursues another with words as he leaves the stage, addressing, so to speak, his retreating back.[4] This one is exceptional in that it contains statements that must on no account be heard by the addressee. Amphitryon's remarks to the retreating back of Lycus (Eur. *H.F.* 726–8), though more defiant than any utterance in the previous dialogue, can be taken simply as a general

---

[1] As often in question clauses, the γάρ of 64 is hard to classify. I do not find Denniston (p. 78) altogether convincing in this instance. Perhaps it signifies (mock) surprise.

[2] In his commentary, Denniston implies that the *autourgos* leaves the stage after speaking the prologue, to return again at 63, and that this explains his question at 64: he was not present when Electra uttered 57–9. There seems to me no justification for this assumption. If he had gone back into his house at 53 (and where else could he go?), he would have met Electra coming out. It is certain that her first entrance is from the house. She tells us she is going to *fetch* water (55–7) and it is clear when she returns she is carrying a newy filled urn (112). Hence the natural inference is that when she first enters carrying this pot (τόδ' ἄγγος 55), she is setting out from the house. It would be pointless to have the *autourgos* exit without motive only to return (again without motive) in the space of ten lines.

[3] 'χρή ϲε θύειν [θύειν cannot be right; see W. Schulze, *Quaestiones Epicae* (Gütersloh, 1892), p. 334, n. 4]: Der Anfang der Rede, während dessen Klytämnestra noch nahe ist, deutet das Bevorstehende an, nachher wird die Rede immer deutlicher', Wecklein.

[4] e.g. Aesch. *Suppl.* 952–3, Soph. *Ai.* 1161–2, Soph. *Phil.* 1259–60 (Soph. *Tr.* 813 is quite different: there the chorus expect an answer from Deianira), Eur. *Alc.* 72 ff., Eur. *Med.* 623–4, Eur. *Suppl.* 284–7, Eur. *Or.* 630 f., 718 ff., Eur. *Bacch.* 358–9, and from comedy Ar. *Lys.* 611–13. One might also adduce Theocr. 14. 36 ff. See also O. Taplin, *GRBS* 12 (1971), 42.

threat that, since the wicked are punished, Lycus will eventually receive his just deserts: they do not give the game away as Electra's words here would if Clytaemnestra heard them.[1]

I.T.

As Iphigenia tells Orestes and Pylades, of whose identity she is as yet unaware, the contents of the letter she wishes one of them to take for her to Argos, she is interrupted by Orestes:

> 774 Ἰφ. κόμιcαί μ' ἐc Ἄργος, ὦ cύναιμε, πρὶν θανεῖν
> ἐκ βαρβάρου γῆc καὶ μετάcτηcον θεᾶc
> cφαγίων, ἐφ' οἷcι ξενοφόνουc τιμὰc ἔχω —
> 777 Ὀρ. Πυλάδη, τί λέξω; ποῦ ποτ' ὄνθ' ηὑρήμεθα;
> Ἰφ. ἢ coῖc ἀραιὰ δώμαcιν γενήcομαι . . .

Iph. Take me to Argos, my brother, from a barbarous land before
I die and remove me from the goddess's sacrifices, at which
I have duties connected with the slaughter of strangers—
Or. Pylades, what am I to say? Where on earth have we been
found to be?
Iph. else I will be accursed to your household . . .

It is obvious that 777 is an aside. Iphigenia continues reciting her letter as though there had been no interruption and completes the sentence begun before Orestes' interruption. This is in contrast with 780 where the exclamation ὦ θεοί, 'gods!', provokes a surprised question from her. It is also remarkable in that Orestes' interruption follows a warning against interruptions made by Iphigenia three lines earlier. Here we have an example of the second type of aside envisaged above (see p. 17)—X talking to Z in Y's presence, but without being heard by Y.

---

[1] 'Amphitryon sagt diese Worte nicht mehr zu Lykos, der sich auf die Tür zu bewegt, aber doch nicht in Hörweite ist, so dass die Drohung auch eine allgemeine Deutung auf Gottliches Strafgericht zulassen muss. Erst wo er den Chor anredet, kann Amphitryon unverblümt sprechen', Wilamowitz. Similarly in *Hecuba*, Hecuba sends Polymestor off the stage with sinister but ambiguous remarks. Once he is off stage, the chorus address him openly:

> 1024 οὔπω δέδωκαc ἀλλ' ἴcωc δώcειc δίκην.

The scholia here wrongly speak of *sotto voce* performance by the chorus (cf. above, p. 18 n. 1, on Aesch. *Cho.* 46).

In Murray's text, 782 is also an aside, but this is one
of the least plausible attempts to interpret a much vexed
passage.[1]

Ion

(a) Bayfield makes Creusa's remarks in 252–4 an aside. Certainly she has turned away from Ion to exclaim 'O wretched
women! O violent acts of the gods! etc.', but Ion clearly hears
what she says. His reaction (255) τί χρῆμ' ἀνερμήνευτα δυσθυμῆι,
γύναι; 'Why do you utter things difficult to interpret in your
despondency, woman?', is much more apt if it takes up 252–4
than if the reference is back to what Creusa said directly before
them. There is nothing 'difficult to interpret' about the latter
passage, whereas ἀνερμήνευτα δυσθυμῆι from the point of view of
Ion is an exact description of the schetliasmus contained in 252–4.

---

[1] Murray there emends L's οὖν to οὐκ, thereby destroying the idiom, and translates 'no need for us to question; we shall hear things marvellous' (a somewhat
similar approach in Donner's translation). This he gives with L to Pylades. It seems
a singularly pointless remark. Jackson has clearly demonstrated (*Marginalia
Scaenica*, pp. 9 ff.) that 782 is in place where it stands as long as we accept Weil's
ἀφίξεται for L's ἀφίξομαι and give the line to Iphigenia. In addition, however, he
postulates a complicated transposition whereby 780–1 follow 769 and are themselves followed by 779. I do not expect he will win many adherents (cf. H. Strohm,
Gnomon 28 (1956), 335, and Schwinge, pp. 238 ff.). Schwinge contests Jackson's
assertion that the most appropriate place for the exclamation ὦ θεοί is directly
after the first mention of the name Orestes and that the most natural place for the
repetition of the name comes directly after this. In the main his arguments are
convincing. The mention of Orestes' name for the second time is perfectly in place
at the end of the résumé of the letter. On the question of whether or not it is appropriate to have an immediate reaction from Orestes at the first mention of his
name, however, if this were a real-life situation, one could not but agree with Jackson. Schwinge tries to minimize the surprise of the mention of the name by reminding us that at least Orestes knows that the letter is to go to Argos. Even so,
to hear one's own name in such circumstances and in such a place would surely
provoke some sort of reaction. Even in the pseudo-reality of drama one would be
hard put to it to find a character so well able to reconcile himself to coincidence
as Schwinge's Orestes. What audience could work out Orestes' reactions by thinking back to 660 ff. where Orestes comments on Iphigenia's interest in Argos and
deduces that she is an Argive? In a modern production, Orestes would begin to
display his reactions as soon as he heard his name, and perhaps he made some
sort of gesture even in an ancient production. As it is, Euripides makes Orestes
choose to take up a point which is even more surprising than the mention of his own
name, the reference to Iphigenia and the assertion that she is still alive. This is
dramatically effective and there is no need to look for psychological explanations
in order to excuse it.

Here again (cf. above, p. 33 on *Hec.* 812 ff.) we have a commentator mistakenly describing an emotional outburst as an aside.

(*b*) During the stichomythia that follows, Creusa confirms that her ancestor was earth-born:

268 Ἐριχθόνιός γε· τὸ δὲ γένος μ' οὐκ ὠφελεῖ.

Yes, Ericthonius—but my ancestry does not help me.

Ion does not take up the second part of this line, but proceeds with another question. This reaction is in contrast with his response to a similarly puzzling exclamation of Creusa later in the scene[1] and one might be tempted to take 'but my ancestry does not help me' as an aside. Ion, however, has already ignored another mysterious reply:

264 τοσαῦτα κεὐτυχοῦμεν, ὦ ξέν', οὐ πέρα.

So far I am fortunate, stranger, no further.

The audience knows what Creusa means by this and by her remark at the end of 268, and a certain amount of dramatic tension is created[2] as a response from Ion is awaited. He reacts, however, in neither case, proceeding with his genealogical questions. I am not certain whether an audience is supposed to apply naturalistic demands here. The spectator, if struck by Ion's failure to take up some of the strange things Creusa says, assumes perhaps that he does not comment because he can make nothing of them.

(*c*) 425 Λοξίας δ' ἐὰν θέληι
νῦν ἀλλὰ τὰς πρὶν ἀναλαβεῖν ἁμαρτίας,
ἅπας μὲν οὐ γένοιτ' ἂν εἰς ἡμᾶς φίλος,
ὅσον δὲ χρήιζει — θεὸς γάρ ἐστι — δέξομαι.

Apollo if he wishes even now to compensate his earlier mistakes would not be a friend in all respects to me, but whatever he desires —he is after all a god—I shall accept.

[1] ὡς μήποτ' ὤφελόν cφ' ἰδεῖν in 286 provokes the question τί δὲ cτυγεῖc cὺ τοῦ θεοῦ τὰ φίλτατα;

[2] 'Dies sachliche Interesse [in the early history of Athens] ist Ion zugeordnet, ist der Faden, an dem er äusserlich das Gespräch führt: Kreusas Antworten aber brechen immer wieder aus: 264 οὐ πέρα 268 τὸ γένος μ' οὐκ ὠφελεῖ— Dieser Gegensatz zwischen dem äusseren Verlauf und der inneren Situation gibt der Stichomythie wie dem ganzen Stück seine dramatische Tension', M. Imhof, *Euripides' Ion— Eine literarische Studie* (Bern, 1966), p. 70, n. 49.

So speaks Creusa just after Xuthus has left the stage.[1] Ion on the other hand is present and within earshot when she speaks the lines. It is clear in fact from the opening of his soliloquy which follows immediately on Creusa's exit that he has been listening to what Creusa has been saying:

> 429 τί ποτε λόγοιςιν ἡ ξένη πρὸς τὸν θεὸν
> κρυπτοῖςιν[2] αἰεὶ λοιδοροῦς' αἰνίςςεται;

Why is the foreign woman for ever abusing the god in obscure terms?

Those who describe 425b–8 as an aside[3] are therefore mis-applying the term. These lines are an emotional outburst similar to 252–4, but there is no suggestion that anything is being concealed from the one person there to hear them, Ion. To the outsider the lines sound obscure and impious, but they do not give away Creusa's position. They could still, at a pinch, be taken as reflecting her indignation over the way Apollo has treated her (fictitious) friend: one could still take the 'mistakes' as referring to what Apollo is supposed to have done to this woman rather than to anything that personally affected Creusa. We may note that earlier when Creusa makes an even more indignant accusation of Apollo, despite her passion, she

---

[1] At 418 he says ϲτείχοιμ' ἂν εἴϲω and then spends four lines explaining his in-tentions and telling Creusa what she is to do. After his command to Creusa in 423–4, we are to assume that he is on the move. It does not matter whether or not he hears Creusa's acknowledgement of his orders ἔϲται τάδ' ἔϲται in 425. He is cer-tainly to be regarded as out of earshot by the time Creusa delivers the lines quoted above.

[2] Cf. Soph. El. 638 and the discussion below, p. 77.

[3] e.g. Mahaffy, A History of Classical Greek Literature, i. 345: 'This feature the aside recurs in the famous dialogue between Ion and Creusa (Ion 424 ff. [sic]) and elsewhere in the play and may belong to the later style of Euripides.' In his book on Euripides he also marks 252–4 as an aside, but does not go on to substantiate the assertion that the aside is a feature of the later Euripides. A. Spira (Untersuchungen zum Deus ex Machina bei Sophokles und Euripides (Kallmünz, 1960), p. 52) speaks of Creusa's remarks 'zur Seite'. All these Ion passages (and many more besides) are signalled as asides by 'H. B. L(ennard)' (The Ion of Euripides now first translated with stage directions, London, 1889) who, encouraged perhaps by the title of his work, set out to supply the play with as many misleading and unnecessary stage directions as possible.

maintains the fiction that she is indignant about the maltreatment of a friend (384–5).[1]

Helen

(a) After Helen's prologue speech comes the unexpected arrival of Teucer who at first takes her for the 'real' Helen. Once she has convinced him that she is not Helen, she begins questioning him about the fate of the various Greeks who went to Troy. The dialogue following Teucer's statement that Menelaus is rumoured to be dead proceeds as follows:

> 133   Ἑλ. ἀπωλόμεcθα. Θεcτιὰc δ' ἔcτιν κόρη;
> Τε. Λήδαν ἔλεξαc; οἴχεται θανοῦcα δή.

Helen   I am done for. But is the daughter of Thestius still alive?
Teucer   You mean Leda? She is dead.

Later when Helen asks about her brothers, the Dioscuri, we hear:

> 138   Τε. τεθνᾶcι καὶ οὐ τεθνᾶcι· δύο δ' ἐcτὸν λόγω.
> Ἑλ. πότεροc ὁ κρείccων; ὦ τάλαιν' ἐγὼ κακῶν.
> Τε. ἄcτροιc cφ' ὁμοιωθέντε φάc' εἶναι θεώ.

Teucer   They are dead and yet not dead. There are two stories about them.
Helen   Which is the prevailing one? O wretched that I am!
Teucer   They say they are gods, made like stars.

ἀπωλόμεcθα, 'I am done for' (133a), and ὦ τάλαιν' ἐγὼ κακῶν, 'O wretched that I am' (139b), seem excessively strong reactions for an outsider (and that is what Helen is pretending to be) on being told of the misfortunes of the Spartan royal family. Despite this Teucer comments on neither exclamation.[2] Instead, on each

---

[1]
> ὦ Φοῖβε, κἀκεῖ κἀνθάδ' οὐ δίκαιοc εἶ
> ἐc τὴν ἀποῦcαν, ἧc πάρειcιν οἱ λόγοι.

(F. W. Schmidt deleted 385). Another example of a character 'covering up' or explaining away an emotional outburst is contained in Eur. El. 290. See below on Eur. Hel. 125, p. 41 n. 1.

[2] Contrast an analogous situation at I.T. 549 f. There, on being told by Orestes of the death of Agamemnon, Iphigenia who, like Helen here, has not revealed her identity, exclaims τάλαιν' ἐγώ. Instead of taking up her questions at the beginning of the line, Orestes asks her why she has reacted so emotionally at the news of Agamemnon's death (τί δ' ἐcτέναξαc τοῦτο; μῶν προcῆκέ cοι;) and Iphigenia is ready in the next line with an explanation which allows her later expressions of pity for the Argive royal house (557) to go by without comment.

occasion, he answers Helen's questions, the first of which is placed after an exclamation, the second before one. The natural assumption is that the audience is supposed to believe that Teucer hears neither of Helen's cries, that is to say that an aside-convention is operating.[1]

Schwinge (p. 328), however, does not accept this. Teucer, he asserts, does hear the words in question, but simply pays no attention to them. Both exclamations are juxtaposed to questions and Teucer must answer these questions before he makes any other comment. This point has no validity: reference to Eur. *I.T.* 549–50 (cited above, p. 39 n. 2) is enough to show that there is no such rule in stichomythia.

Schwinge also argues that it suits Teucer's own purposes to ignore Helen's strange behaviour. He is in a hurry and wishes to terminate the interview as soon as possible in order to leave and find Theonoe. The evidence adduced for this assertion about Teucer's intentions is lines 143 ff.

> ἅλις δὲ μύθων· οὐ διπλᾶ χρήιζω στένειν.
> ὧν δ' οὕνεκ' ἦλθον τούςδε βαςιλείους δόμους . . .
> ςὺ προξένηςον . . .

Enough of talk. I have no desire of double lamentation. But you assist me in the business which brought me to the palace . . .

But this is to make retrospective inferences about Teucer's state of mind. If Teucer had expressed a desire to depart or created an impression of urgency *before* Helen uttered 133a and 139b, one *might* have been entitled to infer that throughout the scene Euripides wished the audience to believe that his main interest was in departing. As it is, there is nothing in the text to explain Teucer's lack of reaction. It is hard to believe that a competent dramatist would keep the audience on tenterhooks as regards the behaviour of a minor character like Teucer—even Schwinge admits that his behaviour is astonishing ('dieses erstaunliche

---

[1] This is a general assumption shared by e.g. Barbieri (p. 107), Wecklein, A. Y. Campbell, Kannicht, Dale, Zwierlein, p. 66, n. 5, and W. Ludwig (*Sapheneia: Ein Beitrag zur Formkunst im Spätwerk des Euripides*, Inaugural dissertation, Tübingen, 1954, p. 57).

Verhalten')—and then ten lines later provide an explanation so that the audience could think back and say 'Ah! That was why he ignored Helen's ἀπωλόμεcθα!'. There is tension and suspense in this scene, but it centres on Helen, not Teucer. Will she or will she not reveal her true identity?[1] The audience must not be distracted from this issue by being required to speculate about Teucer's travelling arrangements.[2]

If one wanted to contest the notion that 133a and 139b are asides, a much more promising approach would be to stress the artificiality of stichomythic dialogue (and perhaps the speed with which it was delivered—the audience scarcely has time to stop and think). One could argue from the analogy of a passage like the one just discussed (*Ion* 268 ff.) where it appears extremely unnatural for one part of a line in stichomythia to be ignored by the interlocutor. This would be an extreme position to take with regard to the *Helen* scene. In the *Ion*, Creusa's mood has been established before the passage in question. The audience is already familiar with her tendency towards passionate outbursts and her (to Ion) mysterious accusations of Apollo. Ion has already commented on her strange behaviour. With such preparation and in such circumstances, it would seem much less remarkable for a mysterious utterance like 268b to go by without comment than it would for Teucer to hear *Hel.* 133a and 139b and not to comment on either of them. There has been no sign up till then of

---

[1] Earlier (125) she invents an ambivalent explanation to cover up for her involuntary cry αἲ αἲ (oddly Barbieri takes 125 as an aside).

[2] In any case some of the evidence Schwinge adduces as evidence for Teucer's state of mind is of dubious value. Teucer's termination of the conversation is supposed to be abrupt, indicating that he is in a hurry. ἅλιc δὲ μύθων· οὐ διπλᾶ χρῄιζω cτένειν might in real life appear abrupt behaviour and brusque language, but it is hazardous to use conventional formulae of transition in tragic dialogue to make inferences about the character or state of mind of the speaker. The conversation between Helen and Teucer must at some stage be terminated: the πρόcωπον προτατικόν must be removed from the stage leaving it empty for the central character to lament (see Kannicht ad loc.). It may be that ἅλιc δὲ μύθων had some additional function, but speculation here is unwise. If indeed one approaches the scene in Schwinge's way, one might ask why, if Teucer is in such a hurry, he is so leisurely in departing. If anyone's state of mind is relevant at this point, it is the poet's. It is time to get rid of Teucer. This is neatly achieved by having him close the stichomythia by raising a topic which both explains why he is here at all and provides a motive for his departure.

emotional disturbance in Helen. This makes Teucer's failure to
react all the more strange.[1]

That the second part of a line in stichomythia should go by
unheard and unanswered, as at *Hel.* 139b, is perhaps more striking than the case of *Hel.* 133a where it is the first part that is
ignored. The formal pattern of reply (or question) followed by
comment not addressed to the interlocutor in patterned[2]
dialogue can be paralleled often in Greek tragedy.[3] In *Andr.* 70,
Andromache asks a question of her attendant and reacts emotionally in the following line. Her attendant ignores the exclamation
and replies to the question. Nothing hangs on whether or not the
attendant is supposed to hear Andromache's expression of dis-
may in 71b—she is sympathetic towards her and Andromache
would feel no compulsion to hide her feelings from her. *Hel.* 139b
displays the same pattern, but a conventional element has been
added.

(*b*) Menelaus, travelling incognito, has just been informed by
the old concierge that Helen is in the house:

> Με. πόθεν μολοῦca; τίνα τὸ πρᾶγμ' ἔχει λόγον;
> Γρ. Λακεδαίμονος γῆc δεῦρο νοcτήcαc' ἄπο.
> 475 Με. πότε; οὔ τί που λελήιcμεθ' ἐξ ἄντρων λέχοc;

Men.   How did she get there? What does this mean?
Woman She came here from Sparta.
Men.   When? Surely my wife hasn't been stolen from the cave?

Whereupon the old woman instead of asking 'what do you mean
by that?' simply replies to the question 'When?' Here the considerations are the same as they were with 133a and 139b. If the
old woman hears 475b, surely she ought to react to it. Commentators are virtually at one in describing 475b as an aside.[4] The

---

[1] Additional confirmation that *Hel.* 133a and 139b are asides is obtained if one
accepts what is said about Ar. *Thesm.* 603b, 604b, below, p. 98.

[2] I borrow this term (and slightly alter its application, using it to include formal
dialogue related to stichomythia such as two lines answering two) from Miss
Bradbrook, p. 97.

[3] Cf. Soph. *El.* 883, 925, 930, *O.T.* 746, 754 f., *Phil.* 1231, Eur. *Hipp.* 342, *Ion*
268.

[4] Barnes was the first. His note on the line (his 482) is: 'reliquam versus partem
secum mirabundus mussitat ut in nostris scaenis fieri saepenumero videmus.' It is

pattern is the same as that of 139b: question plus aside-comment followed by answer which ignores that comment.

It is possible that 473 contains the same sort of aside.[1] In 474 the woman takes account only of the question 'How did she get there?', and the second question is redundant. One might think of it as a mere line-filler, but it is preferable to take it as a surprised exclamation. There are two ways of translating it, either 'What reason is there in this?' (Pearson) or 'How is this to be explained?' (Pearson—'was soll das bedeuten?', Kannicht). Pearson opts for the latter, but the former suits the context better: 'this is absurd' (Kannicht), 'het heeft geen zin, het is absurd' (Italie). On hearing that Helen is in the palace, Menelaus is astonished and asks for confirmation. On being told that Helen, the daughter of Tyndareus, is indeed there, his first reaction is to ask how she got there, his second to exclaim that what he has been told cannot be true. With this interpretation, we are probably justified in calling 473b an aside, exactly parallel to the aside that occurs two lines later. One must allow, however, that 473b is much less in need of a response from the old woman, if she hears it, than 475b. It is after all surprising to hear that Helen is in Egypt and a stranger's surprised reaction to the news will hardly surprise the person imparting it. It is because 475b is so demonstrably an aside that a case can be made out for so describing our line.

(*c*) Two lines in the recognition scene are often regarded as asides:[2]

559   *Με.*   οὐπώποτ᾽ εἶδον προσφερέστερον δέμας.
      Ελ.   ὦ θεοί· θεὸς γὰρ καὶ τὸ γιγνώσκειν φίλους.

odd that several commentators—Barnes himself, Hermann ('submissa voce haec dicit Menelaus'), Paley, Grégoire—signal this line as an aside, but say nothing of *Hel.* 133a and 139b. Perhaps this is because 475b has a more conventional appearance than either of the other two: it looks like an aside that is there for the audience's benefit.

  [1] So Barbieri (pp. 108 f.) and Kannicht.
  [2] So Barbieri (p. 110—he also takes 564 f. in the same way wrongly), Ammendola, and Kannicht. Kannicht takes οὐδ᾽ ἔχω τί φῶ 564b as an aside, but surely Menelaus takes up these words.

Men.   I have never seen a form more like [Helen's]!

Hel.   O gods!—for recognizing a dear one is indeed the equivalent of a god.

These exclamations explain and justify the questions each has
put to the other with regard to the other's identity in 557–8 and
are followed by a more specific question from Menelaus which
sets the recognition in train. Though it would be misleading to
think of either speaker as trying to conceal his or her emotions, it
may well be right to think of them turning away when they
speak: the formal analogies of this kind of 'double aside' are to be
found in New Comedy.[1]

Orestes

During the long speech in which Orestes begs his uncle
Menelaus for help (640–79), he begins to appeal to Menelaus in
the name of the person he himself has most reason to hate,
Helen. He cannot bring himself to name her and breaks off his
appeal in the following manner:

671   ὦ μέλεος ἐμῶν κακῶν,
         ἐς οἷον ἥκω. τί δέ; ταλαιπωρεῖν με δεῖ·
         ὑπὲρ γὰρ οἴκου παντὸς ἱκετεύω τάδε.

(τάδε refers to the supplication in general, not just to what
follows, cf. Eur. *Hec.* 750.)

O wretched me! To what a pass have I come! But what of it? I
must bring myself to endure it. This supplication is on behalf of
the whole household.

After this, he once more addresses Menelaus.

Commentators from the scholia onwards are agreed that
these words constitute an aside.[2] Since it would hardly help

---

[1] See below, p. 162 n. 2. Pearson writes on *Hel.* 1197 'οὐδέν τι χαίρω coîc λόγοιc
τὰ δ' εὐτυχῶ is spoken half-aside; he then addresses Helen directly.' I presume that
here (cf. the use of the term by other commentators, pp. 32, 49) he means that
the second part of the line is an aside ('τὰ δ' εὐτυχῶ dit wordt terzijde gezegd:
Theoclymenus spreekt zijn voldeening niet terstond openlijk uit' Italie). I am not
sure that it is necessary to have Theoclymenus hide his feelings here.

[2] So e.g. Paley, Wecklein, Wedd, Chapoutier, Wilamowitz (*Hermes* 59 (1924),
260 = *Kl. Schr.* IV. 353), Barbieri, and Biehl. The scholion on 671 runs as follows:
τὰ δὲ ἐξῆc ἠρέμα (see above, p. 18) καθ' ἑαυτὸν λέγει οἰκτίρων ἑαυτὸν ὅτι μέχρι

Orestes' cause if Menelaus were to hear them, this is the most natural way of staging the speech. The assumption that Orestes is speaking aside is reinforced if we look back to 670 where Orestes attempts to forestall the charges of hypocrisy and flattery when he begins to speak of Menelaus' love for Helen: 671b–3 confirm that Orestes is insincere, that he is forcing himself for the sake of his whole family to resort to an argument which exploits Menelaus' love for his wife.

This is the first aside we have found in an extended rhesis. Although Orestes' speech is formally a statement of a case before a person who has to be convinced (on the formulaic λέγοιμ' ἂν ἤδη which begins it see Fraenkel on Aesch. *Ag.* 838), Euripides uses the situation to show Orestes' real feelings and to heighten the pathos of the scene.[1] This technique of having a character turn away from his interlocutor in the course of a longish speech is not, as has sometimes been suggested, exclusively a feature of Euripides' 'late' style (*Orestes* was produced in 409). In *Andromache*, a play which on metrical grounds is dated in the 420s, the heroine who is pleading for her life before Menelaus (387 ff.) breaks off and begins to lament her fate:

> 394 οἴμοι κακῶν τῶνδ', ὦ τάλαιν' ἐμὴ πατρίς,
> ὡς δεινὰ πάσχω.

Alas these woes, o wretched homeland, how terribly I suffer!

She continues in this vein, convincing herself that it is useless to go on living, until at 410 she begins once more to address Menelaus. From 394 to 410 we have a kind of soliloquy,[2] but

---

τοσούτου προῆλθεν αὐτῶι τὰ τῆς δυστυχίας, ὡς διὰ τοῦ μεμνῆςθαι τῆς Ἑλένης προς-δοκᾶν βοηθείας τυχεῖν. ἀνάξιον γὰρ ἑαυτοῦ ἡγεῖται τὸ καὶ μόνον μεμνῆςθαι τοιαύτης γυναικός, μήτι γε δοκεῖν cώιζεcθαι δι' αὐτῆς.

[1] Cf. Wilamowitz cited above: 'und nun gibt er sich einen Stoss; einige *a parte* gesprochenen Worte verhelfen uns dazu, die Überwindung zu fühlen, mit der er den verachteten Oheim bei seiner ihm verhassten Frau beschwört und alle Register des Pathos zieht. Wenn das der Schauspieler herausbringt, muss es prächtig werken, freilich ganz anders, als wir es auf der tragischen Bühne von einem Heros erwarten.'

[2] See Schadewaldt, pp. 222 f.

there is no reason to describe Andromache as speaking aside. The element of novelty in the *Orestes* passage is that the content of the soliloquy must not be heard by the interlocutor.

Bacchae

The great scene in which Dionysus leads his willing victim Pentheus to start his journey to Cithaeron and destruction (912–76) raises the same kind of difficulties of interpretation as we found in *Medea*. Much of what Dionysus says to Pentheus is ambiguous. Behind utterances that might sound innocent enough to Pentheus, the audience is liable to detect sinister predictions of what is really going to befall him.[1] There are, however, certain places where it is hard to extract an innocent meaning from what Dionysus says. In these cases editors have tended to draw the conclusion that Dionysus' words cannot be heard by Pentheus, that they must be spoken aside.[2]

The most striking of such passages occur towards the end of the scene in 'distichomythia':

> Πε. καὶ μὴν δοκῶ cφᾶc ἐν λόχμαιc ὄρνιθαc ὡc
> λέκτρων ἔχεcθαι φιλτάτοιc ἐν ἔρκεcιν.
> Δι. οὐκοῦν ἐπ' αὐτὸ τοῦτ' ἀποcτέλληι φύλαξ·
> 960 λήψηι δ' ἴcωc cφᾶc, ἢν cὺ μὴ ληφθῆιc πάροc.
> Πε. κόμιζε διὰ μέcηc με Θηβαίαc χθονόc.

Pe. Yes, I seem to see them [the maenads] in the thickets, like birds caught in the sweetest snares of love.
Di. Well, you are being sent as a guard for this very purpose. You may well catch them—if you are not caught yourself first.
Pe. Take me through the middle of Thebes . . .

Both Sandys[3] and Dodds take 960b 'if you are not caught first

---

[1] See Dodds on 955–6, 963–5, 966–70 and Schwinge, p. 408. Kirk in his translation notes on 940 (a line on which commentators are strangely silent): 'it is difficult to think of a harmless meaning for this verse, one which Pentheus might be expected to place on it.'

[2] '. . . and in the scene that follows, he [Dionysus] directs "asides" to an appreciative audience' (R. P. Winnington-Ingram, *Euripides and Dionysus* (Cambridge, 1948), p. 117). Do the inverted commas round the word 'asides' imply dissatisfaction with the term?

[3] Sandys's alternative explanation, that the words are a warning to Pentheus to remember to go in his present disguise, need not detain us.

yourself' as an aside. Similarly when Dionysus sends Pentheus off
with the words:

971 δεινὸς cὺ δεινὸς κἀπὶ δείν' ἔρχηι πάθη,
      ὥcτ' οὐρανῶι cτηρίζον εὑρήcειc κλέοc.

Wondrous you are and wondrous the experiences you go to meet.
You will find a fame that reaches to the sky,

Dodds sees an address to Pentheus' 'retreating back'.[1]

In both cases what Dionysus says seems too explicit to be heard
by Pentheus. In 960 he hints that Pentheus may be caught; in
971 he seems to assert that Pentheus will undergo suffering. It is
generally agreed, however, by those who have written about this
scene that Pentheus is not in his right mind and that it does not
greatly matter whether or not Pentheus hears what Dionysus
says to him.[2] If that is the case, we should be less eager to find
asides. It would indeed be possible for 960b to be delivered in
such a way as to suggest that it was not meant to be heard by
Pentheus, but it is worth noting that elsewhere stress is laid upon
the daring of the enterprise Pentheus is about to undertake.
cπεύδοντά τ' ἀcπούδαcτα Dionysus says of him as he calls him out
of the palace. Pentheus speaks of himself as τολμῶν τόδε (962). It
is possible that 'if you are not caught first yourself' is, as well as a
sinister hint of what is to happen, which will be picked up by the
audience, an extra piece of titillation for Pentheus, reminding
him of the risks he is taking.[3]

More problematical is 971 f. Against Dodds's interpretation one
may say that it would be a pity if Pentheus were not present to
hear the ostensible striking compliment offered him in the second
of these lines. Perhaps too it is less effective if there is no clear
break between the moment when Dionysus is playing a double
game and the moment when alone on stage he is completely
open. This would most naturally come between 972 and 973. On

---

[1] On this phenomenon see above, p. 34.

[2] Cf. Winnington-Ingram, 'it matters little now what Dionysus says, for Pentheus is past understanding' and Schwinge (p. 407, n. 129), 'er Pentheus hört nur noch, was er will'. See also Kirk on 971.

[3] Roux in her commentary is surely wide of the mark in assuming that Pentheus will take the words as 'une invitation à la prudence'.

the other hand, it is difficult to take the words δεινὰ πάθη as meaning anything other than 'terrible suffering'.[1] Sandys's suggestion that Pentheus is to take the words as referring to the punishment he will inflict upon the maenads is rightly dismissed by Dodds. The problem lies in πάθη[2] rather than δεινά. It is easy enough for that word to be equivocal following δεινὸς cὺ δεινός, in the one sense 'wonderful', in the other 'terrible'. πάθη can refer to something external to the subject of the sentence in which it occurs,[3] but it is hard to extract such a reference from the phraseology here. One would like parallels in tragedy for the word meaning someone else's experiences. That is what I should take its innocent meaning to be here.[4]

Because this scene is so remarkable in its design and effect and because Pentheus appears to be presented in a way that may be thought to conflict with the rational and logical technique of the stichomythic form, we may indeed be justified in arguing that Pentheus does not comprehend what he hears. At any rate, it is my feeling that asides have no place in this scene.

I.A.

(a) Two of Agamemnon's lines in the stichomythia where he first converses with his daughter directly after she and Clytaemnestra have arrived from Argos have been thought to contain asides. As with most questions concerning this play, the text and

---

[1] Cf. Eur. *El.* 1226.

[2] Schwinge (p. 410) goes so far as to assume that Pentheus hears all that Dionysus addresses to him save this one word.

[3] Perhaps Eur. *El.* 1226 is a parallel δεινότατον παθέων ἔρεξας but πάθος is chosen there deliberately to indicate that the doer shall suffer. At Eur. *Or.* 1455 the Phrygian speaks of *seeing* πάθη. πάθαι occurs in a similar context at Soph. *Ai.* 295.

[4] So also Kirk in his translation and Roux in her commentary. C. W. Willink, *CQ* n.s. 16 (1966), 232, supposes that Pentheus 'if *compos mentis*' takes the words as equivalent to μέγαν ἀγῶνα (cf. 964), but surely they are a long way from suggesting that. He also suggests that after 972 Dionysus conducts Pentheus to one of the parodoi and turns back to deliver 973 ff., the asyndeton between 972 and 973 marking a pause for stage movement. This may be correct (although I think it more effective to have Dionysus remaining still on stage while Pentheus leaves), but one should note that asyndeton at the end of a stage conversation is quite normal. At Eur. *Or.* 630 ff. Orestes addresses Tyndareus' retreating back: at 632 he turns to address *in asyndeto* Menelaus. There is no suggestion that the speaker has been moving round the stage.

authorship of the passages in question are in doubt. As regards the sequence of the dialogue, I follow John Jackson in placing 664 before 653 and deleting ll. 652, 665.[1] It does not really affect the argument set out below.

The first alleged aside occurs at 653:

> 664 Ἰφ. μακρὰν ἀπαίρεις, ὦ πάτερ, λιπὼν ἐμέ.
> 653 Ἀγ. συνετὰ λέγουσα μᾶλλον εἰς οἶκτόν μ' ἄγεις.
> Ἰφ. ἀσύνετά νυν ἐροῦμεν, εἰ σέ γ' εὐφρανῶ.
> 655 Ἀγ. παπαῖ· τὸ σιγᾶν οὐ σθένω, σὲ δ' ᾔνεσα.
> Ἰφ. μέν', ὦ πάτερ, κατ' οἶκον ἐπὶ τέκνοις σέθεν.

Iph. You are going on a long journey, father, leaving me behind.
Ag. Saying things I understand too well, you bring me further towards pity.
Iph. I'll say things you can't understand, then, if it will make you happy.
Ag. Alas! I haven't the strength to keep silent, but I thank you.
Iph. Stay at home, father, by your children.

On 653 England comments: 'this verse was perhaps half an "aside".' We have already met this not particularly helpful way of speaking about dramatic dialogue.[2] This line is surely less of an aside or 'half-aside' than most of the lines taken in this way. For one thing it is addressed to Iphigenia. In the second place, it is clear from her reply (ἀσύνετα ∼ συνετά) that she hears it. Presumably England feels that Agamemnon is revealing too much when he says 'you bring me to pity'. Certainly the full import of this expression can be understood only by the audience and it may seem somewhat obscure to Iphigenia. If it does, at least it has already been established that Agamemnon is behaving rather strangely towards her. We have had a series of puzzled questions from her which prepare us for considering her reaction to the various puzzling and sinister remarks that Agamemnon will make in this scene (γέγηθά σ' ὡς γέγηθ' ὁρῶν 649, ἄλλους 659, 667, 673, 675). This degree of preparation is similar to the technique of the

---

[1] *Marginalia Scaenica*, 1 ff. I would not, however, go along with him in accepting all the transpositions he here suggests. The essential point is, as Miss Dale (*JHS* 76 (1956), 115) agrees, that 664 should precede 653.
[2] See above, p. 32.

Ion scene discussed above (p. 37). The audience is free to concentrate on the pathos of the situation and to wonder how far Agamemnon will go in hinting what will happen to Iphigenia. The tension of the scene would be reduced if we had to think of him speaking aside here.

Similarly, we may doubt whether 655, about which there is a much stronger case for its being an aside, is what it appears to be. On this line (his 660) Hermann remarked that Agamemnon turned away from Iphigenia when he said 'Alas! I haven't the strength to keep silent', since he did not want her to hear the words. Hermann has been followed by most commentators.[1] At first sight the words in question do seem to satisfy the prescription for asides given above (p. 17). If she hears what her father says, Iphigenia would be puzzled and distressed. In the following line she seems to take no account of his words. There is also in *Hel.* 133a a firm formal parallel for the type of aside that 655a would be. Nevertheless, I have some hesitation about agreeing with Hermann. If Iphigenia is supposed not to hear the first part of 655, what is the force of δέ in the second part? If, as it is natural to suppose, it takes up τὸ ϲιγᾶν οὐ ϲθένω, what can it mean to Iphigenia, who is supposed not to have heard these words? She can hardly be expected to understand 655b as a reply to her own last words: 'I will speak obscurely if it will make you happy'— 'And (but) I thank *you* for it.' This would be extremely tortuous.[2] It is much easier to assume that Iphigenia hears the whole line (unless we take the whole line as an aside):[3] '*I* haven't the

---

[1] Monk, England, Wecklein, Firnhaber, Vater, and Klotz.

[2] Of course in dramatic dialogue a character may turn aside from the person he has up to now been addressing and address someone else, prefacing his utterance with some part of the second-person pronoun followed by δέ: Eur. *Hel.* 868, *Bacch.* 809, *I.A.* 685, and Ar. *Ran.* 164 f. Such a δέ performs from the point of view of the speaker the function of arranging in order what he has to say. Such a form of address, however, is much more natural when it is understood that the recipient has probably heard what preceded and is aware that the speaker is using the δέ to order his thoughts. The aside which would be the closest parallel for *I.A.* 655, *Hel.* 133a, does not (it should be noted) disrupt the dialogue in the way ϲὲ δ' ᾔνεϲα does. Θεϲτιὰϲ δ' ἔϲτιν κόρη; is a perfectly natural response to the previous line.

[3] As Mr. T. C. W. Stinton suggests to me. There is something to be said for this. Iphigenia's lack of reaction to what her father has just said then becomes explicable. Line 656 can begin a new tack in the stichomythia, 655 marking the end of a section of dialogue (so Schwinge, p. 187).

strength to keep silent, but I thank *you*.' Perhaps τὸ ϲιγᾶν οὐ
ϲθένω explains the cry παπαῖ, 'I cannot stop myself from crying
out.' The audience of course will hear a more specific reference in
ϲιγᾶν than Iphigenia.

Similar problems arise at the end of this dialogue when
Agamemnon sends his daughter inside:

> Ἰφ. ϲτήϲομεν ἄρ' ἀμφὶ βωμόν, ὦ πάτερ, χορούϲ;
> 677 Ἀγ. ζηλῶ ϲὲ μᾶλλον ἢ 'μὲ τοῦ μηδὲν φρονεῖν.
> χώρει δὲ μελάθρων ἐντόϲ . . .

Iph. Will I direct choruses around the altar, father?
Ag. I envy you more than myself because of your lightheartedness.
But go inside . . .

l. 677 has been taken as an aside,[1] but if Iphigenia does not hear
the line, what does she make of the δέ in 'but go!'? In fact, there
is no reason why she should not be able to put an innocent
interpretation on μηδὲν φρονεῖν. On one level it can be understood as 'not having a care' and to refer to her naïve interest in
dancing at a sacrifice at what may be the last time she sees her
father.[2] The audience, however, will realize that Agamemnon
means 'knowing nothing' (cf. Soph. *Ai.* 554), think of Iphigenia's
impending doom, and contrast the girl's eagerness with what
they know to be in store for her.

Editors have tended to find asides in scenes where characters
make ambiguous remarks (compare what has been said on
Med. 899 f., *Ion* 268 f.) and a scene like this where Agamemnon
seems ever on the point of giving the game away is a happy
hunting ground for such a quest. It may be that the scene was
played in the manner editors would suggest, with Agamemnon
turning away from Iphigenia at 655 and 677, but Euripides (or
whoever wrote the scene) has not demarcated these passages with
enough clarity to enable us confidently to interpret them thus or
to be sure that an audience would be surprised if Iphigenia
did not take up the lines. Perhaps, however, they might find

---

[1] So England.
[2] 'The light-heartedness with which the daughter settles how it is all to be
arranged gives rise to the father's next remark' (England).

Clytaemnestra's silence throughout more surprising. Could *she* hear 655 with equanimity?

(*b*) Achilles' speech in reply to Clytaemnestra's plea that he come to her aid in saving Iphigenia contains a curious passage where he turns away from Clytaemnestra and reflects on the injury done him by Agamemnon (959 ff.). This has been found by some (see England ad loc.) to be inconsistent with the impression of his character created by and the sentiments expressed in 926 ff. and it has been suggested that 959–74 be deleted. In fact the tone of the remarks contained in the offending section is not at all surprising in a character like Achilles: pique at personal slights is characteristic of all heroes and peculiarly characteristic of Achilles. The oddity is that the attitude displayed in these lines should follow so closely upon the more generous attitude expressed in 940–1 and that the lines should be spoken in the presence of Clytaemnestra,[1] especially when Achilles actually refers to her by name in the third person (963). These considerations have led some to suppose that part of what Achilles says is spoken aside.[2] If that were the case, the speech would have a kind of parallel in *Or.* 671 ff. (see above, p. 45) where Orestes interrupts his plea to Menelaus to talk to himself.[3] There, however, we had an aposiopesis followed by a relatively brief emotional outburst. We have here a piece of extended reflection.

Against taking the lines as an aside is the difficulty of isolating those parts of the speech Clytaemnestra is supposed not to hear. Lines 959–74 form an indivisible unit, yet, whereas in 963 Clytaemnestra is spoken of in the third person, at 972 Achilles is able to speak of '*your* daughter'. It is far from clear when Achilles is supposed to stop talking to himself and to turn back to Clytaemnestra. Lines 970 ff. cannot be detached from the preceding sentence and that sentence answers to 965 ff. where Achilles

[1] See England. On the alternations of mood in this speech see also D. L. Page, *Actors' Interpolations in Greek Tragedy* (Oxford, 1934), pp. 179 f.

[2] Monk marks off from ἡ Κλυταίμηϲτρα to πόϲει and treats it as an aside. This is impossible. See below, p. 53.

[3] Cf. also, although it is not an aside (see above, p. 27), Eur. *Hcld.* 435 ff.

admits that had he been asked properly by Agamemnon, he would have allowed the deception to proceed, precisely the part of the speech Clytaemnestra ought not to hear. The part she must not hear, then, comes in a sentence which is inextricably linked with 970 ff., where she is addressed directly.

Such incoherency is characteristic of the whole speech and not just of this particular section. It is hard to disagree with Page when he states that 909–1035 are almost entirely post-Euripidean.[1] The particular obscurity of staging discussed here can be added to the heap of arguments against the whole section.

(c) Finally we come to the stichomythic dialogue between Agamemnon and Clytaemnestra which leads to Agamemnon revealing his secret. After he has promised to give an honest answer to whatever she asks him, she asks him directly whether he intends killing Iphigenia. The dialogue proceeds as follows:

> Aγ. ἔα·
> 1132   τλήμονά γ' ἔλεξας, ὑπονοεῖς θ' ἃ μή ϲε χρή.
> Κλ. ἔχ' ἤϲυχοϲ·
> 1133   κἀκεῖνό μοι τὸ πρῶτον ἀπόκριναι πάλιν.

Ag. Ah! Your utterance is grim and you suspect what you ought not to suspect.

Cl. Keep quiet! Answer again what I first asked you.

'It is obvious from the context,' says Page (*Actors' Interpolations*, p. 114), 'that 1132 must be spoken aside.'[2] I do not see that it is.

[1] Page, op. cit., p. 179. Cf. Paley on 942: 'from this verse to the end of the speech W. Dindorf includes in brackets as an interpolation. It does not seem to the present editor in any degree more suspicious than the first part; although it certainly is equally so.'

[2] Page also makes the suggestion (tentatively) that ἔχ' ἤϲυχοϲ has been confected from a stage direction ἡϲύχωϲ in the prompter's copy (Kannicht on *Hel.* 705 suggests that there was a παρεπιγραφή which went Aγ. ἤϲυχοϲ). This seems to me highly improbable (incidentally, there seem to be no examples of ἡϲύχωϲ as distinct from ἡϲυχῆι in the dramatic scholia). We have no evidence for production copies of the plays circulating with lavish stage directions (both Page and Schmid I 4 p. 451, n. 11, greatly over-value the stage directions found in dramatic scholia. Apart from those which reflect Hellenistic staging (e.g. Σ Eur. *Or.* 57, 643) they are obviously built on nothing more than inference from the text (I do not believe for example that Σ Eur. *Hipp.* 701 which Page adduces as an example of a scholion deriving from the prompter's copy is anything more than a guess by a commentator imagining how the scene was played. It is probably misplaced anyway: Wilamowitz

The sentiment Agamemnon expresses in the line formally neither confirms nor denies Clytaemnestra's suspicions, but can be taken as a fervent denial of them, 'what a thing to suspect!'. Clytaemnestra's 'Keep quiet' indicates that she has heard a reply from Agamemnon: she does not want to be distracted from her object by indignant protestations, but demands a straight answer to her questions.

The stichomythia continues:

> 1135   Κλ. οὐκ ἀλλ' ἐρωτῶ, καὶ cù μὴ λέγ' ἄλλα μοι.
>   Αγ. ὦ πότνια μοῖρα καὶ τύχη δαίμων τ' ἐμόc.
>   Κλ. κἀμός γε καὶ τῆσδ', εἰc τριῶν δυcδαιμόνων.
>   Αγ. τί δ' ἠδίκηcαι;[1]   Κλ. τοῦτ' ἐμοῦ πεύθηι πάρα;
>   ὁ νοῦc ὅδ' αὐτὸc νοῦν ἔχων οὐ τυγχάνει.[2]
> 1140   Αγ. ἀπωλόμεcθα. προδέδοται τὰ κρυπτά μου.
>   Κλ. πάντ' οἶδα καὶ πεπύcμεθ' ἃ cù μέλλειc με δρᾶν.
>   αὐτὸ δὲ τὸ cιγᾶν ὁμολογοῦντόc ἐcτί cου
>   καὶ τὸ cτενάζειν. πολλὰ μὴ κάμηιc λέγων.

> Cl. Answer the questions I ask you.
> Ag. O Moira and Tyche and my daimon.

was surely right in referring it not to the nurse's last line, but to Phaedra's reply)). Such marginalia containing stage directions as we have are for the most part readers' additions and do not constitute part of the paradosis. The few παρεπιγραφαί that might go back to the author's time or at least to the Alexandrian editions of dramatic texts were probably transmitted within rather than in the margin of the text like χοροῦ in the comic papyri (or the as yet unexplained ὠιδαί of P. Oxy. 2746): see J. C. B. Lowe, *BICS* 9 (1962), 36. It seems *a priori* unlikely that anyone intending to include this hypothetical παρεπιγραφή in the text should have done so by including it in a remark *extra metrum* rather than a complete line. Monometers are rare in Greek drama: they are more likely to disappear by being transformed into complete lines than to be created in the way Page suggests here (for expansion of an interjection into a complete trimeter see Fraenkel, *Ag.* p. 580, n. 4). Since ἔχ' ἥcυχοc in our text makes perfect sense the only reason for suspecting it is the consideration that, apart from hypermetric exclamations such as ἔα, φεῦ, ἆ, there are no incomplete iambic lines in Euripides (in this he differs from Sophocles— see Kannicht on Eur. *Hel.* 706). When we consider the play in which this monometer occurs this reason does not seem a very compelling one. (Fraenkel's argument that ἔα in 1132 betrays the hand of the interpolator does not seem to me valid. It is not here 'unmistakeably a cry of distress': it is rather the regular Euripidean expression of surprise. Agamemnon is taken aback by the blunt question his wife has put to him.)

[1] This is Matthiae's emendation. LP before correction have τί μ' ἠδίκηcε;
[2] Here England follows LP and attributes the line to Agamemnon. He glosses 'the cleverness that can put such a question is not cleverness but folly', but there is nothing particularly clever about Clytaemnestra's indignant question.

Cl. My daimon and the daimon of this girl too, one fate for three ill-fated ones.

Ag. What wrong have I done you?

Cl. You ask this of me? This idea [that you have not wronged me] is itself devoid of sense [there is a pun on νοῦς which cannot be rendered in English].

Ag. I am done for. My secrets are betrayed.

Cl. I know all and have discovered what you intend to do to me. Your very silence and your groaning is a sign of your guilt. Don't bother to say anything.

In 1136 Agamemnon turns away as he realizes that the truth will inevitably come out. There is no reason to doubt, as England seems to in his note on 1132 ff., whether Clytaemnestra hears it. She obviously takes it up and elaborates on it in the following line. In 1140a we have another such exclamation (for ἀπωλό-μεσθα cf. *Hel.* 133a) followed by an explicit explanation for Agamemnon's distress. Because the line is both explicit and in-organic, it is natural to think of it as being delivered aside.[1] Additional confirmation of this interpretation comes in the ensuing dialogue. Clytaemnestra takes Agamemnon's *failure to reply* and groaning as proof of his intentions.[2] This surely is meant to suggest that she has not heard 1140. It is hard to see what other reference 'your silence' could have than to a failure to elicit a response from Agamemnon at some stage of the dialogue. And at what other place could this failure come than after 1139? Here, then, we have a whole line in stichomythia being delivered aside.

In the continuation, 1144 f., Monk sees in the words following ἰδοὺ cιωπῶ 'See, I am silent' an aside. This is unnecessary. Now that Agamemnon knows that all his secrets are revealed, there is no need to assume that he continues to keep his feelings hidden from Clytaemnestra.

---

[1] So England and Page. England, however, tries to have it both ways. He first describes 1140 as an aside, but later takes the reference to his silence in 1142 as showing that he stopped abruptly after uttering 1140. The point is that for Cly-taemnestra 1140 *is* silence. Schwinge (p. 190, n. 1) seems not to take 1140 as an aside.

[2] In 1142 f. we meet a mixture of motifs. The aside is treated both as silence and (cf. Eur. *Hec.* 740, on which see above, p. 15) as groaning. This does not seem to me particularly competent and may be a further sign of interpolation.

iii

From the preceding pages it can be seen that asides, if they do not play a large part in the *œuvre* of Euripides, are at least to be found in that *œuvre*. The passages which to my mind fully satisfy the definition of an aside given above (p. 17) are: Eur. *Med.* 277–80, *Hec.* 736–8, 741–2, 745–6, 749–51, *I.T.* 777, *Hel.* 133a, 139b, 475b (and possibly 473b), *Or.* 671b–3, and? *I.A.* 1140.[1] Of these the most striking is the block of asides in *Hecuba* where Agamemnon is all the time trying to engage the attention of the aside-speaker, Hecuba. Since Agamemnon does at least seem to be aware that Hecuba is making sounds, albeit inarticulate ones (see above, p. 15),[2] and since it is clear from the text that her back is turned on him, the convention there may be said to be excused in a naturalistic way. Some have drawn from this the inference that Euripides was tentatively introducing the convention to the tragic stage.[3] But the opposite inference is just as likely:[4] Euripides may have wished to treat in a new way a convention that was already familiar to the audiences of tragedy. The sheer number of asides in the scene may have led Euripides to think that some naturalistic apology was necessary. Certainly he achieved a most ingenious effect, inserting a genuine monologue[5] into a passage of patterned dialogue.

---

[1] I include here only those instances I regard as certain. There are, as can be seen from the discussion above, other passages which may well be asides (e.g. Eur. *Hel.* 559 f.) and others, which if not exactly asides, employ a convention similar to that of the aside (e.g. Eur. *Hipp.* 523 ff.). There are no asides in the exiguous remains of satyr drama. Kaibel (*Hermes* 30 (1895), 74) took Eur. *Cycl.* 480–2 as an aside. The lines certainly contradict 478 ff. and ought presumably to be kept from the satyrs, but as Zwierlein has convincingly shown (*Gnomon* 39 (1967), 451) they are without doubt an interpolation. The interpolator may have derived the idea of adding a section beginning with καίτοι from passages like *Med.* 1049 f. and *Ion* 1385 ff. where soliloquies take new and final turnings which lead to decisions. What he has achieved is something indecisive and inept.

[2] Possibly too that she is thinking aloud (see above, p. 15 n. 2).

[3] e.g. Tierney on 658–904.

[4] And if what is said about *Med.* 277–80 is correct, we may assume that the first audience of *Hecuba* was already familiar with the convention since *Medea* in all probability antedates *Hecuba*.

[5] 'Hier ist eine vollkommene szenisch stark bezeichnete, durch vier Phasen bis zum Entschluss und dessen Ausführung geleitete Überlegung', Leo, p. 34. Schwinge (p. 82) thinks that Hecuba's decision is hastened by Agamemnon's presence *and* by the distichs he speaks. There is nothing in the text, however, to suggest that Hecuba

Whether this was a solitary experiment, never to be repeated, we cannot say.

The remaining asides, apart from *I.T.* 777 which is addressed to someone else on stage, are (in varying degrees) emotional outbursts. Five of them occur in patterned dialogue: one (*Or.* 671b–3) occurs within a rhesis. Both phenomena, turning away from one's interlocutor in the course of patterned dialogue and breaking off the argument of a rhesis for personal reflection and expression of one's emotion can be paralleled elsewhere in Euripides (see pp. 32, 33, and 45 above). What sets the passages collected here apart is that the other person or persons who happen to be on stage at the time must be supposed not to hear, or at least not to apprehend, what is being said in them. Frequently turnings away *tout court* are described by commentators as asides (or half-asides).[1] Such descriptions—they are particularly common in Barbieri's thesis[2]—make the logical fallacy of assuming that utterances that are not directed at a particular addressee are co-extensive with utterances that are not meant to be heard by that addressee. This is true neither in life nor in the theatre. It is easy to conceive of asides developing out of such turnings away, but one should remember that it is not the form that determines whether a passage is an aside, but the content considered in the light of the dramatic context. In a large sense everything in Greek drama may be described as conventional[3] and one is entitled to describe emotional outbursts or appeals to the gods in the course of dialogue or rhesis as tragic conventions. If, however, such appeals are to go unheard by others present at the time of their utterance, an added dimension of convention is present. It is this dimension that we must go on to investigate. We must look for passages where actors are supposed to be unaware of what other actors are doing on stage or even unaware of the presence of other actors.

'The presence of other actors', it was said. But what of the

takes note of anything that Agamemnon says. Each of her utterances takes up the preceding one as though there had been no interruption.

[1] See above, pp. 32, 33, 36, and below, p. 79.
[2] See above, p. 17 n. 2, and p. 17 n. 3.
[3] Cf. above, p. 10.

chorus? Are they not actors too as Aristotle prescribed? Leo in his great work on the monologue assumed (an assumption that Schadewaldt was able to show was unjustified)[1] that the major obstacle to the development of the soliloquy in Greek drama was the presence of the chorus. It was only when this obstacle was removed that the soliloquy attained its prominence as a dramatic form, that is to say, it was only when the chorus was excluded from the action in the kind of comedy that was written in the fourth century. Similarly, it is sometimes asserted that the presence of the chorus is an obstacle to the exploitation of the aside-convention in Greek tragedy and this helps explain its relative infrequency in the genre.[2] I doubt whether this was, except in special circumstances, an important consideration to the dramatist. In the first place, it is hard to see why it is any more contrived or conventional for a remark to go by unheard by the chorus of a play in addition to the other actors on stage than for it to go by unheard only by the actors. Secondly, if this is felt to be difficult, the presence of the chorus would only appear to be an obstacle to the delivery of asides in cases where the chorus was not in sympathy with the character who delivered the aside. Of the Euripidean asides, three, those occurring in *Helen*, happen to be delivered when the chorus is absent; the first two of these could equally well have been delivered in the presence of a chorus sympathetic to the speaker. Of the other asides in every case the chorus is 'in the know' about the speaker's circumstances.

Even though we have no examples of asides which could not in any circumstances be heard by a chorus (for example a remark uttered by a character revealing his true intentions before a hostile chorus), I would hesitate before assuming that Euripides would have felt such an aside awkward or impossible. Generalization about the role of the chorus in Greek tragedy is notoriously

---

[1] Schadewaldt, pp. 1–31.

[2] e.g. Mahaffy (*Euripides*, p. 124) who says 'the chorus being the recognized spectators of the action, asides of the actors not intended for their ears do not, I think, occur in any Greek play' and Haigh (*The Tragic Drama of the Greeks*, p. 349) who speaks of 'the comparative infrequency of soliloquies and asides, which were scarcely possible on the Greek Stage, owing to the presence of the chorus' (cf. also Flickinger, *The Greek Theater and its Drama*, p. 312).

perilous. Sometimes it is deeply involved in the action, the confidant of the hero. Sometimes its aid is enlisted or its secrecy enjoined (see Kannicht on Eur. *Hel.* 1387). Yet there are occasions in the plays of, at any rate, Euripides when, for all the notice the actors take of it, we feel it might as well not be there. This certainly applies to plays like *Orestes* and *I.A.* Note how at *I.A.* 863 ff. the old man peeping out of the door of Agamemnon's tent inquires whether Achilles and Clytaemnestra are alone and obtains the following reply from Achilles: ὡς μόνοιν λέγοις ἄν ('I can assure you that you would be speaking just to the two of us'), as though there were no group of Euboean ladies standing by. Consider too a scene like *I.T.* 658–715, where Orestes and Pylades discuss their affairs without constraint even though there is present a chorus of whose support and sympathy they are not as yet certain.[1]

A scene in *Ion* is often adduced as evidence for the awkwardness of a 'private' conversation on stage in the presence of a chorus. After the dénouement when Ion is apprised of his own identity, he calls his mother to him:

1520   τὰ δ' ἄλλα πρὸς cè βούλομαι μόνην φράcαι.
      δεῦρ' ἔλθ'· ἐc οὖc γὰρ τοὺς λόγους εἰπεῖν θέλω
      καὶ περικαλύψαι τοῖcι πράγμαcι cκότον.

The rest I wish to say to you alone. Come here: I want to speak into your ear and to cloak these matters in darkness.

After which a conversation begins which is interrupted only by the appearance at l. 1549 of Athena. This scene, which appears to foreshadow a type of scene frequently to be encountered in New Comedy (see below, pp. 162 ff.), is, on the face of it, a conversation *aside* or *apart* from the chorus. The effect has been thought clumsy. People who are prepared to accept asides delivered apart from two players balk at an aside delivered apart from fifteen choreutai. But did the dramatist mean the conversation to be

---

[1] Contrast Soph. *Tr.* 343–4 where Deianira (and Sophocles) draws attention to the presence of the chorus when the messenger attempts to speak to her alone. Presumably Sophocles felt it implausible for the conversation to proceed unless the man admitted that he was prepared to speak in front of the chorus. I am not so sure that in a similar situation Euripides would have felt such a procedure necessary.

taken in that way? If the presence of the chorus was felt to be a
difficulty in a situation like this, it would surely be inept to draw
the audience's attention to it in the way Euripides is supposed to
be doing here. There is room for doubt whether the audience
would hear a reference to the chorus in Ion's words or feel that
what followed was in any sense an aside. Throughout the whole
scene from the entrance of Ion at 1261, no remarks[1] have been
addressed to the chorus by any of the actors and the only
utterance of the chorus has been a conventional generalization
addressed to no one in particular in a distich (1510–11) the
function of which is purely formal, to divide lyrics from iambic
dialogue. The chorus's presence and influence on the scene is thus
negligible. Suddenly to elevate them to the status of participants
in the action, people from whom secrets must be kept and to feel
disturbed because of the difficulty of *sotto voce* speech in the
presence of a crowd, merely on the strength of 1520 ff. (which
does not in any case explicitly refer to them), is to misconceive
the point of these lines. What has been seen as a bungling
attempt to hold a conversation aside is in fact a neat device for
bringing closer together on stage the two central figures for the
confrontation with the deity speaking from the machine. They
must have become separated at some point during or after the
preceding lyric duet.[2] These lines bring them together again.
They also serve to characterize Ion, showing his embarrassment
at the question he is about to put to his mother. It is natural,
even when two people are alone, for the one who is about to ask
a personal question or to impart confidential information to
behave as if there was a possibility of the conversation being
overheard and to look around and lower his voice.[3] In any case,
Ion, Creusa, and the chorus may not be the only people on stage.
Ion brought attendants when he first came to arrest Creusa
(1266). When she left the altar (1402) he told them to seize her
(λάζυcθε) and bind her arms. After this we hear nothing of

---

[1] Possibly cκέψαcθ' in 1417 is addressed to them, although it is hard to see why
Creusa should at this point cease to address Ion. The plural is unexplained (unless
it takes in the guards as well) and may be corrupt.

[2] Clearly they are embracing at 1437.

[3] Cf. Herondas 1. 47–8.

these men.[1] It may be that they melt imperceptibly into the background and are no longer visible once Ion has established that Creusa is his mother and has embraced her (1437). If, however, they are still on stage and standing in the background when Ion speaks 1520 ff., there is added point to Ion's appeal to Creusa to come near and to his fear of being overheard. One cannot press this point, since the exact movements of non-speaking characters can rarely be tabulated with certainty (in many cases their comings or goings are unimportant)[2], but it seems a valid enough way of envisaging the staging of this scene.

Before we turn to examine the plays of Aeschylus and Sophocles, we should look at a form of stage action in Euripides which implies a convention similar to that of the aside, but which would not properly be called an aside. The aside-convention implies a degree of unawareness about what is being *said* on stage—the actors failing to hear or hear properly what the aside-speaker says. There is a type of entrance frequently to be found in the plays of Euripides where the speaker is unaware that there is anyone else present on stage. The speaker enters talking to himself and after a while notices that he is not alone. This initial lack of awareness seems to me to have affinities with the lack of awareness of the people on stage in the presence of an aside-speaker, the dimension which makes the aside conventional. One would not, however, call such entrance speeches asides,[3] since, if the speaker is not aware that he is being overheard or that there is a possibility of him being overheard, he cannot be regarded as trying to conceal what he has to say. In some cases, however, once he has realized that he is not alone he does not immediately address the other people on stage. Such remarks may well be asides.

At Eur. *Suppl.* 87, Theseus enters (unannounced) talking to himself and wondering anxiously about the sounds of

---

[1] ll. 1404–6 probably imply that they do not succeed in restraining Creusa (see Wilamowitz ad loc.). Ion must at some stage turn away from her so that she cannot see the ἀντίπηξ while she is enumerating its contents.

[2] See Andrieu, *Le Dialogue antique*, pp. 201–4, and Bain, *CQ* n.s. 25 (1975), 20.

[3] Leo (p. 48, n. 1) strongly deprecates the application of the term 'aside' to monologues (*Zutrittsmonologen*) of this type. See also below, p. 183 n. 1.

lamentation which have drawn him to the place. Only at 92 does he notice the presence of others, including his mother, on stage. When he sees them, he exclaims with surprise:

> ἔα·
> τί χρῆμα; καινὰς εἰςβολὰς ὁρῶ λόγων·
> μητέρα γεραιὰν βωμίαν ἐφημένην
> ξένους θ' ὁμοῦ γυναῖκας . . .

Ah! What is it? I see strange occasions for entering into speech, my aged mother sitting at the altar and a crowd of foreign women with her . . .

Finally at 98 he turns to his mother and addresses her: τί ταῦτα, μῆτερ;, 'What is this, mother?'.

At Eur. *H.F.* 523 when Hercules enters (his arrival has been observed by Megara, 513 ff.), the stage is crowded. Megara, her children, and Amphitryon are on the point of being led away by Lycus' attendants. When Megara observes her husband arriving, she tells her children to run over to him and grab hold of his robes. It is at this point that we first hear Hercules speaking:

> ὦ χαῖρε μέλαθρον πρόπυλά θ' ἑστίας ἐμῆς
> ὡς ἅςμενός ς' ἐςεῖδον ἐς φάος μολών.
> 525 ἔα· τί χρῆμα; τέκν' ὁρῶ πρὸ δωμάτων
> στολμοῖςι νεκρῶν κρᾶτας ἐξεςτεμμένα
> ὄχλωι τ' ἐν ἀνδρῶν τὴν ἐμὴν ξυνάορον,
> πατέρα τε δακρύοντα — ςυμφορὰς τίνας;
> φέρ' ἐκπύθωμαι τῶνδε πληςίον ςταθείς.
> 530 γύναι, τί καινὸν ἦλθε δώμαςιν χρέος;

Greetings, o hall and forecourt of my house, how glad I am to see you, coming once more into the light. Ah! What is it? I see my children in front of the house, garlanded as for a funeral and my wife in a crowd of men and my father weeping—for what disaster? Come, I shall go up to them and find out. Wife, what new misfortune has come upon the house?

This speech displays all the features of the previous passage: comment on entry (in the *Supplices* an explanation of why the speaker has come, here an address to the house Hercules has not seen for so long), followed by surprise expressed at seeing that there are others on stage, in each case the phrase ἔα, τί χρῆμα; being employed, and finally a question addressed to one of the people on stage. In *H.F.*, however, we have in addition a formal announcement of the speaker's intention to ask this question φέρ' ἐκπύθωμαι . . . 'come, I shall go up to them and find out', a phrase which has the appearance of an aside (cf. Eur. *Med.* 280). Like Theseus in the *Supplices* Hercules comes upon a frozen tableau. The children do not obey their mother's instructions. They do not rush forward and cling to his robes. Nor does Megara cry out to her husband. Action on one half of the stage reaches a standstill so that all attention may be fixed upon Hercules' soliloquy.[1]

Helen's re-entrance at Eur. *Hel.* 528 follows the same pattern. She returns to the stage reflecting on what Theonoe has told her (the chorus has just preceded her, but she is scarcely addressing them—see Kannicht ad loc.). Suddenly she sees, but does not recognize, Menelaus, exclaiming ἔα, τίς οὗτος; (541). She does not immediately address him, but describes his appearance, guessing that he is one of Theoclymenus' men come to seize her. Menelaus addresses her as she is about to flee to the altar. On his first entrance later in the same play, Theoclymenus first addresses the tomb of his father and then soliloquizes, describing what he intends to do to Helen (1165 ff.).[2] Only later does he notice that there is something amiss on stage:

1177 ἔα·
   ἀλλ', ὡς ἔοικε, πάντα διαπεπραγμένα
   ηὕρηκα· τύμβου γὰρ κενὰς λιποῦσ' ἕδρας
   ἡ Τυνδαρὶς παῖς ἐκπεπόρθμευται χθονός.

Ah! It seems I have found everything awry. Helen has left the altar empty and quitted this land!

He gives feverish instructions to his attendants to make ready for a search (1180–3): then at last seeing the newly entered Helen he calls them off (1184–5) and addresses her. The form is identical

---

[1] Analogy with *Phoen.* 261 ff. should deter one from assuming that Hercules is here addressing the chorus. τῶνδε need not indicate that Hercules is pointing out to the *chorus* the people he intends to approach: it is quite normal for an actor soliloquizing to use the deictic pronoun of the people he has observed on stage (cf. e.g. Aesch. *Eum.* 406).

[2] Between apostrophe and soliloquy comes a command to his attendants (1169–70) to take his hunting equipment into the palace.

with the other entrance monologues we are discussing. In this case, however, the speaker is assuming the presence of someone who is in fact not present (he does not notice Menelaus who is in hiding). Just like the other speakers, he is unaware of what is going on on stage.

Polynices' furtive entrance at Eur. *Phoen.* 261 ff. is another instance. Here, however, the people present on stage are the chorus. After a false alarm when he thinks he hears a noise at 269, Polynices becomes aware of the situation on stage, first observing the altar and then the chorus:

> 274 ἀλλ' ἐγγὺς ἀλκή (βώμιοι γὰρ ἐςχάραι
> πέλας πάρεισι) κοὐκ ἔρημα δώματα.

But succour is at hand (the altar is near by) and the house is not deserted.[1]

Like Hercules at *H.F.* 529, he announces his decision to question the people on stage:

> 276 φέρ' ἐς ςκοτεινὰς περιβολὰς μεθῶ ξίφος
> καὶ τάςδ' ἔρωμαι, τίνες ἐφεςτᾶςιν δόμοις.

Come, let me hide my sword in the recesses of my cloak and ask these women that stand before the house who they are.

After this, as in the *H.F.* scene, we have a direct question.

Finally, at Eur. *Bacch.* 215, Pentheus on entering soliloquizes for thirty-three lines before taking note of the presence of Tiresias and Cadmus:

> 248 ἀτὰρ τόδ' ἄλλο θαῦμα, τὸν τεραςκόπον
> ἐν ποικίλαιςι νεβρίςι Τειρεςίαν ὁρῶ
> πατέρα τε μητρὸς τῆς ἐμῆς — πολὺν γέλων —
> νάρθηκι βακχεύοντα.

But this is another marvel—I see Tiresias the seer in dappled fawnskin and my grandfather, a ridiculous sight, carrying a thyrsus and behaving like a Bacchant.

---

[1] The staging of this scene is discussed by N. C. Hourmouziades, *Production and Imagination in Euripides* (Athens, 1965), p. 79. He points out that one might expect a newly entered actor to be facing the chorus in the orchestra and contrasts this scene with Pentheus' entrance in *Bacchae* where he thinks it easier for the new entrant to miss people standing directly in front of the stage building. As he points out, however, the text (275, 277) seems to indicate that the chorus is at the moment positioned near the stage building (presumably nearer the entrance Polynices does not use).

In this case the speaker turns directly to one of the characters on stage without any announcement of his intention to do so.

These entrance speeches[1] should cause us to look both forward and back. It is easy, looking forward, to see in them a forerunner of a type of entrance monologue of New Comedy.[2] When we look back we find their ancestor in the plays of Aeschylus.[3] There is a temptation to regard them as characterizing Euripides' 'late style' in which the poet is seen to revert to the more formal and severe effects of an earlier age of drama, to cloak in formality the emotions of his characters (within the spoken dialogue at least) and to concentrate on clarity of structure in the composition of scenes.[4] It is significant that Sophocles presents us with no similar entrance speeches. Significant too in support of the contention that such speeches are a mannerism of the late Euripides is the fact that all but two of the speeches come from plays which certainly emanate from the last ten years of the poet's working life.[5] Of the two remaining plays, one, the *Hercules Furens*, should almost certainly also be assigned to this period.[6] One may

---

[1] They are collected by Leo (pp. 70 f.). Slightly different is Eur. *Tro.* 860–79. Menelaus enters and soliloquizes, addressing neither the attendants he brings with him nor the people on stage. At 880 he turns to his attendants and tells them to go inside and fetch Helen. It is only Hecuba's sudden joyous prayer that attracts his attention to the people on stage. The entrances of Agamemnon at Eur. *Hec.* 1109 and the old man at Eur. *El.* 487 are similar. Such passages are less conventional than the ones discussed in the text (cf. too Eur. *Or.* 375 ff. where Menelaus asks the chorus where Orestes is and Orestes saves them the trouble of replying). Almost certainly a fragment of *Andromeda* (fr. 125N) is from a conventional entrance monologue. It marks the stage when Perseus, presumably newly entered, first becomes aware of the presence of Andromeda, the observation being preceded by ἔα (cf. *Suppl.* 92 f., *H.F.* 525).

[2] See Fraenkel, *EP*, p. 211. Schadewaldt (p. 237) describes *Phoen.* 261 ff. as 'einen fast technischen Auftrittsmonolog'. Examples from Seneca are collected by Zwierlein, p. 69.

[3] See below, p. 68.

[4] On 'archaizing' tendencies in Euripides' later work see W. Kranz, *Stasimon. Untersuchungen zu Form und Gehalt der griechischen Tragödie* (Berlin, 1933), p. 232, Gross, *Die Stichomythie*, pp. 52 ff. On recurring formal patterns see Gross, pp. 104 ff., and Ludwig, *Sapheneia, passim* (on *Hel.* 1165 ff., p. 76).

[5] *Troades* was produced in 415, *Helen* and *Andromeda* in 412, *Phoenissae* certainly after 412 and *Bacchae* posthumously.

[6] The *Hercules Furens* comes after *Tro.* in Zieliński's tables: the *Supplices* is directly after *Hecuba* (which contains a similar sort of entrance speech, see above, n. 1) in the plays of 'semi-severe' style. For an attempt to date *Supplices* see G. Zuntz, *The Political Plays of Euripides* (Manchester, 1955), pp. 88–91. G. E. M. de Ste

contrast the types of entrance found in earlier plays such as *Med.* 663, *Alc.* 476, *Hipp.* 790, *Andr.* 881. Of course Euripides did not use one type of entrance to the exclusion of another in the later plays. After the entrance monologue of Polynices which we described above, we have the contrast of his brother's entrance: 446 μῆτερ, πάρειμι, 'I am here, mother.'

Leo asserts, when discussing these passages, that ἔα is the word that ends the monologue. This is true only up to a point. It marks a transition in the speaker's thought, but not, however, the point at which the speaker ceases to talk to himself and begins addressing another person. Theseus (*Suppl.* 92 ff.) spends six lines in describing what he sees before he addresses his mother. Hercules likewise (525 ff.) describes the situation before him and also states his intention of addressing the people on stage before actually doing so. So Helen (*Hel.* 541) does not immediately address Menelaus, but deliberates over his appearance. Theoclymenus does not address anyone after he exclaims ἔα: he explains rather why he has cried out. Similarly in scenes where means other than the cry ἔα are used to make it clear that the speaker has observed the presence of other people on stage, the speaker continues to talk to himself before turning to address the other people present (*Bacch.* 248, *Phoen.* 276). This portion between recognition and address has some claims to be called an aside,[1] particularly the passage in the *Phoenissae* where Polynices says he will *hide* his sword.

Croix (*The Origins of the Peloponnesian War* (London, 1972), p. 356, n. 1) argues against Zuntz. I do not believe it is possible to date the play with reference to contemporary military and political events.

[1] So Barbieri, p. 116. G. M. A. Grube, *The Drama of Euripides* (London, 1941), p. 357, also regards Polynices' speech as 'in a sense an aside', but he mistakenly includes in this category not just 276 but also the part preceding it.

3. Aeschylus and Sophocles

i

THERE is no passage in Aeschylus comparable to Eur. *Hec.* 736 ff. or even Eur. *Hel.* 133a, 139b. Aeschylean actors, it is true, often turn away from their companions on stage to address the gods or the elements.[1] They never do so, however, in situations where the plot requires that what they say be concealed from other actors who may happen to be present. Often the dramatic effectiveness of such turnings away would be greatly reduced if we were meant to suppose that what was said in them was to be regarded as unheard by the actors present. One cannot agree wholeheartedly with Fraenkel when he comments on Aesch. *Ag.* 1646 ff.:

> ’Ορέcτηc ἆρά που βλέπει φάοc
> ὅπωc κατελθὼν δεῦρο πρευμενεῖ τύχηι
> ἀμφοῖν γένηται τοῖνδε παγκρατὴc φονεύc.

Orestes is surely still alive to come back if fortune is kind and prove an àll-powerful slayer of these two,

‘1648 shows how this sentence is to be played . . . the coryphaeus has turned away from Aegisthus and is speaking (in the language of the modern stage) “aside” or (in terms of Aeschylean ideas) to the gods to whom alone such a prayer or wish can be addressed.’ No one would quarrel with the second half of this statement, but surely the coryphaeus’s words are in *no* sense an aside. There is no hint that a convention is operating whereby the speaker’s remarks are to go by unheard by his interlocutor. The coryphaeus at this point does indeed interrupt a conversation with Aegisthus and go on to speak of him (and of Clytaemnestra) in the third person, but that does not mean that he is trying to

---

[1] See Schadewaldt, *passim* (index, s.v. ‘Selbstäusserung’). Cf. also Fraenkel (*SBAW* 1957, pp. 55–6) on Aesch. *ScT.* 653 ff.

conceal his hopes from the two of them. The wish that Orestes may return and kill Agamemnon's murderers is of a piece with the defiant and insulting question put by the coryphaeus directly before it and squares with the chorus's belligerent attitude throughout this whole scene.

What we do find in Aeschylus relevant to the topic of our inquiry is a type of entrance speech foreshadowing the type found regularly in the later plays of Euripides discussed in the previous chapter. There are occasions when characters enter and deliver long speeches which seemingly take little or no account of the other people present on stage.[1] So the herald in *Agamemnon*, on entering, at first ignores the chorus and delivers a speech of thanksgiving for his safe return from Troy. He begins by addressing the land of Argos (503) and goes on to address the royal palace (518 ff.). Only at 522 does he take note of the chorus, referring to them in general terms as 'all those present here'.[2] Similarly, later in the play Agamemnon, when he enters, prefaces his reply to the chorus's greeting with a long section (810–29) addressed to Argos and the local gods. When Aegisthus enters (1578), he ignores the chorus and Clytaemnestra, beginning with an apostrophe ὦ φέγγος εὖφρον ἡμέρας δικηφόρου 'O kindly light of day that has brought justice'. This leads to a speech of self-justification during which at some point Aegisthus addresses the chorus leader (ὡς ὁρᾶις, 1597, shows that he is no longer soliloquizing) : Fraenkel suggests that he has turned to the chorus by the time he speaks l. 1583.

The form and extent of these entrance speeches, rather than any implication within them that a convention is operating when they are delivered, has led scholars to see in them anticipations of the type of entrance monologue which became so common in New Comedy, the 'Auftrittsmonolog'.[3] The Euripidean entrance speeches discussed above are much more obviously conventional.

---

[1] See Fraenkel on Aesch. *Ag.* 829.

[2] Commentators differ on who is addressed in the continuation. Fraenkel takes ἀσπάσασθε (524) as addressed to the chorus: Denniston and Page believe that the herald continues his address to the palace. I believe that 538–9 supports their view.

[3] Leo, p. 8, Wilamowitz, *Aischylos Interpretationen* (Berlin, 1904), p. 169, Fraenkel on *Ag.* 729.

In the Aeschylean passages it is of no importance dramatically whether or not the new entrant takes immediate note of the presence of other people on stage. Nor is there present that clear demarcation to be found in Euripides between self-absorbed soliloquy and soliloquy where the speaker is aware of the presence of others: there is no startled phrase (like ἔα· τί χρῆμα;) to make this division clear. Some of Aegisthus' speech is certainly meant for the chorus,[1] the herald moves on to mention obliquely the presence of the chorus, and one might argue (though this is probably reading too much into the particle) that Agamemnon's μέν in the first line of his speech presupposes that he will eventually reply to the advice the chorus has just given him.

There is, however, in Aeschylus one passage closer to the Euripidean speeches, one place where a character enters unaware that the stage is already occupied and expresses surprise on finding that it is. Athena at *Eum.* 397 arrives to find a stage already occupied by Orestes and his pursuers, the furies. She does not, however, take immediate notice of their presence, but delivers a speech which explains her arrival and describes where she has come from. Only at 406 does she signal that she has seen the furies:

καινὴν δ' ὁρῶσα τήνδ' ὁμιλίαν χθονὸς
ταρβῶ μὲν οὐδέν, θαῦμα δ' ὄμμασιν πάρα.

Seeing this group newly arrived in the land, I am not at all afraid, although it is a remarkable sight.

After this she turns to them to ask them who they are.

This is surely a close parallel for the Euripidean type of entrance monologue.[2] Of course the calm way in which Athena reacts to the unexpected sight of the furies contrasts with the

---

[1] Leo p. 30, n. 4: 'die Rede des Aegisthos Aesch. *Ag.* 1577 die einen ähnlichen Anstrich [to the Eur. examples] hat, ist doch von ganz andrer Art: Aegisthos erzählt zwar, aber dem Chor, um seine Tat als Resultat gerechter Überlegung und des auf Agamemnon ruhenden Fluches zu erweisen.'

[2] Schadewaldt (p. 53, n. 2) distinguishes this passage from the Euripidean entrance speeches because what Athena says is, in contrast to them, 'bühnenbewusste "Mitteilungen"' and one cannot therefore speak of Athena as self-absorbed in the way Euripidean characters are. This seems an over-fine distinction in an area where drawing distinctions is hazardous (see below, p. 185), but in any case it is the formal similarity that I wish to stress here.

surprise and, on occasions, near panic which some of the Euripidean characters display when they realize that they are not
alone. One would not expect a goddess to react like that. And the
reasoned and unhurried description of her feelings is of course
characteristically Aeschylean.[1] However, given these qualifications, it is not a very long step from the technique found here,
the rational description of a character's emotions on seeing others
present on stage, to the kind of conventional statement of the
actor's intention once he is aware that he is not alone that is to be
found at Eur. *H.F.* 429 and *Phoen.* 276–7. In addition, we may
note that an entrance like that of Athena here (and to a lesser
extent those entrances in *Agamemnon* mentioned above) so to
speak freezes the stage action. All those on stage must wait
inactive and unnoticed until the speaker brings them back into
the action. An audience that is accustomed to such a technique is,
at least in some degree, prepared for a convention like that of the
aside where one actor communicates his private thoughts without
the other people on stage taking note of what he is saying. In such
a case there is also a kind of freezing of the action, with all attention concentrated on one actor to the exclusion of the others.

ii

The plays of Sophocles contain some passages that are highly
relevant to our inquiry.[2] They are set out below.

Antigone

(a) The guard expresses the hope that the person who buried
Polynices may be caught:

> 327 ἀλλ' εὑρεθείη μὲν μάλιστ'· ἐὰν δέ τοι
> ληφθῆι τε καὶ μή, τοῦτο γὰρ τύχη κρινεῖ,
> οὐκ ἔcθ' ὅπωc ὄψηι cὺ δεῦρ' ἐλθόντα με.
> καὶ νῦν γὰρ ἐκτὸc ἐλπίδοc γνώμηc τ' ἐμῆc
> cωθεὶc ὀφείλω τοῖc θεοῖc πολλὴν χάριν.

Well I hope he is caught, but whether he is or is not—this depends
on chance—you can depend on it that you won't see me coming
here. As it is, I owe thanks to the gods for this unexpected reprieve.

---

[1] See Schadewaldt, pp. 38–9.
[2] For doubt as to whether fr. 690N is an aside, see above, p. 19.

In the scholion on 327, we meet the suggestion that the lines were delivered aside 'since these words could not be spoken in the presence of Creon'.[1] This comment is fair: the tyrant of Thebes is scarcely meant to hear the guard's garrulous expression of relief in 329 f. The scholiast, however, has failed to envisage properly the movements of the actors in this scene. The lines can only be an aside if Creon is present within earshot when they are spoken. We know from 386 f., where we are informed that he is coming out of the palace, that he must have left the stage at some point before the choral ode which begins at 332. Obviously he leaves *directly* after he has addressed the guard in 324–6. These are the lines of a man taking leave and expecting no answer:

κόμψευέ νυν τὴν δόξαν· εἰ δὲ ταῦτα μὴ
φανεῖτέ μοι τοὺς δρῶντας, ἐξερεῖθ' ὅτι
τὰ δειλὰ κέρδη πημονὰς ἐργάζεται.

Go ahead and make fine distinctions about 'opinion', but unless you show me the culprits, you will agree that greed creates woes.

Whom then is the guard addressing in 329 (οὐκ ἔσθ' ὅπως ὄψηι), if Creon is out of earshot? Theoretically there are three possibilities. Either he is addressing the coryphaeus or the departing (but out of earshot) Creon or else—and this is surely a more remote possibility—ὄψηι is generalized and he is addressing no one in particular. Of these alternatives, the second is by far the most likely. Up to this point the guard's dealings have been exclusively with Creon. We have already collected many examples of actors continuing conversations with another actor who has just left or is leaving the scene.[2]

(b) 740 ὅδ' ὡς ἔοικε τῆι γυναικὶ συμμαχεῖ. 'This man, it appears, fights his wars with the woman as ally.' Creon passes

---

[1] ἀπιὼν ὁ θεράπων καθ' ἑαυτὸν ταῦτά φησιν· οὐ γὰρ δυνατὸν ἐπὶ τοῦ Κρέοντος ταῦτα λέγεσθαι ὡς καὶ ἐν τοῖς κωμικοῖς. Porson emended τοῖς κωμικοῖς to τοῖς Καμικοῖς comparing Phot. Lex. 413, s.v. Πέρδιξ (Suda, s.v.) = Soph. fr. 300N (323P), where the manuscripts read Σοφοκλῆς δὲ ἐν κωμικοῖς. If this was correct, it would on the face of it be an attestation of an aside in Sophocles. The emendation is, however, unlikely and unnecessary. Asides after all are predominantly associated with comedy (see below, pp. 87 ff.). For οἱ κωμικοί compare the scholia on *Phil.* 25 and *O.C.* 17 and for the phraseology, οἷόν τι καὶ παρὰ τῶι κωμικῶι (Σ Eur. *Or.* 168).

[2] See above, p. 34.

this comment about his interlocutor, Haemon, during stichomythia. Lines like this, where the dialogue partner is spoken of in
the third person, have the appearance of being asides.[1] Clearly,
however, this particular line is not an aside since it does not go by
unheard: Haemon immediately takes up the point his father has
made with the words εἴπερ γυνὴ cύ, 'if you are a woman'.

To whom is 740 addressed? The obvious answer might be
thought to be the chorus, the third party present as witness to
this altercation. To interpret the line in this way would obscure
an idiom of real-life conversation that Sophocles is here reproducing. To speak of Haemon to his face in the third person is a
method by which Creon expresses his exasperation with him, it is
almost a way of advancing the argument. Formally it constitutes
an appeal to witnesses, and, as it happens, there are on this
occasion witnesses present, but I doubt whether we need suppose
the line to be specifically directed at them. Odysseus in Eur. *Cycl.*
is alone with the chorus of satyrs when he exclaims of them in
exasperation:

642   ἄνδρες πονηροὶ κοὐδὲν οἷδε cύμμαχοι.

These men are no good, hopeless as allies

(a line which is not an aside since the satyrs, like Haemon in our
passage, take up what the speaker says).[2] For a passage in
Sophocles comparable to *Ant.* 740, we may quote *Tr.* 1238 where
Hercules in the presence of his son Hyllus and in response to his
son's threatened disobedience speaks of him as ἀνὴρ ὅδ' 'this
man'.[3]

[1] See above, p. 31.
[2] It might be argued that the line is addressed to the audience, but there is no
evidence that (in the fifth century at least) satyr drama differed from tragedy in
regard to the dramatic illusion: see Bain, *CQ* n.s. 25 (1975), 23 ff.
[3] Further examples of 'third person address' in Greek drama are: Soph. *O.T.*
429 (Dawe, *Studies on the Text of Sophocles* (Leiden 1973), p. 230, arguing in favour
of Enger's transposition of 404–7 to follow 428 says that with the transposition it
becomes immediately intelligible why Oedipus first addresses his remarks to the
chorus, referring to Tiresias in the third person. The passages collected here show
how common it is for speakers to turn away from their interlocutors and speak of
them in the third person. It seems to me quite inappropriate to have Oedipus wait
for four lines before his outburst and mechanical to assume that because Oedipus
is speaking of Tiresias in the third person he is addressing the chorus), Soph. *Phil.*
910 f., Eur. *Hipp.* 1038 f., Eur. *Suppl.* 426 (note the ironical γε as in *Bacch.* 800 f.),

O.T.

(a) A word perhaps is necessary on the famous confrontation between Oedipus and Tiresias. If we consider the scene from the point of view of strict logic and forget for the moment that it is from a play, what happens in this scene and the behaviour of the two characters are at times past comprehension.[1] Some have found Oedipus' lack of reaction to portions of the information imparted by Tiresias so incredible that they have tried to explain it by assuming that Oedipus does not hear some of the remarks that Tiresias addresses to him, that is to say that an aside convention is operating.

Given that Oedipus has been told by Apollo that he is to kill his father and marry his mother, given too that he believes himself to be an incomer to Thebes and can recall that he killed an old man when first on his way to Thebes, it is indeed incredible that Tiresias' utterances at 366 f., 413 ff. (particularly the mention of the ἀμφιπλὴξ ἀρά of his mother and father), and 452 ff. do not call any of these data to mind and provoke further cross-examination of the seer. On this reasoning, either Oedipus is strikingly unintelligent or else he does not hear what the seer says. In fact it is only the last and most explicit of Tiresias' predictions that provokes no response from Oedipus. He does react to 366 f. by asking whether Tiresias thinks he can say such things with impunity. He has a similarly angry response to the more extended predictions of 413 ff.: ἦ ταῦτα δῆτ' ἀνεκτὰ πρὸς τούτου κλύειν; 'who could bear to listen to such words from this man?' (429). This surely rules out of the reckoning the possibility that any part of Tiresias' utterances is delivered aside. There is nothing in

---

Phoen. 920 (like the Antigone passage, this comes in stichomythia), Or. 1587, Bacch. 800–1. D. Tarrant, CQ n.s. 8 (1958), 159, provides some examples from comedy (cf. also Men. Epitr. 60, Dysc. 480, Peric. 87, Plaut. Most. 38, and Theocr. 15. 89). Cf. Plato's use of οὗτος ἀνήρ (Gorg. 467b1 and 505c3). See J. Svennung, Anrede-formen (Skr. k. hum. Vetenskapssamfundet, Uppsala 42, 1958), p. 420—Of course there are occasions when a speaker appeals to the chorus as witness: the effect is the same as that of the short exclamations we are discussing, but the speaker is allowed to go on at greater length (cf. Soph. Ai. 1093 ff. and Ant. 473 ff., on which see H. F. Johansen, General Reflection in Tragic Rhesis (Copenhagen, 1959), p. 29, n. 42).

[1] See, especially on Tiresias' motivation, Tycho von Wilamowitz, pp. 75–9.

the text to make it clear that Oedipus is supposed by convention not to hear them.[1]

To 452 ff., however, Oedipus does not reply. It seems absurd to suggest that he does not reply because he has already left the stage. If that were the case, Tiresias' predictions would be cast into empty air. The effect would be grotesque (because the speaker is blind) and pointless. Oedipus must be present surely to hear 460 ff. (καὶ ταῦτ᾽ ἰὼν | εἴcω λογίζου κτλ.). By giving the seer the last word in this scene, by having Oedipus exit silently, as it were obedient to the seer's command at 460 f., Sophocles has so to speak made Tiresias the victor and Oedipus the loser in this confrontation. The first shadows have been cast over Oedipus.

That the play proceeds on a tack different from that demanded by logic and probability, that as yet Tiresias' dark hints which become ever clearer about Oedipus' association with his family are not immediately taken up by Oedipus or by the chorus troubles the reader more than the spectator. The reader is disturbed by Oedipus' failure to react on these crucial occasions because he is aware of the outcome of the play and approaches each scene with all the relevant facts about Oedipus in his head. The spectator, however, while probably well enough aware of the outline of the Oedipus story has not the time for leisurely reflection on Oedipus' behaviour. He can take note only of what the dramatist emphasizes. Only one of the 'relevant facts' has been put before the audience before the Tiresias scene, and that only in an oblique way. From 103 f. they are in a position to infer that Oedipus is a late-comer to Thebes. The incident at the cross-roads and the prophecy that Oedipus has been carrying with him from his youth are pieces of evidence that are only presented as part of Oedipus' consciousness later in the play (725 ff., 774 ff.). If they had been mentioned by Oedipus or anyone else *before* his encounter with Tiresias, there is no doubt that an audience

---

[1] I do not understand why W. M. Calder III, *CW* 13334 (1969), 20, singles out 372–3 as an aside, a prediction much less likely to touch Oedipus than those that mention his family connections. In fact Oedipus takes up the lines, replying in a distich—he takes up the threatening element in 372–3 (N.B. τάχα and compare the idiom discussed by Fraenkel on Aesch. *Ag.* 1649): 'you may say this but in your blindness you cannot hurt me or anyone else who sees the light.'

would find Oedipus' behaviour extremely strange. As it is, the audience are not meant to think (at least initially) about Oedipus' consciousness of the past in this scene: their attention is focused on a conflict between two men who become increasingly angry and upon the dark utterances of Tiresias. To pause to wonder that Oedipus is slow to work out the implication of these utterances and connect them with his own situation is tantamount to wondering why Apollo has delayed so long in demanding expiation for the murder of Laius. Admittedly the last extended utterance of Tiresias is bound to strike a chord with anyone who has ever heard the name Oedipus, and an audience might have wondered what Oedipus' reaction would be, but the arrangement of the scene is such that the audience is prevented from pondering on this. Oedipus disappears from their sight and the chorus moves to sing an ode which ignores the topic of incest so that, when Oedipus returns, the audience's attention is directed elsewhere. Had he remained on stage after Tiresias' exit, things would have been different.[1] The effect that Sophocles has achieved here could hardly be described as realistic: no one would deny that it is dramatic.

(b) Iocasta's last words in the play run as follows:

1071 ἰοὺ ἰού, δύστηνε· τοῦτο γάρ ϲ' ἔχω
μόνον προϲειπεῖν, ἄλλο δ' οὔποθ' ὔϲτερον.

Iou! Iou! Wretched man! This is all I can say to you, later nothing.

As she departs the chorus comments:

1073 τί ποτε βέβηκεν, Οἰδίπους, ὑπ' ἀγρίας
ἄιξαϲα λύπηϲ ἡ γυνή; δέδοιχ' ὅπωϲ
μὴ 'κ τῆϲ ϲιωπῆϲ τῆϲδ' ἀναρρήξει κακά.

Why ever has the woman rushed away, goaded by fierce grief? I fear that troubles may erupt from this silence of hers.

Nauck objected to the word ϲιωπῆϲ 'silence' and emended to ἰυγῆϲ 'crying iou'.[2] One can see his point since the chorus appears to be describing Iocasta's impassioned cry, followed by the

---

[1] Cf. above, p. 29.   [2] *Hermes* 10 (1876), 124 f.

allusive explanation of it, as silence. An alternative way of ob-
viating the difficulty is to assume that 1071–2 are not heard by
the chorus or by Oedipus, that Iocasta's exit like those of Eury-
dice in *Antigone* and Deianira in *Trachiniae* is a silent one, silent at
least for those on stage: the audience will hear her speaking
aside.[1] The ϲιωπῆϲ of the chorus would be paralleled by Eur. *I.A.*
1142. I do not like the idea of introducing asides into this scene.
The poignancy is greatly reduced if Oedipus is to be thought of as
not being able to hear rather than not being willing to listen to
what his wife says. ϲιωπῆϲ must, I think, refer to the second part
of 1072. The chorus is saying that Iocasta's refusal to say anything in the future portends ill.

(*c*) When the old herdsman who gave Oedipus as an infant
to the Corinthian shepherd is cross-questioned by that shepherd
and is told that the child was Oedipus, the king who stands
before him, he exclaims angrily to the Corinthian:

> 1146　οὐκ εἰϲ ὄλεθρον; οὐ ϲιωπήϲαϲ ἔϲηι;

Go to Hell! Won't you keep your mouth shut?

On this line Jebb comments: 'the situation shows that this is not
an "aside". The θεράπων while really terrified could affect to
resent the assertion that his master had been a foundling.' Jebb
is correct in his assertion that the line is not an aside, but his
reasoning seems to me over-subtle. The line is not an aside,
because Oedipus' interruption that follows it shows that he has
heard it. There is no need here to seek an ambiguous meaning for
the line, as Jebb does, so that it could be heard with equanimity
or at least without too much suspicion by Oedipus. Jebb's
attempt makes too great a demand of the audience. How could
an audience guess that the old man was 'affecting resentment' or
any other emotion when he delivered the line? There is nothing
in the text to tell them. If an audience does speculate—and there
is scarcely much time for speculation in the course of stichomythia
—on the motives of the old man in saying what he does and in

---

[1] Roussel in his commentary (Paris, 1940) takes it in this way: he is followed
by Barbieri, p. 83.

trying to halt the inquiry, they will surely decide that the old man knows full well the truth of the situation and wants to prevent the truth from coming out.[1] A moment's reflection on the part of anyone placed in his situation would have told him that it was too late to suppress the truth, that the messenger had already said too much and that any attempt to try to shut him up would only make Oedipus suspicious and more eager to press on with the inquiry. Unfortunately at times of crisis, characters of tragedy are no more wont to pause for reflection than real people in real times of crisis. Jebb's interpretation takes the emotion away from the scene and makes the old man's behaviour unnaturally calculating.

Electra

(a) Clytaemnestra begins her prayer to Apollo as follows:

> 637 κλύοιc ἂν ἤδη, Φοῖβε προcτατήριε,
> κεκρυμμένην μου βάξιν. οὐ γὰρ ἐν φίλοιc
> ὁ μῦθοc, οὐδὲ πᾶν ἀναπτύξαι πρέπει
> πρὸc φῶc παρούcηc τῆcδε πληcίαc ἐμοί . . .

I beg you now Apollo to hear my 'hidden' utterance. My speech is not among friends and it is not fitting to uncover and bring to light everything when she [Electra] is nearby.

Some have misunderstood this and assumed that the prayer which follows is spoken in such a way that Electra cannot hear it.[2] Clytaemnestra's prayer is hidden in the sense that she will not utter out loud to Apollo all her wishes because of Electra's presence: the god is expected to guess her unexpressed wishes and see them to fruition. There is nothing in the prayer which is uttered aloud which could not be heard by Electra. If the speech really was concealed from Electra, one would expect it to contain

---

[1] It is possible that the old man might deliver the line in such a way as to suggest that he was trying to keep what he said from Oedipus.

[2] Lewis Campbell writes on 655 'this part of the prayer is merely formal, and is uttered in a loud voice, the rest having been spoken aside'. Kells's notes on 638 and 643 imply that he takes it in this way. Schneidewin correctly notes 'verhaltenes Reden, das nur verstohlen auf das worauf es hinaus will deutet'. Barbieri, p. 85, does not think that there is an aside here.

a specific wish for the death of Orestes rather than the allusive generality of 648–9.

(b) On hearing the report of Orestes' death in a chariot race at the Pythian games, Clytaemnestra reacts as follows:

766 ὦ Ζεῦ, τί ταῦτα, πότερον εὐτυχῆ λέγω,
ἢ δεινὰ μέν, κέρδη δέ; λυπηρῶς δ' ἔχει,
εἰ τοῖς ἐμαυτῆς τὸν βίον cώιζω κακοῖς.

Zeus, what is this? Am I to call this fortunate, or dreadful, but all the same a gain? It is a painful state of affairs if I save my life with my own woes.

It was Leo's belief (p. 12) that Clytaemnestra's words constituted the first aside in Greek tragedy.[1] One may agree that the lines in question are not addressed to anyone on stage and that they show little awareness of the presence of other people,[2] but it is hard to see why the poet should wish Clytaemnestra's feelings to be kept secret from the other people on stage. In fact what the paedagogus says next suggests that he is supposed to have heard her: τί δ' ὧδ' ἀθυμεῖς, ὦ γύναι, τῶι νῦν λόγωι;[3] It is just possible to extract from the words a comment on Clytaemnestra's appearance and demeanour rather than on anything she may have said, but that is not a natural interpretation (τί δ' ὧδ' ἀθυμεῖς looks as if it takes up λυπηρῶς δ' ἔχει; cf. Oedipus' reaction to Tiresias' entrance speech O.T. 319 τί δ' ἔςτιν; ὡς ἄθυμος εἰcελήλυθας). Clytaemnestra's remarks should be categorized as 'Selbstäusserung':[4] they are not an aside.

(c) Orestes, after hearing Electra's speech addressed to what she believes are the remains of her dead brother and

---

[1] Few would now confidently assert that Soph. El. preceded Eur. Hec.

[2] Nothing could be further from the truth than the view found in the scholia and taken up by some commentators that Clytaemnestra is insincere when she delivers these lines. For a refutation see Kaibel, ad loc., Tycho von Wilamowitz, p. 188, n. 1, K. Reinhardt, Sophokles (Frankfurt³, 1947), p. 163, n. 277.

[3] Schaffner's tentative suggestion (p. 7) that τῶι νῦν λόγωι means 'your present utterance' would make it quite clear that the old man was supposed to have heard her: unfortunately it cannot be accepted. Nor can we accept Kaibel's demand that we take νῦν with ἀθυμεῖς. It is based on a quite arbitrary notion of what the old man should have said and despite Kaibel's suggested parallels the word order surely rules it out.   [4] So Schadewaldt, p. 30, n. 2.

after hearing the chorus address her by name as Electra (1171), exclaims:

1174 φεῦ φεῦ, τί λέξω; ποῖ λόγων ἀμηχανῶν
ἔλθω; κρατεῖν γὰρ οὐκέτι γλώccηc cθένω.

Ah! What am I to say? What words can I resort to in my distress? I can no longer master my tongue.

Again I quote Jebb: 'Orestes, deeply moved speaks to himself loud enough for Electra to hear. A similar aside (if it can be so called) *Phil.* 895.' Again the term 'aside' is used when it does not really apply. What we have here is an emotional utterance spoken with no hint of concealment and clearly overheard by the other character on stage. As we have remarked before, the aside occurs only when such remarks are demonstrably not heard by the other person present. It was open to Sophocles to use the aside-convention here: he chose not to. Orestes' remark is there to attract Electra's attention and begin the dialogue which leads to recognition. Its main function is to make it plain to the spectators that this is the point at which Orestes realizes that he is in the presence of his sister.[1] It is probably because Jebb assumes that Orestes has known all along that he is confronted by Electra that he toys with the word 'aside' in describing 1174–5. If one believes that Orestes is playing a part, pretending to be a messenger, and is fully aware of Electra's identity, one feels that he may wish to keep up that role and as a consequence that he does not mean Electra to hear the lines in question.[2]

Orestes' loss of control here is of immense significance dramatically (see the quotation from Tycho von Wilamowitz below, n. 1). What we have is something much simpler and grander than the elaborate pretence envisaged by Jebb. Again, as so often, self-expression is mistaken for an aside.[3]

[1] Tycho von Wilamowitz, p. 206: 'durch diese Worte der Verwirrung, die aber nicht als Beiseite gesprochen gelten soll, wird genau so wie durch die ganz ähnlichen des Neoptolemos (*Phil.* 895, 897) der Umschlag anschaulich gemacht'.

[2] Barbieri's contention (p. 91) that Orestes would like his thoughts to go unheard because he does not as yet know the attitude of the chorus raises an issue that would never occur to an audience.

[3] And again (cf. above, p. 19, on Soph., fr. 690N, and p. 30, on Eur. *Hipp.* 1060) commentators are seduced into taking lines as asides because the speaker says he cannot remain silent.

Phil. 895 is an exact parallel. At an equally crucial stage in the course of the action, when Neoptolemus is on the point of success in his deception of Philoctetes, the play takes a new course, as he reveals that up to now he has been deceiving Philoctetes. This revelation is prefaced by two agonized 'turnings away' on the part of Neoptolemus:

895   παπαῖ· τί δῆτ' ἂν δρῷμ' ἐγὼ τοὐνθένδε γε;[1]

Ah! What should I do now?

897   οὐκ οἶδ' ὅποι χρὴ τἄπορον τρέπειν ἔπος.

I do not know where to direct my faltering words.

Neither of these is an aside.[2] On both occasions Philoctetes reacts with questions. Similarly later in the scene, when Neoptolemus once more expresses his dilemma (908–9), Philoctetes comments on what he says, although this time he too turns away and speaks of his dialogue partner in the third person (see above, p. 72).

(*d*) After brother and sister are reunited and they have expressed their joy in a lyric duet, someone[3] observes that there is someone coming out of the palace. At this point, Electra begins to

---

[1] Diggle's attempt to keep the λέγε of LB (*CR* n.s. 16 (1966), 263) is misconceived. It is hardly appropriate to have Neoptolemus turn to Philoctetes and say 'Oh god, what am I to do now [sc. about Philoctetes]? You [Philoctetes] tell me.' See also C. Austin–M. D. Reeve, *Maia* n.s. 22 (1970), 4 f.

[2] Barbieri (p. 91) concedes that Neoptolemus' remarks are overhead, but believes that he is trying to speak aside.

[3] According to the manuscripts it is Orestes, but one is inclined to follow the τινές mentioned in the scholia who give 1322–3a to the chorus. The chorus (or rather the chorus leader) is wont to counsel silence on the impending entry of a new character (cf. Soph. *Ai.* 1040 ff., *Tr.* 178–9, *Ai.* 975 f., *O.T.* 631–3, *Phil.* 540–2). Dawe (*Studies on the Text of Sophocles*, p. 198) uses the notice in the scholia as support for a suggestion that 1322–5 belongs in its entirety to the chorus. His reasons seem to me frivolous and he completely mistakes the point of εἴσιτ' ὦ ξένοι ... as delivered by Electra, failing to observe that she is assuming a role because she fears the presence of enemies. His argument that the ἀντιλαβή of 1323 has nothing to recommend it does not hold water. At a moment of high tension in Sophocles ἀντιλαβή is quite in place (see W. Köhler, *Die Versbrechung bei den griech. Tragikern* (Diss. Darmstadt, 1912) section I—surprisingly, to my mind, Köhler classifies this instance as 'ohne Motivierung durch starke Erregung').

dissemble. She addresses Orestes and Pylades as if she were unaware of their real identity :[1]

1323 εἴσιτ' ὦ ξένοι,
ἄλλως τε καὶ φέροντες οἷ' ἂν οὔτε τις
δόμων ἀπώσαιτ' οὔτ' ἂν ἡσθείη λαβών.

Go in strangers, especially since you are carrying a burden no one would reject from the house and no one would be glad to receive.

In fact it is no enemy who emerges from the house, but the trusted old family retainer who enters and rebukes the young people for forgetting the danger of their situation. This highly effective piece of stage action where tension is built up and then reduced when, contrary to expectations, it is a friend that comes on the scene deserves mention here in that it displays a phenomenon one might almost call the reverse of an aside. The actor is speaking for the sole purpose of being heard by someone whom he affects not to have noticed. In this and in the motif (found more explicitly at Eur. *Ion* 515–16 and *Hel.* 859–60) where the new entrant is *heard* coming on to the stage via the stage building, Sophocles seems to foreshadow the techniques of New Comedy.[2] This might be added to the heap of evidence suggesting a late dating for *Electra*, although it should be remembered that *Electra* is a play of intrigue and such plays are the ones in which one would most expect to find asides and phenomena like asides no matter the stage of the dramatist's career at which they may have been written.

Philoctetes

The pseudo-merchant whom Odysseus said he would send, if Neoptolemus seemed over-long in returning to the ship (128 ff.),

---

[1] She behaves in fact exactly like the girl in Demeas' narrative in the *Samia* who whispers to the nurse that Demeas is in the house and then (257) παρεξήλλαξέ τι and says aloud something meant to sound innocent and meant for Demeas' ears (for παρεξήλλαξε compare the stage direction 'he shifteth his speech' in Marston's *Malcontent* I. iv. 44).

[2] For someone deliberately giving misinformation and affecting to be unaware of another's presence in New Comedy see Ter. *Eun.* 942 ff. (see below, pp. 173 ff.). For the phenomenon of hearing the door open and for its relation to tragedy see Fraenkel, *QS*, pp. 60–3.

duly arrives (542) announced by the chorus. He immediately addresses Neoptolemus and proceeds to tell him how he comes to be on Lemnus, warning him that the Greeks are pursuing him. Neoptolemus cross-questions him and asks why it is that Odysseus is not among the pursuers (568 f.). The merchant says that Odysseus and Diomedes have set off on another mission, to fetch another man (570 f.). When Neoptolemus asks who this man is, the merchant begins to tell him and it is at this point that he makes it clear that he is aware of Philoctetes' presence:

> 573   ἦν δή τις — ἀλλὰ τόνδε μοι πρῶτον φράσον
> τίς ἐστιν· ἂν λέγηις δὲ μὴ φώνει μέγα.

There was a man—but tell me first who this man is. But whatever you say, speak quietly.

Neoptolemus answers his question:

> 575   ὅδ' ἐσθ' ὁ κλεινός σοι Φιλοκτήτης, ξένε.

This is the famous Philoctetes, stranger.

To this the merchant agitatedly replies that Neoptolemus is to ask him nothing further, but should get away from Lemnus as quickly as possible. Now Philoctetes, thoroughly suspicious, interrupts and asks Neoptolemus:

> 578   τί φησιν, ὦ παῖ; τί με κατὰ σκότον ποτὲ
> διεμπολᾶι λόγοισι πρός σ' ὁ ναυβάτης;

What does he say, son? Why ever is he selling me down the river to you with dark words?

Neoptolemus says that he does not know what the man means, but that he must speak out openly. This the man, after a further show of reluctance, agrees to do. He tells his story to both of them and leaves.

Lines 573–81 are of great interest for the history of conventions in Greek tragedy. The merchant attempts to converse with Neoptolemus *sotto voce*[1] and to some extent succeeds in his aim: it

---

[1] For μὴ φώνει μέγα in 574 cf. μικρὸν λέγειν 'to speak quietly' and μεῖζον λέγειν 'to speak up'. For examples see W. L. Lorimer, *CR* n.s. 10 (1960), 7–8, Kassel on

is clear from Philoctetes' remarks in 578 (τί φηϲιν . . . κατὰ ϲκότον) that he has not properly heard what the man is saying, that he is aware only that he is *talking* to Neoptolemus. Now when we use words like *sotto voce* or 'in lower tones' in describing a stage. action, we must remember that we are applying a naturalistic term to something almost wholly conventional. In real life two people may converse in the presence of a third and by lowering their voices go partially unheard by him. On stage what actors say must be heard by the audience and, if speech is audible to the audience, it is bound to be audible to whoever else is on stage. It is only by convention (mitigated in cases like this no doubt by the relative positions of the actors on stage) that a third actor can be excluded from a conversation which the audience hears. Hence we are justified in calling 573–4 and 576–7 asides.

The matter is not, however, completely settled once one has said this. There is a complication. This whole scene is founded upon a falsehood. The merchant is in disguise, his story is, in as far as it concerns Neoptolemus and Philoctetes, a lie, and the intention is to deceive Philoctetes. It is easy when reading the play to keep this in mind. But when one tries to analyse the point of these machinations and in particular the part Neoptolemus has in them, one encounters many difficulties.[1] It is easier to analyse the scene in terms of the kind of reaction the poet is trying to

---

Men. *Sic.* 202 and in *Eranos* 63 (1965), 10, n. 21, and C. Austin, *CR* n.s. 18 (1968), 21. To these may be added Arist. *Rhet.* 1403b, 27 where reference is made to different degrees of φωνή, μεγάλη, μικρά, and μέϲη.

[1] See, above all, Tycho von Wilamowitz, pp. 281 ff. An issue like this raises the widest possible disagreement about the nature of Sophoclean dramatic technique. I regret that I have only space here to take up a dogmatic and one-sided position and ignore the many distinguished contributions of those who have written on this topic in disagreement with Tycho von Wilamowitz and his approach to Sophocles. In this particular play, I think the emphasis in the scenes I discuss is on Philoctetes and his reactions to Neoptolemus' noble behaviour. Those who wish to concentrate the dramatic interest on Neoptolemus will naturally find it easier than I do to see him as play-acting throughout. However one takes the scene, it is interesting that Sophocles does not use the device which would have removed any ambiguity. He does not allow the dissembler or alleged dissembler to explain his conduct to the audience aside. There are other such scenes where this would have been a way of removing an ambiguity—e.g. the 'Trugrede' of Ajax. Contrast Shakespeare's approach (see above, p. 17).

evoke from the audience with regard to Philoctetes. If one does this, one begins to doubt whether an audience is supposed to concentrate on the course of the intrigue and to work out the role of the parties in it. Are they really expected to remember that all the while Neoptolemus is merely taking up τὰ cυμφέροντα τῶν ἀεὶ λόγων (131)? Commentators assume that Neoptolemus is 'acting' all the while. Jebb and Schneidewin believe that Neoptolemus *deliberately* enunciates 575 loud enough for Philoctetes to hear it. That he speaks the line aloud is certain,[1] but I find it less certain that he can communicate to the audience that he is 'play-acting' and that the audience can take this point. It seems easier, however, for them to see through the deception practised by the merchant. One assumes that, since the man's entrance has been predicted earlier in the play, when he does enter, the audience accepts that he is a deceiver. It is questionable, however, whether Sophocles wished the audience to have this uppermost in their minds in the scene that follows his entrance. The purpose of the by-play in 573–81 is hardly to hasten Philoctetes' departure (I am speaking in terms of Sophocles' rather than Odysseus' plan): Philoctetes is on the point of leaving with Neoptolemus when the man arrives. One can of course apply real-life standards and say that this is meant to be an accident, Odysseus by sending the man has unwittingly delayed Philoctetes' departure, but this is something not alluded to in the text and therefore irrelevant. The obvious dramatic function of the scene is not so much to deceive Philoctetes as to put him in possession of the facts, to let him know that his presence or perhaps the presence of his bow at Troy is essential if Troy is ever to be taken and that an attempt will be made to remove him from Lemnus, an attempt involving his deadly enemy, Odysseus. In other words it is the 'true' part of the merchant's story that matters. From this follows Philoctetes' impatience to leave Lemnus and his increased trust in the man who has forced the truth out of the merchant, Neoptolemus. This, if one were to regard it as a preconceived plan by Odysseus, would be absurdly complicated. If we were intended to see the scene as a consistently worked-out deception, surely

---

[1] ὅδ᾽ . . . ὁ κλεινός indicates a kind of public utterance.

the truth or anything like the truth should have been kept from Philoctetes.

Throughout the deception scenes in *Philoctetes* it is difficult to keep in mind that Neoptolemus is a deceiver, and one may doubt (with Tycho von Wilamowitz) whether Sophocles wished, until the crucial scene where a turning-point is reached (895 ff.), the audience to regard him in this light. During the by-play of 573–81, if we apply real-life standards—and there are difficulties if we do[1]—and investigate what Neoptolemus' conduct should be if indeed he is carrying out Odysseus' instructions, one would conclude that 575 was deliberately spoken out loud in the same way as we have seen *El.* 1323b–5 to be. Since, however, it seems to me unlikely that an audience at this point in the play is meant to speculate about Neoptolemus' motives or those of the merchant, I would take 573–7 at its face value, as a genuine attempt to converse aside. The effect is thus somewhat less complicated than the commentators would have us believe: it is distinct from *El.* 1323 ff. and from a type of deception scene which we will frequently encounter in New Comedy.

Soph. *Phil.* 573–81 has aroused surprisingly little comment or discussion.[2] Yet the lines provide clear evidence that Sophocles was by 409 prepared to use the aside-convention, a convention that most books on Greek drama attribute to Euripides alone of the tragedians (and for those who see more in this scene than I do, it provides evidence of Sophocles using the convention in a highly sophisticated way). The type of aside he uses is, it should be obvious, different from anything attested in Euripides. We may note the absence from Sophocles of the type of aside found predominantly in Euripides, the emotional outburst by a character hiding his feelings from the people present on stage. There are scenes in Sophocles where we might have expected to find such an aside. Significantly Sophocles, when he wishes his characters to

---

[1] If this were real life and if Neoptolemus, in conjunction with the merchant was putting on an act in order to deceive Philoctetes, would not Neoptolemus, unless there had been some sort of rehearsal, take μὴ φώνει μέγα at its face value, as an attempt perhaps to transmit some secret instructions from Odysseus? The same sort of problem arises at Eur. *Hel.* 1196, on which see Kannicht.

[2] Barbieri ignores it. Zwierlein, p. 65, n. 5 notes that the passage contains an aside.

express their true feelings (as for example at *Phil.* 895), does not avail himself of the convention, preferring to have such emotional outbursts overheard by the other people on stage. To such emotional outbursts, as often was the case with similar outbursts on the part of Euripidean characters,[1] scholars have been too ready to apply the term 'aside'.

[1] See above, p. 33, on Eur. *Hec.* 812 ff., and p. 37, on Eur. *Ion* 252–4.

4. Old Comedy

i

To judge from the stage directions with which editors of Aristophanes like van Leeuwen or translators like van Daele equip their texts, Old Comedy was as conventional as Victorian Melodrama, so frequently are the words 'secum' and 'à part' inserted in the margin. In fact this is an entirely false picture of Old Comedy in production and there are very few genuine dramatic asides to be found in Aristophanes.

Schaffner in his dissertation on asides in comedy came nearer than most scholars of his time to appreciating the true state of affairs with regard to asides in comedy and provided a useful starting-point for discussion by distinguishing three phenomena in Aristophanes relating to that convention.[1] First he noted the 'bomolochic'[2] turning away. A character says something irrelevant to the topic under discussion or offensive to the person who has been speaking which apparently goes by unheard by that person. Such remarks were, according to Schaffner, addressed to the audience 'ioci causa'. An example would be the series of comments made by Dicaeopolis at Ar. *Ach.* 65 ff. Secondly there are cases where a speech is interrupted and after the interruption the speaker continues without taking up the interruptor's point. This type of interruption is, like the bomolochic aside, 'ad

---

[1] I have not attempted to discuss all the passages adduced by Schaffner (or Barbieri) and have chosen for each category the examples which best support his case or at least make it clear what he is trying to demonstrate rather than those which he himself puts in a prominent position. Nor have I searched Aristophanic commentaries systematically for references to asides. The reason for this latter omission should be obvious from what is said in the text.

[2] I agree with Wilamowitz (*Hermes* 64 (1929), 471, n. 1 = *Kl. Schr.* IV 489, n. 1) that 'Der typische βωμολόχος ist schon in seinem Namen eine besonders unglückliche Erfindung'. When I reproduce the adjective 'bomolochic' I am merely quoting Schaffner. Any character in Aristophanes is capable of making jokes that might be called 'bomolochic', not just the putative *Ur-Charakter* of comedy, the βωμολόχος.

spectatores ioci causa'. Thirdly there are occasions when the man
who turns away is genuinely self-absorbed. This type of utterance
Schaffner dignifies with the name 'Homeric soliloquy' pointing
out that it contains the essential ingredients of the monologues
in Homer discussed by Leo, these being self-absorption and
deliberation. An example would be Ar. *Eccl.* 947–8.

This classification goes some of the way towards giving a
clearer picture of 'turnings away' in Aristophanes, but it has its
drawbacks. First the distinction here drawn between bomolochic asides and 'interruptions' is scarcely perceptible and
Schaffner wastes a great deal of ink in attempting to put into
distinct categories essentially similar phenomena.[1] He does not
succeed in finding criteria sufficient to sustain such a distinction.
Secondly—and this in part may explain why he got into trouble
over his first two categories[2]—he never properly confronts the
problem of the illusion in Old Comedy.[3] He does not account for
instance for those passages where actors say things to each other
quite openly, things which would be quite incredible if we
imagined the situation in the play transmuted into real life.
Dover (*AC*, p. 60) gives a perfect example of this when he draws
attention to Ar. *Thesm.* 936–8. There the speaker demands a favour
and at the same time insults the person of whom he asks that
favour. In real life such gratuitous insult would almost certainly
ensure that the favour was not granted, but real-life standards do
not apply here. The audience does not have time or inclination to
speculate on why the person insulted does not react to the insult:[4]

---

[1] For this reason I can bring no example of *interloquium* to set beside the examples
of bomolochic aside and Homeric soliloquy quoted above.

[2] When you say as he does that some scenes in Old Comedy are (p. 23) 'libere
et laxe compositae' in a way that makes it easy for the man who is interrupted to
pass over in silence the interruptions of the bomolochus, you remove the need to
posit an 'aside' convention at all in the case of such remarks.

[3] Neither does Barbieri in his discussion of asides in Old Comedy (pp. 124 ff.).

[4] It is, I suppose, possible that he makes a gesture. Dover aptly compares the
technique of the knockabout comedian found particularly in Marx Brothers' films
where Groucho insults in the most outrageous way people whom the plot of the
film requires he should impress, cajole, or persuade. The reaction of such in-
dividuals is, if anything, a momentary flicker of either disapproval or more likely
bewilderment: they make no verbal comment. Since classical scholars are pro-
verbially insatiable for parallels, here is an extract from *Duck Soup* to illustrate
Dover's point:

it spoils the joke if we assume that the insult is not expressed aloud.[1]

In view of such passages, one hesitates to call most of the passages adduced by Schaffner under the heading of bomolochic asides or 'interloquia' asides at all. Perhaps Schaffner felt a similar hesitation and was consequently induced to demand a category distinct from his bomolochic aside, but he was too constricted by the illusionistic view of drama that prevailed at the time he was writing to press the point home.[2]

The technique whereby the comic actor interrupts a character who is trying to be serious and adds to, or subtracts from, what this man says hardly needs exemplification in Aristophanes. One further point may be made which perhaps argues against using conventional terms to describe it—that is to say against asserting that the audience is supposed to assume that the person interrupted is somehow looking away and unaware that he is being interrupted—and that is this. While many such interruptions which often include the grossest of insults (e.g. Ar. *Ran.* 947 f.) go by without comment and affect not at all what the person interrupted is saying—he just takes up where he left off—there are occasions when the interrupted speaker does take up what the interruptor has said. For example, Agathon who is not deflected from his speech by two such 'bomolochic' interruptions from Euripides' kinsman (Ar. *Thesm.* 152, 157–8) stops to agree (171) with the third. One may concede that the first two

Margaret Dumont: 'As chairman of the reception committee I welcome you with open arms.'
Groucho (as Rufus T. Firefly): 'Is that so? How late do you stay open?'
Groucho's reply is ignored by his interlocutrix.

[1] It is interesting to note the change in standards of realism evidenced by the disappearance of this type of joke in New Comedy. In an analogous situation, one person hoping to get some benefit from another, Men. *Dysc.* 425 ff., editors are obviously right in feeling disquiet that one of the possible emendations there suggested would seem to produce an instance of the beneficiary biting the hand that fed him (see below, p. 128).

[2] e.g. in his discussion of Ar. *Ach.* 457 and 461 (p. 23) he says that the lines are addressed to Euripides while the spectators 'obliquis quasi oculis'. Unfortunately he spoils this essentially correct interpretation by treating the lines as one would lines in tragedy that seem to give the game away (cf. above, p. 23, on Eur. *Med.* 899 f.) by saying that Euripides must take the lines at their face value and not perceive that they are ironical.

interruptions are crude and personal, but it seems arbitrary and artificial to suppose that they were delivered in a way that differed from the way in which the interruptor delivered the third.

To speak of the futility of applying normal standards of psychological probability to the action of Old Comedy and to assert that characterization is discontinuous therein is not, however, the same as believing, with Sifakis,[1] that there is no illusion in Old Comedy. Leaving aside the occasions we have been discussing where people are being manipulated for the sake of the joke, there are some dramatic situations where one *is* justified in applying more or less the same standard to comedy as has been applied to tragedy. Schaffner was conscious of this when he posited a category distinct from the bomolochic joke interruptions, 'the Homeric soliloquy'. His distinction, however, is based predominantly on the difference of addressee, the one category of 'aside' being addressed to the audience, the other being 'genuine' soliloquy. The distinction one should draw in this instance is between the kind of joke interruptions which are outside the dramatic action and situations where it is imperative that the speaker's remarks go unheard by another party since otherwise the course of the action would be different. In other words one should apply the criterion for defining an aside which was suggested above (p. 17) with reference to tragedy. Of course there is no suggestion that in Old Comedy such dramatic situations are in any way more 'serious' than the jokes which we decided not to call asides. In such situations where the dramatic illusion obtains, the dramatist is simply using a different technique, a different means of amusing the audience.

One such dramatic situation is that of the eavesdropping scene. For example in *Pax*, Trygaeus having announced his withdrawal at 234 makes several comments aside as he watches the activity of Polemos and Kydoimos (238–41, 244–5, 248–9, 251, 253–4, 257a[2], 258). Since Trygaeus is supposed to be in

---

[1] See above, pp. 3 ff.

[2] I follow Hermann and Dindorf in giving ὡς δριμύς to Trygaeus rather than to Kydoimos.

hiding, it is reasonable for us and for any audience to suppose that any of these remarks, if overheard by Polemos or Kydoimos, would make a difference to the ensuing action: the two of them would realize that there was an intruder present. In fact there is no response from either of the people on whom Trygaeus is eavesdropping. We are surely entitled in a case like this to describe what happens in terms of the operation of an aside-convention: an audience is to take it that the other parties do not react because by convention they do not hear. As it happens, most, if not all, of Trygaeus' remarks are addressed to the audience and this raises a question which will be dealt with below. For the moment, however, we may note that the use of asides in eavesdropping scenes is a convention that is unattested in tragedy. Tragedy has eavesdropping scenes of a sort. Characters observe others coming on stage and then withdraw telling us that they will watch and listen to what follows.[1] But there are no ancient tragic analogies (the ancestor of such scenes is obviously Roman comedy) for scenes like the opening of Marlowe's *Edward the Second* where Gaveston after announcing his intention to eavesdrop[2] interrupts with aside comments Edward's conversation with the dissident nobles or for *Othello* IV. i. 92 ff. where Othello in hiding comments on a conversation between Iago and Cassio. The aside by the eavesdropper in Greek drama is, as far as we know, confined to comedy. Indeed I should be surprised if the tragic poets were found to have written scenes which included eavesdropping asides. 'Eavesdropping scene' is to some extent a misnomer for the two most notable scenes so to have been described in tragedy, Aesch. *Cho.* 20–212 and Eur. *El.* 109–220. In an eavesdropping scene of the sort we find in comedy attention is divided between the eavesdropper and his victims. In the two long tragic scenes the eavesdroppers are out of sight and an audience is not

---

[1] See Leo, p. 69. Hecuba at Eur. *Hec.* 1054 announces her decision to withdraw in a way that foreshadows New Comedy (ἀλλ' ἐκποδὼν ἄπειμι κἀποστήσομαι), but one can scarcely call what follows an eavesdropping scene since the new entrant Polymestor is blind. Eur. *Hel.* 515 ff. is a kind of eavesdropping scene, but there is no comment from Menelaus telling us he is going to withdraw (see Kannicht ad loc.).

[2] 'Here comes my lord the king and nobles,
From the parliament. I'll stand aside.'

expected to be conscious of their presence. Attention is concentrated rather on the new entrant.[1] It is only when they break cover that the eavesdroppers become significant again.[2] There is no need and little inducement to see paratragedy whenever we encounter an eavesdropping scene in comedy.[3] Although Aristophanes may on occasion allude to the way tragedians introduce scenes where characters announce their intention of leaving the stage in order to observe the new entrants,[4] it did not need a scene like Aesch. *Cho.* 20 ff. to make comedians interested in the motif of eavesdropping and Fraenkel surely goes too far in suggesting that the eavesdropping scenes in Old Comedy derive from tragedy. Long before there was drama there were eavesdroppers and there were no doubt plenty of them in fifth-century Athens.[5]

Another type of aside in a dramatic situation where the action would surely proceed differently if the line was not regarded in

[1] If in either of these tragic cases Orestes was present and in some way visible to the audience, the audience would surely be distracted by his presence, particularly at the point when the new entrant makes it clear that she is Electra (Aesch. *Cho.* 106, Eur. *El.* 115 f.). In Soph. *El.* it is the mention of Electra's name that provokes the first emotional reaction by Orestes (see above, p. 79). It would be incredible in the scenes of the other two dramatists if Orestes were present and did not react to the information that the woman before him was his sister. This problem does not arise since in both cases Orestes and Pylades are out of sight and out of mind.

[2] I suppose that Eur. *Hipp.* 601–68 is a case where the eavesdropper's presence is significant. An audience can hardly avoid attending both to Hippolytus and to Phaedra in this scene, watching the effect his words have upon her. Because this is tragedy, Phaedra is given nothing to say; her silence is much more effective than any asides she might have been given. It is notable that she does not proclaim her intention to eavesdrop.

[3] P. Rau, *Paratragodia: Untersuchungen einer komischen Form des Aristophanes*, (*Zetemata* 45) Munich, 1967, p. 100, n. 9, does not regard such scenes as paratragic as such, but believes their form to be derived from tragedy.

[4] I see nothing tragic about *Ach.* 239 f. and there is room for doubt about *Thesm.* 36 and *Ran.* 315. See Fraenkel, *Beobachtungen zu Aristophanes* (Rome, 1962), pp. 22–4. Fraenkel's case rests on πτήξας (cf. ὑποπτήξας in Eur. *Hel.* 1203) being a word of elevated diction. The phonology of πτήςςω shows that it was not native to Attica and in fact it is not attested in prose before Xenophon (see J. Wackernagel, *Kleine Schriften* ii, 1047), but I am not sure how else one could express the notion of crouching in ambush in fifth-century Athens. Euripides uses the more neutral ἐζώμεςθα in the analogous situation of Eur. *El.* 109.

[5] Leo describes eavesdropping as 'ein natürliches, auf μίμηςις des Lebens beruhendes Motiv'. For allusions to real-life eavesdropping see Herod. 8. 130, Ar. *Ran.* 750 ff. (description of the behaviour that Athenians thought typical of their slaves), Xen. *Cyr.* 5. 3. 56, 8. 2. 10, Dem. 19. 288, Arist. *Pol.* 1314b, 14, Strabo 14. 644, and Plut. *Mor.* 522f–523b. See also above, p. 10.

this way occurs in *Vespae*. It is vital for the action that Bdelycleon's intended victim should not hear Bdelycleon when he
utters line 992: ἐξηπάτηται κἀπολέλυκεν οὐχ ἑκών. 'He has been
deceived and has voted for an acquittal although he did not
want to.'

The subsequent action shows that Philocleon does not hear his
son. He goes on inadvertently to acquit the dog which is on trial
and thus commit an act so contrary to his nature that in his
shaken state he is ready to listen to his son's advice.

In *Thesmophoriazusae* too we find 'dramatic' asides. These turn
out to be most akin to the type of aside we found to predominate
in Euripides. Euripides' old kinsman during the scene of the
women's assembly is trying to keep his identity concealed from
the other people on stage. When Clisthenes interrupts this
assembly with the news that there is a male spy in disguise
present and then with the women's permission begins to interrogate the women in order to find the impostor, the old man is
naturally anxious. As the interrogation works its way round to
him, he three times gives vent to his emotions:

ποῖ τις τρέψεται; (603b) Where is one to turn?
κακοδαίμων ἐγώ. (604b)[1] Wretched me!
διοίχομαι. (609b) I am done for!

After this last comment he turns to run away, but is stopped by
Clisthenes and the interrogation begins.[2]

[1] I do not believe that Maas's transposition of 603 and 604 and his consequent
emendation of 604 ζητητέαι (in a *marginale* reported in his *Kleine Schriften* he suggests
ζητητέον) τἄρ' are necessary or right (*RhM* 68 (1913), 358–9 = *Kleine Schriften*
57–8). Against him one might note that κακοδαίμων ἐγώ is a stronger phrase than
ποῖ τις τρέψεται; and might be thought better coming second.

[2] In the sequel, *Thesm.* 625 does not contain an aside:

Κη. ἡ δεῖν' ἔμοιγ'. Κλ. οἴμοι τάλας. οὐδὲν λέγεις.

Although it is an easy enough change (see J. C. B. Lowe, *BICS* 9 (1962), 29) to
follow Scaliger and others in giving οἴμοι τάλας to the old man so that he delivers
a fourth interjection, the above attribution, the one to be found in the Ravennas, is
certainly correct (in the Ravennas there are no attributions by name and the
dicolon that follows ἡ δεῖν' ἔμοιγ' might just possibly be interpreted as an indication
that what follows is an aside. In that case, however, we would have to assume
the loss of a dicolon before οὐδὲν λέγεις and in any case the *scriptio plena* of ἡ δεῖν'
ἔμοιγε surely makes it clear that a change of speaker was intended). Clisthenes is
exasperated by the unsatisfactory answers he has been receiving from the old

In a situation like this we are justified in assuming that an aside-convention is operating. An audience will take it ill that no one reacts to the old man's cries unless they assume by convention that no one else on stage hears them. This is different from the kind of bomolochic insult where nothing hangs on whether or not the person insulted hears what is said.

These asides are formally akin to the kind of emotional outburst we found in the first scene of Eur. *Helen* (see above, pp. 39 ff.), a play produced a year before *Thesm.* and extensively parodied in it. There Helen twice exclaims aside during her dialogue with Teucer (Eur. *Hel.* 133a, 139b), exclamations which would lead to her true identity coming to light if Teucer heard them. The same considerations which lead us to consider these cries asides apply to the cries of the old man here. Whether there is a closer link between the two passages will be discussed below.

ii

Asides of the type we have just discussed, where it makes a difference to the action whether or not what a speaker says is heard by the others on stage, are not common in Old Comedy. The notion that asides are extremely frequent in that genre is due largely to observation of 'bomolochic' remarks—and these we have argued are quite different from asides—and to a second consideration, the possibility of the audience being addressed directly, a possibility that does not exist in tragedy. This latter consideration has led people to interpret as asides directed at the audience

---

man, his persistent stream of δεῖνας, and interrupts before he can produce some more in the manner of 621 ff. (this point is missed by C. O. Zuretti, *RFIC* 39 (1901), 563, in his defence of the attribution of οἴμοι τάλαc to the old man). The tone of οἴμοι τάλαc. οὐδὲν λέγεις is similar to that of τάλαιν' ἐγώ, φλυαρεῖς at 559 and to οἴμοι τάλαc, οἵοις πιθηκιςμοῖς με περιελαύνεις *Equit.* 887 (also the angry Aeschylus at *Ran.* 926. *Av.* 1260 which van Leeuwen adduces as a parallel is somewhat different. Peithetaerus is scarcely 'ira excandescens' when he says οἴμοι τάλαc to Iris. He is pretending to be afflicted with physical desire (cf. 1253 ff.). Schroeder's comment 'im Gefühl der Übermacht, ironisch' hits the nail on the head). A. C. Moorhouse, *CQ* n.s. 13 (1963), 24 rightly adheres to the Ravennas' attribution. His suggestion that οὐδὲν λέγεις contains an etymological pun is ingenious but perhaps over-subtle. I do not think the lines 'lacking in point' if we decline to accept his suggestion.

remarks that are mere exclamations.[1] One should only consider asides those remarks which cannot with equanimity be heard by other characters, only words which the speaker seeks to conceal and keep to himself. From this point of view van Leeuwen's description of a line like Ar. *Nub.* 492 as an aside is highly questionable.[2] Socrates reacts thus to a particularly stupid remark by his prospective pupil Strepsiades:

ἄνθρωπος ἀμαθὴς οὑτοcὶ καὶ βάρβαρος.

This man is stupid and a barbarian.

Nothing in the dramatic context demands that Strepsiades fail to hear these words. Indeed Socrates' next words which are directly addressed to Strepsiades express his dissatisfaction in just as strong terms:

δέδοικά c᾽, ὦ πρεcβῦτα, μὴ πληγῶν δέει.

I'm inclined to think that you need a beating, old man.

The natural way to play this passage would be for Socrates to address the world in general with an exasperated shrug of the shoulders when he spoke 492. What we are dealing with here is not so much a stage convention as a reflection of real-life behaviour.[3] This is the way a real fifth- or twentieth-century Athenian would react when confronted with an interlocutor as obtuse as Strepsiades. He would appeal to witnesses even if none were there to hear him and would not give a fig whether or not the object of his exasperation heard what he said. It is only the form of Socrates' utterance (the reference to Strepsiades in the third person and the use of a deictic pronoun) and the possibility of audience address that exists in comedy (and of course in the broadest sense this line is addressed to the audience since it is meant to be heard by all the world) that have led people to take it as an aside. To do so is to obliterate the subtle distinctions of tone that exist in Old Comedy. At one moment the poet may call

[1] Barbieri criticizes Schaffner for classifying 'Affektäusserungen' as asides (p. 167).

[2] Schaffner, who criticizes van Leeuwen's 'secum', wants Socrates to speak to the coryphaeus 'clam Strepsiade'.

[3] See above, p. 72, on Soph. *Ant.* 740.

the audience into play, but he is not obliged at *every* moment to remind them that they are watching a play. The transition from audience address to action involving the actors can be as swift as the poet wishes and such transitions may be bewilderingly frequent.[1] There is no need to impose regularity upon Aristophanes in a scene like *Pax* 236 ff., where Trygaeus' asides are sometimes explicitly addressed to the audience or at least take note of them (244, 276 ff., 286), but on another occasion he addresses a 'bomolochic' remark to the people on stage which is not meant to be heard by them (252 f.) and on others he exclaims without addressing anyone in particular (238 ff., 248 ff.). To treat all three types of remark in the same way and to describe them all for instance as 'interloquia ioci causa' addressed to the audience is far too rigid an approach. The actor should be allowed to play the lines in different ways even though they come close together in the same scene. To assume a uniformity of delivery is to forget that actors have both voices and bodies.

Apart from the various 'bomolochic' remarks which we have already discussed, the majority of remarks taken as asides by commentators are simply instances where characters are talking to themselves. There is no more reason for calling them asides than there was to do so with the analogous instances in tragedy. When Socrates re-enters at *Nub.* 731 to examine Strepsiades' progress under the blanket, he talks to himself:

> φέρε νυν ἀθρήςω πρῶτον, ὅτι δρᾶι, τουτονί —
> οὗτος καθεύδεις;

Come now, let me see first of all what this fellow is doing—Here you, are you asleep?

Such a passage tells us nothing about the aside-convention: it is quite possible for someone in real life to talk to himself. Stage dialogue exaggerates the extent of this human activity so that it occurs with improbable frequency and improbable length. Only in a theatre where the actors had been schooled in melodrama, however, would anyone try to deliver as an aside or make much of a line like *Nub.* 731. The same holds true of passages like *Vesp.*

---

[1] For such transitions in New Comedy see below, pp. 185 ff.

826, *Thesm.* 757 f., *Ran.* 1399 (here the speaker is clearly thinking *aloud* since one of the other actors finishes off the thought for him), and *Eccl.* 811.[1]

iii

Whereas, with most other aspects of dramatic technique and form, the tendency has been to regard comedy as the beneficiary of tragedy where there exist elements common to both genres, with the aside, the case is different. It is commonly assumed that asides in tragedy came into being because there were asides in comedy. The relationship was the reverse of the usual one, tragedy or more particularly Euripides being the beneficiary of Old Comedy. This view is to be found at any rate in one of the standard histories of Greek literature.[2]

In an area like this one can speak only of hypotheses; proof is out of the question. Nevertheless there are good reasons for rejecting this view of the ancestry of the aside and for regretting that it has virtually become dogma. It rests upon no real evidence, but rather on a misconceived association of ideas. First because the 'bomolochic aside' is so constant a feature of the genre and because it is treated as an aside, it is easy to associate asides *tout court* with comedy.[3] Secondly, because it is natural to associate the

[1] Schaffner classes these examples under different headings. On *Ran.* 1399 he is surely wrong in saying that Euripides is addressing Dionysus. Euripides is thinking aloud and the second speaker interrupts and makes up his mind for him as he racks his brains for an appropriate line. φέρε which Schaffner uses to support his interpretation of course proves nothing either way. Obviously it *may* be used when one is encouraging someone to answer one's question (e.g. Ar. *Lys.* 1161), but it can equally well be used when one is asking a question of oneself (e.g. Ar. *Thesm.* 768). Its usage is indistinguishable from that of φέρ' ἴδω (compare for both the cases envisaged in the previous sentence, *Vesp.* 762 and *Ach.* 4) which it seems to have supplanted in comic dialogue (the last instance of φέρ' ἴδω accompanied by a question is *Thesm.* 630).

[2] Lesky, *Geschichte der griechischen Literatur*, p. 741, n. 1: 'a parte gesprochene Stellen sind bei Euripides selten. Es dürfte Einfluss der Komödie vorliegen'. He repeats this view in *Die tragische Dichtung der Hellenen*³ (Studienhefte zur Altertumswissenschaft Heft 2) Göttingen, 1972, p. 334. Barbieri (p. 168) also criticizes Lesky's assertion, seeing two distinct developments in the history of the aside, the technical aside originating in comedy, the emotional aside arising from life and presumably coming into comedy and tragedy independently.

[3] Σ Soph. *Ant.* 327 cited above (p. 71) which treats asides as typical of comedy (of course it is possible that the ancient commentator meant to refer to New

idea of asides with audience address,[1] it is an easy step to the
assumption that the aside originated in that form of drama which
is replete with audience address.[2] We have already dismissed the
notion that the 'bomolochic aside' is an aside at all. With regard
to the second point, we may point out that not all asides need be
addressed to the audience: even in comedy there are, as Schaffner
noted, passages of genuine soliloquy. Also tragedy and comedy
are quite distinct with regard to audience address: the illusion in
tragedy is consistently maintained.[3]

When we discard bomolochic 'asides' and examine the few
genuine dramatic asides to be found in Old Comedy, a different
picture of this aspect of the relationship between the technique of
comedy and tragedy begins to suggest itself. We may recognize
that all things are possible and that Euripides or whoever it was
that introduced the aside to the tragic stage was influenced by the
kind of dramatic aside we found in Old Comedy, but we may
well consider it more probable that the reverse happened. If we
discard asides in eavesdropping scenes (these would, I believe,
form the majority of dramatic asides in Old Comedy)—which do
not exist in tragedy—the most notable dramatic asides in Aristophanes are those mentioned at the end of Section i. For the three
involuntary exclamations by Euripides' kinsman in *Thesmophoriazusae* we have, as was said above, good tragic analogues in the
Euripidean play produced a year previously, *Helen.* Confronted
by the two sets of passages, who can be certain that Aristophanes

Comedy. If not, I would suggest that the ancient commentator has shown the same
failure to appreciate comic technique as did Schaffner). Koerte *RE*, s.v. 'Komödie',
1272, derives the aside (he is speaking of the aside in New Comedy) from the right
of the Old Comedy bomolochus to break the illusion.

[1] Miss Bradbrook (p. 122) notes 'the Elizabethan asides . . . were not meant
simply to reveal the inner feelings of the character, but practically always showed
some consciousness of the audience to whom they were addressed.'

[2] Such direct address and mention of the audience are to be found also frequently in the fragments of Old Comedy as well as in Aristophanes (it is always
possible in some instances where we do not have the context that the chorus itself
or a group of men on stage is being addressed): e.g. Cratinus fr. 169, fr. 323?, fr.
347, Eupolis fr. 286, fr. 357, *Demoi CGF* 92. 61, Pherecrates fr. 95 (an offer of
drink to the audience), Plato fr. 90, Diocles fr. 14?, and ? Aristophanes *CGF*
58. 4.

[3] For a discussion of this topic see my article 'Audience address in Greek tragedy',
CQ n.s. 25 (1975), 13 ff.

is leading and Euripides following?[1] Most asides in tragedy are after all outbursts of emotion, particularly expressions of grief. There are no tragic analogies for Bdelycleon's expression of glee[2] as his victim steps into his trap at *Vesp.* 992, but it is easy to think of situations in tragedy where a successful plotter might have expressed his satisfaction in the presence of his victim.[3]

This is mere speculation, but it is surely at least as likely that tragedy influenced comedy in respect of the aside-convention as that the reverse was true. It would be hard at any rate to think of any other aspect in which tragedy was to any significant extent influenced by comedy.

[1] I am not suggesting that we have complete tragic parody in any of these passages. The diction certainly rules this out in the case of *Thesm.* 604b. Only διοίχομαι is above the level of comic diction. What I suggest is that Aristophanes has borrowed a motif familiar to him through tragedy.

[2] Schaffner here debates once more whether this remark is addressed to the audience or the speaker is talking to himself. MacDowell (like Barbieri, p. 31, n. 53) thinks 992 a kind of reminder to the spectators in case they did not follow the business of 987–91. Surely the explanatory function of the line is only incidental. It is an imposing line which ought to be played with a note of triumph. There is no need to seek a particular addressee.

[3] It is natural to think of such lines as Eur. *Bacch.* 848 ἀνὴρ ἐς βόλον καθίσταται delivered as Pentheus leaves the stage but is by convention out of earshot. Possibly [Eur.] *Rhes.* 640–1 is relevant here.

5. From Aristophanes to Menander

So far we have surveyed the drama of the fifth century. Our findings have been various. There are asides in Euripides and at least one in Sophocles, but the aside is not an important feature of tragedy. Nor for that matter does the dramatic aside, as distinct from the joke comment made by a speaker who does not care who hears him, play much of a part in comedy. In tragedy there is a phenomenon, however, which might be considered to be related to the aside, that is the entrance of a speaker to an already occupied stage apparently unaware of the presence of others.

When we turn to the remainder of Greek drama, the comedies of Menander and his contemporaries, we find a picture that is, on first inspection at least, strikingly different. New Comedy appears to have a well-developed and extensive range of conventions quite unlike those of tragedy or for that matter Old Comedy. It is desirable to take a closer look, to see if the one genre is really so different from its predecessors and if there are connections between the older genres and the younger one.

Unfortunately the evidence for the period of transition is meagre. After the light of 388 B.C. we are plunged into the darkness of the second volume of Kock, to re-emerge some sixty or so years later. Nevertheless it is possible to say a little about the conventions of the drama which preceded New Comedy, the later plays of Aristophanes and 'Middle Comedy'.[1] Even with such slender evidence we are able to trace a degree of continuity from the fifth century through to the age of Menander.

The last two plays of Aristophanes are, it must be admitted, disappointing in the results they yield with regard to the kind of

[1] Middle Comedy is not an entirely happy term (see K. J. Dover in *Fifty Years (and twelve) of Classical Scholarship* (Oxford, 1968), p. 145). I use it as a convenient short way of describing the comedy coming after the death of Aristophanes and preceding the first production of Menander.

phenomena we are discussing. Although in other respects they provide plenty of evidence that comedy was undergoing a change (a change perhaps guided by Aristophanes himself), as regards the aside, they differ not at all from his fifth-century plays. There is, however, a passage in *Plutus* which does concern us. At 332 the chorus observes and announces the entrance of a new character, Blepsidemus. This man arrives and it becomes clear from his words on entering why he has come:

> 340 ἔστιν δέ μοι τοῦτ' αὐτὸ θαυμάσιον, ὅπως
> χρηστόν τι πράττων τοὺς φίλους μεταπέμπεται.
> οὔκουν ἐπιχώριόν γε πρᾶγμ' ἐργάζεται

It's this especially that I find remarkable–that he should invite his friends when he is doing well. He's not behaving like a native Athenian.

Chremylus who is present on stage and has heard all this announces that he will conceal nothing (ἀλλ' οὐδὲν ἀποκρύψας ἐρῶ μὰ τοὺς θεούς) and in the next line addresses Blepsidemus directly.

This is strikingly different from other scenes of entrance in Aristophanes. The new speaker, a character about whom nothing has been said hitherto, is announced by the chorus. He enters soliloquizing and does not appear to notice that the man of whom he is speaking is in fact present on stage. Chremylus, the man whom he has come to see, hears this soliloquy and says (presumably to himself) that he will conceal nothing. Only then does he address Blepsidemus and only then does conversation between the two of them begin. The affinities of the technique displayed here with those of the 'conventional' entrances found in the later Euripides are obvious.[1] This Aristophanic example differs from most[2] of the entrances in tragedy in that it is someone on stage who interrupts the new speaker's reverie and starts the conversation. In the majority of examples found in tragedy, the new entrant himself observes that there is someone present on stage and then decides to address him. Both ways of setting the dialogue in motion are, as we shall see, extremely common in New Comedy.

---

[1] See above, pp. 61 ff.   [2] See above, p. 65 n.1

After *Plutus* there is very little to be gleaned about the conventions of comedy until we meet our first Menander play. It is clear that direct address of the audience persists.[1] It is clear too that what Schaffner called the bomolochic aside is still alive in Middle Comedy. The examples he collects (pp. 19–21) from the fourth-century fragments scarcely merit the name aside. They are for the most part exclamations designed to break up long speeches.[2] The actor who finds himself on the receiving end of a *narratio convivialis* or a boastful cook's speech makes some sort of comment on the man delivering the speech. So in Alexis' *Milesia* (fr. 149K) a man comments on what his interlocutor has been saying to him :[3]

> 14   εἰc τοὺc coφιcτὰc τὸν μάγειρον ἐγγράφω.

I enroll the cook among the sophists.

In *Odysseus Weaving* (fr. 155K) by the same poet, one character comments maliciously on the present fastidious attitudes of the man he is talking to :

> 4   †οὗτοc πρότερον κεφαλὴν εἰ λάβοι θύννου†
> ἐνόμιζεν ἐγχέλεια καὶ θύννουc ἔχειν

Previously this man, if he got the head of a (?), thought he was eating eel or tunny.

These two examples show the same technique as the kind of 'aside' found so frequently in Aristophanes which was discussed in the previous chapter. One may observe that in the first of them the cook takes no notice of what has been said but goes on with what he has been saying. I expect that the same happened in the second example. In neither case are we really expected to believe that a failure to respond was a result of a failure to hear. In Antiphanes fr. 222 a man who has hired a cook exclaims in

---

[1] e.g. in the request to the audience not to express their disapproval found in Timocles, *Icarii*, *CGF* 222(b).6. It is difficult in the case of book fragments of Middle Comedy to be sure on occasions when one meets masculine second person plurals whether the audience or the chorus is being addressed. See below, p. 190 n. 4.

[2] See below on Men. *Dysc.* 102, p. 128.

[3] All the examples alluded to in the text are taken by Barbieri (pp. 170 ff.) as asides.

exasperation at the man's persistent questioning[1] ἀπολεῖ μ' οὑτοσί, 'this man will kill me!' Such an exclamation is not to be regarded as an aside: it is a spontaneous and undisguised burst of emotion.[2]

Neither these passages nor any of the others Schaffner[3] adduces (some of the ones he adduces are in any case more likely to come from New rather than Middle Comedy)[4] have anything in common with the type of aside found in Euripides and occasionally in Aristophanes where it would make a difference to the action if the person about whom the remark was uttered heard the remark. There are no occasions in Middle Comedy where we have enough context to say for sure that such and such a remark *must* go unheard by the person in whose presence it is spoken, that is to say we are never able to point to what I call a dramatic aside. Consequently the aside-technique of the genre (if it can be called a genre) remains obscure.

[1] This, the interpretation of Meineke (giving φημί in 2 to the householder), makes best sense of the passage and presents us with a familiar motif, the man who has hired a cook complaining of the cook's persistent questioning (cf. Men. *Sam.* 283 ff.).

[2] See above on Soph. *Ant.* 740, p. 72.

[3] Barbieri (p. 171) adduces Alexis, fr . 173 3b–4a (after Edmonds) ποδαπὸς οὑτοσί | ἄνθρωπος, which comes between τί λέγεις cύ; and οὐκ ἐπίcταcαι ζῆν—a good instance of third-person address. Other passages he adds to Schaffner are too fragmentary and too dependent on supplementation to require discussion (e.g. *CGF* 253. 7, which is in any case almost certainly New Comedy, and *CGF* 265).

[4] I see no reason (nor does Barbieri) for regarding Antiphanes fr. 169. 1 as an aside. The other passages discussed by Schaffner are unlikely to come from Middle Comedy. There is no good reason for treating here the asides found in *CGF* 244, 350 ff., or in *CGF* 257. Athenion fr. 1. 27 καινὸc πάρεcτιν οὑτοcὶ Παλαίφατοc, a third-person exclamation, parallel to the type discussed in the text, interrupting a cook's speech, is unlikely to come from a play written in the mid-fourth century (the author may even have been a contemporary of King Juba—see Jacoby *FGrH* 275 F86 who accepts Müller's identification of this man with the man named in F104). Euangelus who provides us with a similar exclamation ὡc ἀλαζὼν ὁ κατάρατοc (fr. 1. 7K) is just as likely to be a poet of the New as of the Middle Comedy. Even Alexis is of doubtful warrant for the techniques of Middle Comedy since his career extends well into the era of the νέα. Only when we are sure of the date of a particular play can we use a fragment from it as evidence for the practices of Middle Comedy. The title *Odysseus Weaving* certainly suggests Middle Comedy. Of the *Milesia*, the only evidence we have with regard to its date is the reference to Tithymallus (fr. 151K). Since we do not know what kind of reference was made to him (whether as a living contemporary or as a dead, but semi-proverbial, personality), all that we can say of the play is that it could have been produced any time after 350. For plays mentioning Tithymallus see T. B. L. Webster, *CQ* n.s. 2 (1952), 22.

The absence of dramatic asides is probably, however, a mere accident of the tradition. Our quotations from Middle Comedy are rarely rich in action, most of them not even containing dialogue. It seems reasonable to suppose that in this as in other aspects of technique New Comedy is developing what had already come into being in the early and middle fourth century.[1] We may note for instance that the expository prologue is found in both Middle and New Comedy and that there are prologue speeches by deities in both genres.[2] We find both Alexis and Menander varying the stereotyped first announcement of the chorus's entry by adding to it an apostrophe of the chorus.[3] And with regard to the way in which a Middle or New Comedy might end, we may note the strikingly similar ways in which the actors of Antiphanes' *Anthropogonia* and Menander's *Samia* take their leave of the audience.[4]

[1] One aspect of New Comic technique which so far seems to have no antecedent is the device where a character enters speaking back into the house from which he has emerged.

[2] Prime evidence for expository prologue speeches in Middle Comedy is Antiphanes fr. 191. 20 ff., which clearly implies that comic characters spoke such prologues (on the interpretation of this fragment see below, p. 189 n. 1). Old Comedy already knew the type of prologue spoken by a divinity. Calligenia spoke the prologue of Aristophanes' second *Thesmophoriazusae*. Compare too Philyllius fr. 9K, the wording of which strongly suggests a prologue speech (cf. Men. *Asp*. 147–8). For Middle Comedy we have a speech delivered by Rhea (*CGF* 215).

[3] Alexis fr. 107K ~ Men. *Asp*. 247–8. Since we cannot be sure of the relative dating of Alexis' *Kouris* and Menander's *Aspis*, the possibility exists that here Menander is the forerunner of Alexis. It is far from certain that Alexis in fr. 108 of this play is alluding to the comic poet Timocles and even if he was we would not be compelled to presume the priority of the Alexis-play.

[4] Antiphanes fr. 3, *CGF* ~ Men. *Sam*. 734.

6. Asides in New Comedy: I

THE evidence for the stage technique of New Comedy comes from three sources. The first is the by now fairly extensive Menandrean corpus, the second the group of papyrus fragments which obviously belong to the genre but have not as yet been convincingly assigned to a particular author (*CGF* 239–86), and the third the *palliatae* of Plautus and Terence. Interpretation of the evidence provided by this third source brings its own special problems. For the moment we will treat that of the first two together and examine the papyrus fragments of New Comedy to see in what respects the technique there employed diverges from what we know of the technique of Old Comedy and to discover what if anything that technique owes to tragedy. An attempt will be made to characterize Menander's technique with regard to conventions. After this we will turn to the Roman adaptations of New Comedy. In the case of these plays, we will try to discover whether or not they contain technical devices or conventional situations that are not present in Greek drama and to decide on the value of such devices as evidence for Greek stage technique.

Our first concern is with the questions we put with regard to the drama of the fifth century. This chapter and the following one will discuss the types of *dramatic* aside (as well as look for the kind of 'joke' turnings away that were such a prominent feature of Old Comedy) in New Comedy. The chapter after that will look for conventional patterns of entrance.

There are basically two situations in which dramatic asides may occur. If someone who is eavesdropping comments on what he sees and if the victim takes no note of his remarks, we must speak of eavesdropping asides. Alternatively there is the situation where two people are in conversation (or at least have acknowledged each other's presence) and one of them breaks off the conversation to comment apart from his interlocutor who shows no sign of hearing him (or, if he does hear, of understanding what the man is saying). This second type we will call the 'aside in conversation'. For the moment we will deal with the first kind, listing those passages which may be thought or have been thought to contain such asides and appending comment where necessary. The term 'eavesdropping aside' is not here confined to occasions of deliberate eavesdropping, since formally there is little difference between asides which occur in a scene where one character has chosen to eavesdrop on another and asides in which a character comments when the other character just happens to be unaware of his presence.

Men. *Asp.* 465 ff.

> Σμ. ἦ που φέρουϲιν αἱ γυναῖκεϲ ὡϲπερεὶ
> ἐκ πολεμίων. ἐπιτάττεται τοῖϲ γείτοϲι
> διὰ τῶν ὑδορροῶν. Δα. θορυβήϲω τουτονί.
> ἀλλ' ὅπερ ἔπραττον . . .

Smicrines	I expect the women are plundering as though from enemy territory. Instructions are being given to the neighbours through the drains.
Daos	I will throw him into confusion. Well, as for what I was (they were?) doing . . .

The point of Smicrines' words in 465–7a has not yet been satis-factorily elucidated.[1] It is clear that he is conjuring up a picture (such is the force of ἦ που) of what is going on inside Chaere-stratus' house. It remains in question whether he is speaking ironically or with genuine misgivings and this has some bearing on how we take Daos' aside in 467b (obviously θορυβήϲω τουτονί is an aside, as the person who wrote ἡϲυχῆι *supra lineam* in the papyrus recognized).[2] Is this Daos' first utterance on re-entering or is he present to hear all of 465 ff.? In the latter case we would be justified in calling 467b an eavesdropping aside.

---

[1] The most extended discussions of the problem are to be found in D. Del Corno, *ZPE* 6 (1970), 223, K. Gaiser, ibid. 8 (1971), 194 ff. and *Grazer Beiträge* 1 (1973), 135 f. I do not find the aside conversation suggested by Del Corno at all probable. All that I would take for granted about this passage is that φέρουϲιν does not have as an object to be understood Chaerestratus. διὰ τῶν ὑδορροῶν remains inscrutable.

[2] On this see below, p. 132 n. 2.

One cannot be certain about the movement of the actors in this fragmentary scene. Before 467b, the last point at which we can be assured of Daos' presence was at 432 where he was again quoting Euripides, this time to hurry the pseudo-doctor inside. After this line, Smicrines began to soliloquize, which makes it likely if not completely certain that he was alone on stage.[1] When the papyrus resumes, Smicrines is conversing with the pseudo-doctor and there is no indication that Daos is present. On the surface, then, it might appear more likely that θορυ-βήcω τουτονί in 467b are the words of Daos returning to the stage[2] after the departure of the doctor.[3] This will be the first time we have seen him since he ushered the doctor inside at 432.

Nevertheless it might be thought a more effective piece of stage action if Daos heard or rather made it clear to the audience that he had heard 465 ff. Whatever the precise meaning of this utterance, it appears most likely that it reflects Smicrines' anxiety. In view of the way he is depicted elsewhere in the play, one would expect him at this juncture to be extremely keen to see that none of the property which he imagines is coming to him should be removed from Chaerestratus' house before he can get his hands on it. After all, the intrigue that Daos has set on foot depends entirely on knowledge of Smicrines' character and in no small part on the predictable reaction he will show when he hears that his brother is on the point of death.[4] A mixture of greed and

---

[1] In 436 he seems to be justifying his previous conduct to the audience in a way that seems to recall the monologue which begins at 149 (N.B. ἄτοπον which occurs at 160 and ? ἐπηρόμην ~ 149 f.).

[2] 'Daos may have come out with the doctor, but it is perhaps more likely that he appears here' Sandbach ad loc.

[3] προάγωμεc, παῖ in 455 makes it clear that the doctor intends to leave the stage and not return to his patient (cf. Men. Sam. 690, Dysc. 87, Dis Ex. 14–15). The impression perhaps is being given that there is no point in the doctor's attendance; the patient is as good as dead. If we wanted the doctor to play a further part in the play and make an immediate return to the house, we would have to read παράγωμεc (there might be some support for this in δεῦρ' ἀπὸ τῆc θύραc ἔτι 457 which could be taken as suggesting that the doctor had moved towards the door intending to re-enter. H.-D. Blume (Menanders Samia Darmstadt, 1974, p. 106, n. 47) may be right, however, in explaining this as motivated by Smicrines' natural secretiveness).

[4] Gaiser (Grazer Beiträge) stresses this.

fear that he may be cheated will lead him to rush into Chaerestratus' house and lay claim on everything inside it (319 ff.,
356 ff.). In this way he will be trapped.

I would guess that 465 ff. demonstrate Smicrines' fears and
perhaps even show him on the point of rushing in. Daos' θορυ-
βήcω τουτονί indicates that Daos is going to play on these fears to
ensure that he does take the fateful step. If this is the correct
interpretation, it would be neater for Daos to be present while
Smicrines is expressing his misgivings so that he might know
how to agitate further an already agitated Smicrines.[1] The verb
ἔπραττον might in that case be third person, referring to the
women and taking up φέρουcιν, the beginning of a fictitious
account of what the women are doing inside, or rather what they
were doing when he left. The main objection to this interpretation apart from its purely hypothetical nature—and any interpretation must be hypothetical until we have a convincing
interpretation of Smicrines' words and until we have the
whole of 468—is that the text gives no indication of Daos'
presence before 467b. It is possible to show, however, that
Menander was not always completely explicit about the entrances
and movements of characters,[2] so that Daos may have entered
silently while Smicrines was speaking or else have come out
with the doctor and failed to return to the house when the
doctor left.

However we interpret it, θορυβήcω τουτονί is an aside for the
audience's benefit (what Schadewaldt and Barbieri would call
a 'technisches Beiseite') advising them how to take what follows.
It should, I believe, be followed by a full stop.[3] Possibly ἀλλ'
ὅπερ ἔπραττον was not addressed to Smicrines (I think it unlikely
it is a continuation of the aside) but was the beginning of a faked
entrance monologue (and in such a case it might be thought more
likely that ἔπραττον was first person).[4]

---

[1] Cf. Plaut. Amph. 295: timet homo: deludam ego illum.

[2] See below, p. 139.

[3] Cf. Ter. Phorm. 351 where Phormio explains 'iam ego hunc agitabo' and then
proceeds to put on an act ('pro deum immortalium' etc.) pretending not to have
noticed Demipho while at the same time meaning every word to be heard by him.

[4] On faked entrance monologues see below, pp. 171 ff.

Men. *Dysc.*

Cnemon's first entrance monologue is twice interrupted by timorous comments from Sostratus at 168b and 171a (for a discussion of the text of these remarks see Sandbach on 168–71), the second of which leads to a direct address of Cnemon. These are not strictly eavesdropping asides since Cnemon has just become aware of Sostratus' presence (167 f.). There is no indication that any kind of conversation has begun, however, or that Cnemon hears or is supposed to hear either of the remarks. The formal pattern is the same as that of Sostratus' asides considered in the next paragraph.

The entrance speech of Cnemon's daughter is interrupted by aside comments[1] from Sostratus who remains unseen until he addresses her at 199:

191   ὦ Ζεῦ πάτερ
       καὶ Φοῖβε Παιάν, ὦ Διοσκόρω φίλω,
       κάλλους ἀμάχου.

O father Zeus and Phoebus the healer! O dear Dioscuri! What unsurpassed beauty!

194b   ἄνδρε[ς ∪ ⏓,[2] Gentlemen . . .

A little later Daos, emerging from Gorgias' house and on the point of leaving for the fields, chances on this confrontation between Cnemon's daughter and Sostratus. Twice he comments aside, first when the girl is given the pitcher by Sostratus, exclaiming τί ποτε βούλεται οὑτοcὶ | ἄνθρωποc; 212b–13a 'what is this man up to?' and then when Sostratus is alone on stage soliloquizing,[3] interrupting the soliloquy with words that take up

---

[1] In some editions οὐ cχολὴ ματ[_ ∪ _ is given to Sostratus as well (196b). There is, however, no paragraphus under the line and it is difficult by supplementation to give Sostratus an utterance with any point. It seems best, then, to give the words to the girl and adopt a supplement like Gallavotti's μάτ[ην λαλεῖν. See Sandbach ad loc.

[2] τί δρῶ; has become the vulgate here (Sandbach prints Barigazzi's τέραc)— the elevated tone suiting the situation (so Schäfer, p. 120). Recently S. L. Radt (*Mnemosyne* iv. 25 (1972), 138) has attacked it. I am not sure that he is right to argue that δρᾶν could *only* be used in a paratragic context. Possibly the combination of an archaic word recalling the language of tragedy with the audience address ἄνδρεc would be meant to have a humorous effect.

[3] For the correct staging and division between speakers here (now in Sandbach's text) see E. Grassi, *A&R* 6 (1961), 144 and H.-J. Newiger, *Hermes* 91 (1963), 127.

what Sostratus has just been saying κατὰ τρόπον τί; 215 'what does he mean by "all right"?'

During the hectic scene of the entrance of Sostratus' mother and her party, Knemon unseen in the background makes a couple of comments expressing his disgust (431b–2a, 435a on which see Sandbach ad loc.).

The distraught entrance speech of Simiche is interrupted several times with malice by Getas who remains unseen and continues to comment unnoticed even after the entrance of Cnemon (575–6a, 581 ὀρθῶc,[1] 583, 586b?[2] 587–8a, 591b–3).[3] His final suggestion (599b–600a) is overheard and brings an angry rebuke from Cnemon. This is clearly distinct from the other remarks in that it is a genuinely helpful suggestion (καὶ μάλα δικαίωc in 602, 'it's my own fault for being generous', surely proves this)[4] so that we cannot entertain the idea that it was played like the other, unrealistic suggestions as an aside but this time overheard by Cnemon.[5]

Callippides' entrance leads to a short conversation aside between Gorgias and Sostratus (777b–9a). After this Callippides sees Sostratus and addresses him.

Men. *Epitr.*

The soliloquy of Smicrines with which the papyrus fragments of the play begin is interrupted several times by an eavesdropper

[1] This is generally given to Getas against the attribution in the papyrus and Sandbach argues that it must be restored to Simiche (Gomme–Sandbach, p. 224).

[2] That is if we accept Barrett's suggestion that καὶ . . . θύραν be given to Getas (see Schäfer, p. 133).

[3] Those who give 593 to Getas are certainly right: it suits him much better than Cnemon who is not given to explanations. Short utterances characterize Cnemon's anger in this scene (ποῦ 'cτιν ἡ τοιχωρύχος, βάδιζε δὴ | εἴcω, δήcαc καθιμήcω cε). It remains in question whether we follow Lloyd-Jones in assigning 592b to him also. I am not sure that Sandbach is right in assuming that Cnemon hears this comment and is reminded that the rope is rotten (Gomme–Sandbach, p. 226).

[4] Compare Men. *Sam.* 389.

[5] Ritchie gives ὦ 'Ηράκλειc in 612 to Getas too, a surprised comment on *Gorgias'* impolite πάντ' ἔχομεν, this too against the papyrus. I think Sandbach is correct in adhering to the division in the papyrus. There is no point in Getas remaining on stage to the end of the act without making contact with his master; 611a is his exit-line and he has no interest, as a town slave, in mixing with the yokels his master has brought with him (ἀλλά . . . γάρ in 607 indicates that Getas intends to withdraw—see Denniston, pp. 103 f.).

who comments aside (5b–7a (7?),[1] 11b–12, 14b–15). After this
last comment a new character enters and we learn from the
ensuing conversation that the first eavesdropper was Chaerestratus. The new entrant is surely Habrotonon (see Del Corno and
Gomme–Sandbach ad loc.). The two of them begin a conversation whose length the lacunose state of the papyrus does not
enable us to gauge. It is clear, however, that Smicrines is still on
stage while they are speaking. After the papyrus resumes we hear
him (25–7) deciding to enter Charisius' house and observe him
do so. Habrotonon and Chaerestratus are still there and it seems
most likely that Smicrines has completely failed to notice them.[2]

Little is clear about *Epitr.* 433 ff., but it seems likely that
during this scene Smicrines happens to hear the cook Carion
entering and remains on stage commenting aside unnoticed at
first by Carion and whoever else is on stage (see Del Corno and
Gomme–Sandbach ad loc.).

Epitr. 536–7a is a brief comment addressed by Habrotonon to
the child she is holding. As the ensuing action shows, it is not
heard by Pamphila. The only question is whether when Habrotonon speaks the lines she is aware of the presence of Pamphila
or she is merely continuing her entrance soliloquy. Gomme–
Sandbach evidently think the latter and restore accordingly.[3]
They object to the restoration printed in Koerte which implies
that Habrotonon has just seen and recognised Pamphila, that
Habrotonon is not yet certain of Pamphila's identity: 'that
certainty comes only at 860 [540], when she has seen her face to
face.' But it is quite possible for Habrotonon to be practically
certain when she sees the girl and to exclaim joyfully to the child
before she is completely certain (I do not see much point in the
emotional address to the child here unless it is the result of
Habrotonon seeing the mother). Line 540, it should be noted, is

---

[1] It seems to me that the balance of probability is with those who give the whole
of this line to the eavesdropper. One of Arnott's arguments that this must be the
case (*CQ* n.s. 18 (1968), 226) is answered by W. J. Verdenius (*Mnemosyne* iv. 27
(1974), 18) but his case as a whole is strong.

[2] I agree with Kassel (*ZPE* 12 (1973), 6) against Gomme–Sandbach that
Smicrines is not addressing the eavesdroppers at 24.

[3] ὦ φίλτατον τέκνον, πότ' ὄψει μητέρα; (Fraenkel) as against ὦ φίλτατον παιδάριον,
ὄψει μητέρα. (Koerte).

not Habrotonon's *first* reaction on seeing the girl. She it is that calls on Pamphila to wait and to look at her face to face (538–9). Line 536 will be Habrotonon's first emotional reaction to the sight of Pamphila: line 540 comes more by way of confirmation.[1]

Men. *Carch.*

On hearing a door being opened (ἐψόφηκεν), one character announces his decision to withdraw (ἐπανάγω) and at 9 f. is clearly commenting aside on the speech of the new entrant:

> τουτὶ τὸ κακὸν τί] ἐcτι; περὶ τίνος λαλεῖ
> ὁ τρισκακοδαίμ]ων; οὗτός ἐcτιν οἰκέτης ...

What is this trouble? Who is the wretch talking about? This is a slave ...

Obviously the speaker goes on to say whose slave the man is. It looks as though he broke cover fairly soon after this: l. 14 (ὅτι λέγεις λέγε) seems to be addressed by him to the slave.

Men. *Mis.*

Exactly as in the previous passage, a character announces his intention to withdraw when he observes someone coming on to the stage; ἐπανάξω. ψοφεῖ ... says Demeas (206) as Crateia makes her entrance. When she is on stage and talking to her old nurse, he exclaims (210 f.):

> ὦ Ζεῦ, τίν' ὄψιν οὐδὲ προσδοκωμένην
> ὁρῶ;

O Zeus! What unexpected sight do I see?

which Crateia does not hear. Possibly the old nurse (who does not have a speaking part) is supposed to hear this. From Crateia's words at 211 f. we gather that the old woman has seen Demeas and is trying to draw Crateia's attention to him.

In the highly conventional and farcical scene[2] where the excited slave Getas wanders round the stage pursued by Clinias yet failing to observe him, there are several remarks by Clinias

---

[1] On 540 see below, p. 125.
[2] For a more extended discussion see below, pp. 141 ff.

which must be accounted asides (289b, 290a, 296, 300–1, 311a).
Getas is so completely self-absorbed that he fails to hear not just
the asides, but two attempts by Clinias to converse with him
(286, 312).

Men. *Per.*

Sosias on first entering observes Doris emerging from Polemon's and comments on her appearance (62–4a) before leaving
(on this see below, p. 118).

Sosias returns from Polemon at 164 and goes into Polemon's
house at 170. He comes out again at 176, talking back into the
house angrily. His movements here are not unobserved. Someone
comments on his arrival (171–5) and when he returns that same
person comments again (177–8, 181–2) this time aside since
Sosias is present. In 177–8 the speaker's intention of withdrawing
and eavesdropping is probably proclaimed (it looks as if 178 ended
with ὑπαποcτήcομαι). After the second comment, Sosias, still not
aware of the presence of an eavesdropper, decides to knock on
the door of the house where Moschion lives. After this he is
addressed by Daos. The majority of editors (though not the two
most recent) give the comment on Sosias' return and the eavesdropping asides to Doris and assume that she remains on stage
unseen by the others until 207. There are clinching objections to
this;[1] all these lines belong to Daos.

The recognition scene is perhaps the locus classicus for eavesdropping asides in Menander. From 338 we are presented with
the picture of Glycera and Pataecus examining the recognition
tokens. The first hint of Moschion's presence comes with 344 ff.,
five lines which are incomplete at the beginning. Some have taken
them as a comment by Moschion on the situation he sees before
him, that is to say as an eavesdropping aside.[2] There are many

---

[1] See P. W. Harsh, *CPh* 28 (1933), 205, and *AJPh* 62 (1941), 104, and Gomme–
Sandbach ad loc.

[2] Sudhaus, Capps, Coppola, Webster (*Studies in Menander*, p. 12, n. 3), and most
recently P. Flury (*Liebessprache bei Menander, Plautus und Terenz* (Heidelberg, 1968),
p. 48) are for an aside here. The suggestion put forward by Jensen and van Leeuwen
that Moschion is conversing with Daos is refuted by Arnott, *CQ* n.s. 18 (1968),
p. 238, n. 3.

arguments against such a view and in favour of regarding the lines as an entrance monologue spoken in ignorance of the presence of other people on stage.[1] Not the least of these is the sheer length of Moschion's utterance if it is meant to be an aside.[2] The content of the lines although they cannot be restored with absolute certainty betrays a tone that is much too unemotional given the dramatic situation and a form that is much too long-winded for an aside. What we have is a fairly leisurely piece of reflection ending with a conditional sentence 'if this is the case, then I'm done for'. This is the form of utterance one expects in a monologue. Also it is much easier to regard 353–4, however the lines be restored, as Moschion's first reaction to the situation he sees on stage than as the second or possibly third of a series of comments on what he has seen Glycera and Pataecus doing.[3]

During the remainder of the scene, Moschion makes several comments aside (353–4, 357, 362–3, 389, 394–6). At some point after his entrance monologue he must observe the presence of the other two on stage and begin eavesdropping. It is after 352 that he first expresses his reaction to what is going on on stage. In that line Glycera says of the recognition tokens that she was found in

---

[1] Among those who favour an entrance monologue here are Koerte, Del Corno, Sandbach, Fraenkel (*EP*, p. 204, n. 1), Schaffner (pp. 11 f.), E. Ulbricht, *Kritische und exegetische Studien zu Menander* (Diss. Leipzig, 1933), 51, E. Schwartz, *Hermes* 64 (1929) 13 = *Gesammelte Schriften* ii. 204, and Gomme, *CQ* 30 (1936), 68).

[2] See below, p. 151.

[3] An additional argument is the difficulty of staging the scene with only three actors (on the three-actor rule in New Comedy see below, p. 120 n. 3) if 344–8 is not the entrance speech of Moschion. If these lines are an aside, we must assume that Moschion's entrance occurred in the lacuna between 337 and 338 (there is nothing to be said for Capps's view that he is present at 301). If that were the case, the actor playing Doris, who would have to return to the stage as Moschion if we suppose that only three actors were available, would have to make an extremely quick change. Doris is asked to go inside at 333 f., but is still being addressed at the beginning of 335. This point we may mark as the beginning of her exit. Clearly, however we envisage the scene, she is no longer present after the lacuna which precedes 338. We must assume that the lacuna contained her re-entrance with the κιϲτίϲ and her subsequent return to Polemon's house. After this the actor would have to change costumes and return as Moschion. If the lacuna was a mere seven lines, all this movement would be extremely compressed. From these lines we would probably have to deduct two lines for Doris' re-entry and dismissal and at least one line indicating Moschion's entrance. (Some reconstructions of the play assume that Doris does not in fact re-emerge during the lacuna. This possibility is discussed in the excursus at the end of this chapter.)

them when a child. Moschion reacts to this with a start. It would be interesting to know how the actor playing Moschion filled in his time between finishing his entrance monologue and speaking his first aside here. He must surely begin eavesdropping before 352.[1] It is characteristic of Menander that there is no conventional announcement of his first sighting of the people on stage or of his intention to eavesdrop on them.[2]

This scene of course is not just remarkable for the number of eavesdropping asides it contains. The tone of 349 ff. is quite different from that of the preceding section, the metre and prosody suddenly aspiring to the stricter rules of tragedy and the diction likewise showing tragic inclinations.[3] There are other places in Menander where tragic prosody is employed[4] and where the diction and formal pattern of tragic rhesis and dialogue are exploited, but there is nothing to set beside this scene. The narrative of the demesman in *Sic.* is fairly strict in metre but far from being consistently tragic in its diction[5] (I cannot believe that the first Didot-rhesis has anything to do with Menander).

It is often asserted that Moschion is a comic figure in this scene and that he displays less 'real emotion' (whatever that may mean) than either of the other two actors on stage.[6] I suspect this arises from the belief that asides are *tout court* comic or even

---

[1] l. 353 is too strong a reaction if Moschion has merely *seen* Glycera and Pataecus for the first time.

[2] See below, p. 139.

[3] See the classic article of Paul Maas in *RhM* 68 (1913), 361 f. (= *Kleine Schriften*, pp. 78–80). The distinction between the part preceding 349 and the part following is not quite as clear cut as Maas made out. Sandbach has shown (*Ménandre*, pp. 126 ff., 130, and in Gomme–Sandbach, p. 523) that after 380 the tone and level of diction subside.

[4] e.g. Men. *Epitr.* 148, *Mis.* 214, *Sam.* 517, *Sic.* 169. See Wilamowitz, *Schiedsgericht*, p. 65 and Sandbach, *Ménandre*, p. 125.

[5] See Sandbach, *Ménandre*, p. 129.

[6] Capps speaks of Moschion's asides as 'bomolochic', M. Andrewes, *CQ* 18 (1924), 5, says that 'except for the comic asides of Moschion, the *Perikeiromene* scene is almost wholly tragic', and Coppola compares Moschion's interventions to those of Gripus in the recognition scene of Plautus *Rudens* ('Moschion's complaints are in complete contrast with the seriousness of the scene'). He at least tries to adduce evidence to support his view. S. Zini (*Il linguaggio dei personaggi nelle commedie di Menandro* (Firenze, 1938), p. 19) says 'Moschion ci averte che questa scena non è tragedia ma commedia', but does not find that Moschion is distinguished from the other characters with respect to language. Schaffner (p. 12) does not find anything comic about Moschion's asides.

'bomolochic'. This is, as has been shown, not always the case.[1] However there are some indications in the language that Moschion is given that he is on a different plane from the other two. The plums of tragic diction go to Glycera and her father.[2] With the possible exception of 353–4[3] his diction is less coloured than that of the other two and one or two things he is given to say are prosaic or distinctly untragic.[4] One would do well not to exaggerate the distinction in language[5] or to be over-confident in allotting marks for seriousness to characters in comedy.[6] One may

[1] See above, p. 56. It is the scene *after* 349 that I am discussing. Moschion's utterance on entering (344–8) certainly contrasts as regards both diction and metre with what follows. See Sandbach in Gomme–Sandbach, p. 520.

[2] We may note τἀπίλοιπα 349 (cf. Soph. *Phil.* 24), 358 a parody of a famous Euripidean line, χὤ 368, 379 a Euripidean confection, ὦ θεοί 397 (cf. Eur. *Hel.* 72 and Ar. *Thesm.* 1098 parodying Euripides' *Andromeda* although Sandbach may be right in suggesting that this represents the beginning of a trochaic tetrameter) and the various clichés of Euripidean stichomythia: πέραι]ν' 350 (cf. Eur. *I.T.* 781), cήμαινέ μοι 355 (Eur. *Phoen.* 1324, 1355), τίνος χάριν; 371 (Eur. *Or.* 95). It may be that the form of 375 was influenced by lines like Soph. *El.* 1112 (on this see above p. 42). For further discussion of paratragedy in this scene see now Lloyd-Jones *ZPE* 15 (1974), 212 f.

[3] ῥοθ[in 353 suggests ῥοθίωι (or possibly ῥόθωι), a word one associates with tragedy. The 'fifth foot anapaest', however, would seem to work against any tragic parody occurring here (see now in favour of ῥόθωι H. Lloyd-Jones, *ZPE* 15 (1974), 212).

[4] The most notable non-tragic features of his language are τουτί 357 (Maas points out that immediately before the 'Stilwechsel' both Glycera and Pataecus use pronouns ending in -ί) and cύccημον 362 (see D. B. Durham, *The Vocabulary of Menander*, Princeton, 1913, p. 95 and C. Mahlstedt, *Über den Wortschatz des Aineias Taktikos*, Diss. Jena, 1910, p. 73). One might argue that ἐπάναγε cαυτὸν μικρόν in 353 was somewhat bathetic. The second person address is admittedly more emotional than a first person announcement of an intention to withdraw (e.g. ὑπαποcτήcομαι), but μικρόν seems rather to detract from this (contrast Men. *Dis Ex.* 23). l. 357 is an extremely matter-of-fact line (so Sandbach, *Ménandre*, p. 127, although see Lloyd-Jones, *ZPE* 15 (1974), 212 f., who compares Aesch. *Eum.* 589 and suggests reading πάλαι rather than ἐμοί), μέν reducing the emotional level. For its form compare Σ Ar. *Thesm.* 80 τοῦτο τῶν ζητουμένων ἐcτί. I see no reason to follow Coppola in regarding ποῦ πότ' εἰμι γῆc; in 363 as tragic. δηλαδή a prosy word frequent in comedy (three occurrences in tragedy, Soph. *O.T.* 1501, Eur. *I.A.* 1366, *Or.* 789, these last two at the beginning of trochaic tetrameters and to be added to Ulbricht's list, p. 10) is found at the end of 388. This might argue that Moschion is speaking, but if Sandbach is right in assuming a drop in the level of the language around here one of the more serious characters may have relapsed into more ordinary diction.

[5] Euripides would not have used παιδίον (372, 381) which occurs in lines spoken by the 'tragic' characters. I do not think that anyone would have thought of tragedy hearing Glycera's τάλαιν' ἔγωγε τῆc τύχηc (ἔγωγε in this context makes a difference: this is much less elevated than Men. *Dysc.* 189 on which see Handley ad loc.).

[6] See Sandbach, *Ménandre*, pp. 126 ff., and in Gomme–Sandbach, p. 520.

note that Menander might have effected a stronger contrast between Moschion and the others if he had allowed him an anapaest or two within his lines. This he may do on one occasion,[1] but otherwise Moschion is not distinguished from the others by means of metre.

Men. *Sam.*

In the famous scene depicted on the Mytilene mosaic,[2] where Demeas drives Chrysis and the infant he believes hers from his house, watched all the time by the inquisitive cook, there are probably some asides by the cook. Initially the cook had got in the way of Demeas as he rushed inside to seize Chrysis. When he hears him returning (τὴν θύραν πέπληχεν 366 f.) the cook announces his decision to eavesdrop (μικρὸν ὑπαποστήσομαι 368). During the ensuing confrontation between Demeas and Chrysis, the cook makes several comments aside. First of all at 375 he says τοιοῦτ' ἦν τι τὸ κακόν, μανθάνω 'that was what the trouble was about. Now I understand.' Then at 383 he remarks τὸ πρᾶγμ' ὀργή τις ἐcτί 'the affair is some sort of outburst of anger' and decides to intervene, προcιτέον 'I had better approach'. The first attempt to do so meets with a rebuff. The second and equally unsuccessful intervention is prefaced by the aside remark οὔπω δάκνει 'he's not yet biting'.[3]

These, then, are the passages in Menander containing eavesdropping asides or asides where one of the actors is unaware of the presence of the aside-speaker. Other passages of Menander[4]

---

[1] In 353. In the section before the 'Stilwechsel' he breaches Porson's law (345, a line without a caesura).

[2] See †S. Charitonidis, L. Kahil, R. Ginouvès, *Les Mosaïques de la maison de Ménandre à Mytilène* (*Antike Kunst*—Beiheft 6 [Bern, 1970]), pp. 38–41.

[3] For the attribution in 385–6 see Sandbach in Gomme–Sandbach. τί ἐcτιν; is probably another such aside from the cook.

[4] Fraenkel, *EP*, p. 175, n. 3, thought that the second speaker in fr. 97 Koerte–Thierfelder (*Deisidaemon*) was not observed by the first so that one might consider 4b–6a an eavesdropping aside. I do not think it wise without further context to accept this. Del Corno may well be right in seeing the presence of an eavesdropper in *CGF* 257. 14–19.

or of the anonymous fragments[1] which have been thought to contain asides are either too fragmentary or obscure for us to be certain of the staging (e.g. Men. *Her.* 60 ff. where I think Webster is probably right against Koerte in arguing that we have a dialogue with no third party present)[2] or else have been misinterpreted. The latter holds good of the two instances discussed below.

(1) Men. *Per.* 68–70:

> εὐφρανθήςεται
> κλάουcαν αὐτὴν πυθόμενος νῦν. τοῦτο γὰρ
> ἐβούλετ᾿ αὐτόc.

He will be glad to hear that she is weeping now. That's exactly what he wanted.

These words are enclosed by double points in the papyrus and have sometimes been taken as an aside spoken by Sosias eavesdropping on Doris who is in the meantime knocking on Myrrhine's door. But is Sosias on stage to speak them? Five lines previously after commenting on the appearance of the newly entered Doris, he told us he would go (πορεύcομαι δέ). Presumably he means to go into his master's house to fetch a cloak (he has this in his possession when next we see him at 164 ff.), the ostensible purpose of his present visit (59–60). If he speaks 68–70, we encounter the oddity of him saying that he will go and yet for no apparent reason remaining.[3] How too could he tell from what Doris says when first she enters that Glycera is crying? If one wants him to speak the lines in question, one must assume that

---

[1] There is a book fragment which might possibly preserve the end of an eavesdropping scene, the point at which the eavesdropper breaks cover:

> μὴ κατακούcειεν δέ μου
> ὁ Κωρυκαῖοc. :: ἀλλὰ μὴν κατακήκοα
> coῦ κατακολουθῶν ἔνδοθεν
> (Dioxippus fr. 2).

For the proverbial Κωρυκαῖοc see Men., fr. 137, Call., fr. 191. 82, and Strabo 14. 644. Possibly, however, the first speaker has just come out on to the stage.

[2] *Studies in Menander*, 33 f.

[3] The contrast between this and other scenes where characters announce their intention of withdrawing but fail to do so is stark (cf. Men. *Epitr.* 537). There is no reason why Sosias having announced his intention should not adhere to it. It is not as if he has not already seen and commented on Doris' entrance.

Sosias speaks them on re-emerging from Polemon's house carrying the cloak.[1] He has entered as he said he would and he has seen for himself that Glycera is weeping. Against this it might be argued that the visit is a very short one even by the conventions of comedy[2] for him both to collect the cloak and observe Glycera weeping. The lines are quite suitable in the mouth of Doris.[3] She has already been complaining about Polemon and his like. While she awaits an answer to her knocking, she imagines Polemon's reaction if he saw Glycera now. The technique of inserting a remark between addresses to the doorkeeper can be paralleled by Men. *Dysc.* 461 ff. The double dots enclosing Doris' remark are used here, as elsewhere, to mark change of addressee rather than change of speaker.[4] With this attribution, Sosias will re-enter in the lacuna that follows 70, after Doris has entered Myrrhine's house.

(2) Stark[5] detected an eavesdropping scene in the anonymous fragment P. Oxy. 2329 (*CGF* 256). His reconstruction flouts too many of the conventions of New Comedy to be taken seriously. He assumes in fact that we have a dialogue between mother and son (this is true of 5 ff.) which is overheard by two separate sets of eavesdroppers, a couple who are speaking when the fragment begins and who leave after line four and, as well as them, by a slave Dromon who is speaking when the fragment ends. Such a scene would be without parallel in Greek comedy. Not only does it demand that five actors with speaking roles be on stage simultaneously, but that the two sets of eavesdroppers be unaware of the other's presence. In addition the conversation aside at the

---

[1] So Ed. Schwartz, *Hermes* 64 (1929) 6 (= *Gesammelte Schriften* 2. 190), Webster, *Studies in Menander* 7, Ulbricht, *Kritische und exegetische Studien*, pp. 43 f., and Del Corno.

[2] Sandbach, however, in Gomme–Sandbach provides parallels.

[3] I think both Del Corno and Sandbach are hyperlogical in arguing that the words are more appropriate to Sosias. When Doris exclaims 'he'll be glad to see her weeping now; that's what he wanted', she is not concerned with the question *how* Polemon will get to know of Glycera's state (I wonder whether it would be better to give an extra touch of bitterness by emending αὐτός to αὐτό, 'that's the very thing he wanted', cf. Ar. *Nub.* 1499. αὐτός as it stands must be 'the master').

[4] Cf. Men. *Dysc.* 177–8. For examples of this in the Cairo Codex see Koerte's introduction p. xii (cf. Lowe, *BICS* 9 (1962), 33, and Sandbach, *CR* n.s. 12 (1962), 28–9).

[5] R. Stark, *RhM* 100 (1957), 131 ff.

beginning of the fragment would be of unparalleled length,[1] at least a line more than the four we have since on Stark's interpretation ἔχ' ἥcυχ[οc ἔτ]ι μικρόν[2] is an instruction by one of the eavesdroppers to his partner telling him to keep silent and would imply an utterance immediately preceding it by this man. The correct inscenation of this fragment was first seen by Del Corno[3] and is accepted by Austin. The first four lines of the fragment are a soliloquy containing self-apostrophe. The character who speaks it then exits leaving the stage empty for the two new entrants. ὅπερ λέγω δή 'as I was saying' (5) is obviously that form of entrance so common in New Comedy[4] where we are to imagine the actors continuing a conversation that was begun off-stage. It is clear that there is no eavesdropper present during this scene.

[1] See below, p. 151.

[2] 'On grounds of space ἡcύχ[ωc is more likely than ἥcυχ[οc', Roberts in the *editio princeps*. But what about grounds of idiom?

[3] *Proceedings of the Twelfth International Congress of Papyrology* (Toronto, 1970, *American Studies in Papyrology* vol. vii), p. 107, n. 26. The inscenation proposed in the *editio princeps* demands four actors. Two people exit to be followed without break by another two. At the present moment there is no positive evidence that there were more than three actors in the company that performed New Comedy (see Sandbach in Gomme–Sandbach, pp. 16 ff. The evidence of *CGF* 281 is disconcerting but it should not outweigh the evidence of better preserved plays) and the strict adherence to this restriction in the number of speaking parts that is observable in the extended fragments of Menander strongly supports this (on one interpretation Men. *Mis.* 257 ff. would provide a parallel for two actors exiting followed by two new actors entering, but see below, p. 133).

[4] See Legrand, p. 459 (cf. Men. *Epitr.* 294).

EXCURSUS

The movements and reactions of Doris
in Men. *Per.* 331 ff.

In the discussion of the recognition scene in *Periciromene*, some assumptions were made about the role of Doris which are not universally shared.[1] Koerte[2] has a different explanation of the way in which Glycera's γνωρίϲματα are produced. It is not Doris who produces them by entering Polemon's house and fetching them out. Rather Pataecus happens to be carrying on his person the ξυϲτίϲ,[3] having picked it up among the finery which Polemon had earlier shown him in his desire to demonstrate how well Glycera had been treated. On Koerte's theory Doris is summoned from Polemon's house[4] and told to fetch the garment but she enters weeping because she knows that it has disappeared. During the lacuna following 337, Pataecus produces it and the recognition scene begins.

This theory has its attractions. It is to the credit of Menander's οἰκονομία that Polemon's seemingly irrelevant invitation to Pataecus

[1] Sandbach shares them. See Gomme–Sandbach, p. 518.
[2] His final statement of his view is to be found in the introduction to the third edition (p. xxxiii). He first put forward the theory in 1909, but changed his mind in his Pauly article (*RE*, s.v. 'Menandros' 746).
[3] It makes no difference to the argument what object we decide to restore as the recognition token. In this section I refer to a ξυϲτίϲ because this is what Koerte thinks Doris was asked to bring (with Sandbach I think κιϲτίδ' a much more likely restoration in 333). One could as easily secrete a κιϲτίϲ as a ξυϲτίϲ about one's person.
[4] Koerte is surely correct in assuming that Doris comes out of Polemon's house rather than Myrrhine's.

   i. She is Polemon's property (Schwartz, p. 5) and Glycera has no legal claim on her when she abandons Polemon. Demeas in *Sam.* regards himself as generous in allowing Chrysis to leave with her θεράπαιναι (Men. *Sam.* 382).
  ii. Doris emerges from Polemon's house at 207 although by then Glycera is installed in Myrrhine's house (212 would have been phrased differently if she had come out of Myrrhine's house).
 iii. Glycera wants *Pataecus* to see about fetching her tokens from Polemon's house (324 ff.). This implies that she cannot send Doris because Doris is there already.

to come into the house and inspect Glycera's finery has crucial significance for the plot. There would be an analogy in the situation in *Misumenus* where Demeas happens upon the vital recognition object, a sword, in the house of the man who has invited him to dinner.[1] Nevertheless it would be a pity if Koerte's theory were to become dogma since there are several cogent objections that can be brought against it.[2]

Pataecus' behaviour when confronted by Glycera is really quite remarkable if he has in his possession a garment of Glycera's which has led him to suspect that Glycera may be his daughter or at the least may be able to tell him something about the fate of his daughter. He forbears to make any inquiry about the matter. Instead he resolutely acts as advocate for Polemon. Even more remarkably, when Glycera goes so far as to mention some γνωρίϲματα of her father and mother, he is reluctant to take up her request and persists in his advocacy (322, 325, 329).

Secondly, if Doris is distressed at the loss of the γνωρίϲματα (and we may note with Webster and Ulbricht that she is distressed *before* Glycera mentions the object), one might have expected her to say so when asked by Glycera why she is weeping (335). Instead of a reply from Doris, we hear a comment from Pataecus. It is simpler to assume that Doris' tears are brought about by general distress at Glycera's condition[3] and because she regards the demand for the γνωρίϲματα as an indication that the break between Glycera and Polemon is to be final. The question Glycera puts to her does not receive an answer because it is obvious to the audience why she is crying or else, and this may be thought to be more likely, because it is not so much a demand for information as a reproof.[4]

Most important of all is a third point. When does Pataecus cease to be Polemon's lawyer and begin to act like a man personally concerned at what is happening on stage? At 335, at the point after he has heard Glycera *mention* the recognition token, he says πέπονθά τι 'something has come over me' (this is stressed by Schwartz, p. 13). It is much easier to take this as the comment of a man who has been taken aback

---

[1] See Men. *Mis.* 176 ff.

[2] See especially H. Sauer, *de Circumtonsae Menandreae argumento Klass. Philol. Studien* (Berlin, 1922), pp. 40–1, and Ulbricht, *Kritische und exegetische Studien*, pp. 48 f.

[3] So Webster, *Studies in Menander*[2] (Manchester, 1960), 14 n. 1 (he allows, however, that Pataecus may have *seen* something inside) and Sandbach, *Gnomon* 39 (1967), 768.

[4] Cf. Men., fr. 87 and Soph. *El.* 829.

by something completely unexpected than that of a man who hears the object that he has in his pocket being mentioned by the person whom he must assume to be its owner.

No restoration of a fragmentary play can be completely secure and likewise no rejection of a restoration. It may be that the objections raised against Koerte's theory would be explained away if we possessed the play in a better state. In the present state of knowledge, however, it is surely preferable to assume that Doris comes out of the house with the recognition tokens and that it is at this point that the recognition scene begins.[1]

[1] It is certain, at any rate, that the object(s) is actually visible during this scene. This is proved by the use of present-tense verbs in connection with Glycera's recognition tokens as against past-tense verbs describing Moschion's γνωρίςματα which neither party has with them at the time of speaking. Note too οὑτοcί 338 and τουτί 341.

7. Asides in New Comedy: II

WHAT follows is an examination of asides which occur when one actor turns away from the other actor with whom he has been conversing or who is (at least) aware of his presence. This is the type I called 'asides in conversation'. The examples are arranged in three categories, those which to my mind certainly contain asides of this sort, those where the issue is less clear cut, and those where the term aside has been misapplied.

The following seem to me certain examples of the type of aside in question.

Men. *Dysc.*

After the girl has given Sostratus the pitcher and told him to hurry up, he exclaims:

> 201
> ἐλευθερίως γέ πως
> ἄγροικός ἐcτιν. ὦ πολυτίμητοι θεοί,
> τίc ἂν ἐμὲ cώcαι δ[αιμόν]ων;[1]

Country girl though she is, she has the manners of a lady. O gods! What god could save me now?

This is clearly an aside. We know that the girl is still present when Sostratus speaks the lines since, immediately after he has spoken them, we hear her exclaiming in distress as she hears, so she imagines, the door of her father's house opening. She could hardly be expected to hear what Sostratus has just said without comment and it is scarcely admissible to argue that comment was forestalled because she heard the door opening. Sostratus' remarks here continue a sequence of asides commenting on the appearance and behaviour of the girl. The previous ones, however, all occurred before he had addressed her and she was aware of his presence (see p. 109).

---

[1] For the attribution see Schäfer, p. 120, and Sandbach in Gomme–Sandbach.

Men. *Epitr.*

Pamphila is about to leave the stage when Habrotonon who has lately entered tries to attract her attention:

539 ἐναν]τίον βλέπε. Παμφ. [ἦ μ]ε γινώςκεις, γύναι;[1]

'Look at me face to face.' 'Do you know me, woman?'

Habrotonon does not give an immediate reply to Pamphila's question, but comments aside αὐτή 'ςτιν[ἣν] ἑόρακα 'This is the girl whom I saw', making it quite clear to the audience why she had earlier joyfully exclaimed to the baby (536–7) about the prospect of it seeing its mother.[2]

Men. *Mis.*

In the scene where Getas unwittingly tells Clinias what has been going on inside Thrasonides' house, contact is finally made between the two parties:

323   χαῖρε, Κλεινία.
     π[όθεν πάρ]εςθ'; (cf. *unde haec advenit?* Ter. *Hec.* 81.)

     Greetings, Clinias. Where did he come from?

πόθεν πάρεςθ';, if that is the correct restoration, is a surprised comment aside.[3]

Men. *Sam.*

In reply to Moschion's question about the reason for Chrysis' departure, Demeas says:

454]πρεςβεύεταί τις πρὸς ἐμέ· δεινόν . . .

Someone is sending an embassy to me—this is dreadful.

He then addresses Moschion and tells him it is not his business. At 456 he asks τίς ὁ φλύ]αρος; δεινὸν ἤδη. cυναδικεῖ μ' οὗτος, 'What is this nonsense? This is really dreadful. He too is wronging me,' and continues, probably after an interruption by

---

[1] For the supplement and attribution see R. Merkelbach, *MH* 23 (1966), 184.
[2] See above, p. 111.
[3] See also below, p. 141.

Moschion, (457) περιφα]νῶc· τί γὰρ προcέρχεται ὑπὲρ ἐκείνηc;
'I am certain. For why does he approach me on her behalf?'[1]
All these utterances, with the possible exception of τίc ὁ φλύαροc;,
are part of a soliloquy and, since Moschion takes no account of
them[2]—he follows the last of them with the question 'What will
your friends say when they hear of it?'—we may justifiably regard
them as asides, although it is possible that τί φήιc; implies that
Moschion knows that Demeas is speaking.[3] Later in the same
scene Demeas' angry outbursts *are* heard by Moschion, 461b–2a,[4]
which brings the response 'you shouldn't give over everything to
anger' and 473b–5 where Demeas turns and addresses Apollo
Agyieus once more and is asked by Moschion 'What do you
mean?'[5]

Men. Sic.

While Pyrrhias is handing over or pointing out to his master
the guarantees of the letter he has brought back from Sicyon,
Stratophanes' parasite Theron prays aside to Athena:

144   ὦ δέcποιν' Ἀθηνᾶ, τουτονὶ cαυτῆc πόει
              ἵνα λάβηι τὴν παῖδ', ἐγὼ δὲ Μαλθάκην.

O mistress Athena, make this man one of your citizens so that he
may marry the girl and I may obtain Malthace.

Stratophanes takes no notice of this, but tells Pyrrhias and Theron to get going (δεῦρο Θήρων may indicate that Theron was some
distance from the others when he delivered the aside).

---

[1] The rest of Demeas' utterance is probably also aside. See for restoration Sandbach in Gomme–Sandbach.
[2] See below, p. 157 n. 2.
[3] Alternatively τί φήιc; may take up οὐχὶ cόν . . . παντελ[ῶc ἐμόν and not 456.
[4] On the addressee here see below, p. 191 n. 2.
[5] Before leaving *Samia*, I should mention 690 φλυαρεῖc where Austin notes 'for-
tasse pressa voce hoc dicit Parmeno.' One may note, however, that Parmeno is
already treating his master somewhat contemptuously when he dismisses him with
the words πρόαγ' ὅποι μέλλειc. Sandbach in Gomme–Sandbach contemplates
giving φλυαρεῖc to Moschion. I see no reason to do this. All that it means is 'you
are behaving nonsensically' cf. τίc ὁ φλύαροc 456. H.-D. Blume, *Menanders Samia*,
Darmstadt, 1974, p. 183, takes 469 f. as an aside. This is possible, but it may be
that Moschion simply does not understand the lines.

Men. *Fab. Inc.*

Cleaenetus enters from his house having heard a noisy debate taking place outside his door (20 f.) : τίϲ ὁ βοῶν ἐϲτίν ποτε | πρὸϲ ταῖϲ θύραιϲ; 'Whoever is shouting at my door?' The text of what follows does not permit us to say for sure whether or not either of the persons on stage gave him an answer. However that may be, the two people who were on stage when he entered, Laches and Chaereas, continue to converse apart from him after they have become aware of his presence (εὔκαιροτ in 21 probably indicates that they are aware that he is present).[1] They do so for at least four lines before addressing him.[2]

I now move to cases where the issue is less easy to decide.

Men. *Asp.*

At long last Chaerestratus understands the point of the plan his slave Daos is outlining. When he says so, Daos before continuing comments εἰ μὴ πέτρινοϲ εἶ 353 'unless you are made of stone'. I find it impossible to decide whether Daos says this under his breath with a patient shaking of his head[3] or whether he says the words aloud to Chaerestratus' face. Either way would be effective. Daos is a well-behaved slave with a sense of humour. Perhaps if he is speaking aloud he has for the moment lost patience with the slowness of the free man. It would be out of character for him to speak such a line gloatingly like a Plautine slave or some of the cheekier slaves in Menander.

Men. *Dysc.*

The comment ὡϲ ὀργίλωϲ 'How angrily!' which interrupts Pyrrhias' description of Cnemon's behaviour at 102 might be described as an aside, particularly if we take it as referring not to

---

[1] Cf. Men. *Dysc.* 668.

[2] Much remains uncertain with regard to the attribution here. I feel that Chaereas ought to have 25b–6; he is convinced by the older man's authority and undertakes to do what he asks. He may then be interrupted by Cleaenetus (τί βοᾶιϲ; would be a suitable supplement even if it cannot be read; it could refer to the strong oath νὴ τὸν ῞Ηλιον) and then Chaereas will begin his explanation with the words ἄκουε δή μου.

[3] So H. Lloyd-Jones, *GRBS* 13 (1972), 184 (approved by Gaiser, *Grazer Beiträge* 1 (1973), 127).

Cnemon but to Pyrrhias' attitude towards him. It does not matter, however, whether or not Pyrrhias hears the words. Menander is using a technique frequently to be found in comedy whereby narratives of some length are enlivened by interruptions from the person or persons to whom the narrative is addressed.[1] Often (as for example at Men. *Asp.* 33) the interruptions serve to characterise the person who speaks them, but their prime purpose is to avoid monotony. Their ancestor is the 'bomolochic' aside.[2] Henceforward I will only note such interruptions where it makes a difference whether or not they go by unheard.[3]

The malicious hope Daos expresses at 371b–374 might be a soliloquy (so Lloyd-Jones in the *actio* printed below his text) or it might be addressed to Gorgias. It does not make any difference whether or not Sostratus hears the lines and their length perhaps argues against their being an aside. I would accept Lloyd-Jones's αὐτόν in 371 and take what Daos says as a reply to Gorgias' question.[4]

At 425 we read

ἐπαινέτης οὖν εἰμι coῦ καὶ τῆς τέχνης
ἔγωγ' ἀεί ποτ' — οὐχὶ πιcτεύω δ' ὅμωc.

I am accordingly always praising you and your art—but I don't trust you.

For the incomprehensible οὖν 'accordingly' in 425 some read μέν which would mean 'on the one hand'. This brings with it a difficulty. Sicon has promised to feed Getas. With this emendation (printed in Lloyd-Jones's text), Getas seems to be reducing his chances of obtaining this meal by insulting Sicon. Obviously οὐχὶ πιcτεύω δ' ὅμωc is an aside that qualifies and detracts from the compliment of the previous line: it cannot be intended for

---

[1] See above, p. 102, and Fraenkel, *QS*, pp. 88 f.

[2] See above, p. 89.

[3] Here the exclamation is followed by a request to Pyrrhias to continue (the question of attribution cannot really be decided on objective grounds—for discussions see Schäfer, p. 116, and Sandbach in Gomme–Sandbach whose treatment assumes that the question in 103a is connected with the exclamation rather than a request for further information). This makes what had become by Menander's time a purely formal device more lifelike and natural. Pyrrhias' pause is motivated too by the implicit suggestion that Pyrrhias is out of breath.

[4] See against this Schäfer, pp. 126 f. and Sandbach in Gomme–Sandbach.

Sicon's ears. If, however, Getas begins to compliment Sicon with the words ἐπαινέτης μέν he is, by using the word μέν, already indicating some kind of reservation and, as it were, inviting the cook to remain and listen to a point of criticism.[1] There is a way out of this difficulty. It is possible to assume that Sicon hears neither of the lines, that they are in fact addressed to his retreating back.[2] It seems clear that Sicon enters the stage-building before Getas. He takes the lead throughout this scene, Getas always lagging behind. When first we see him, he is commenting on how far back Getas is (401). At 419 he tells Getas to pick up the baggage and go into the shrine. Seeing the slave looking glum, he gives him a word of encouragement and then goes in. The slave will naturally take longer to enter the shrine since he is carrying more than the cook. However, the problem need not arise if we adopt the suggestion of Griffith modified by Jacques (and printed by Sandbach) and read in 425 ἐπαινέτης coῦ τ᾽ εἰμὶ καὶ τῆς ⟨cῆς⟩ τέχνης. Whether in this case we should call οὐχὶ πιcτεύω δ᾽ ὅμωc an aside is questionable. I would assume that Sicon is in the shrine by the time Getas speaks the words.

One might regard Getas' exit lines at 479b–80 as an aside.[3]

> ὦ πολυτίμητοι θεοί,
> ἔχιc πολιὸc ἄνθρωπόc ἐcτιν οὑτοcί.

Ye gods! This man's a grey snake.

It makes little difference, however, whether or not Cnemon hears them, especially since he is leaving the stage in any case. For the form compare above, p. 102.

Men. *Epitr.*

After Syriscus has asked Smicrines to arbitrate, Daos reflects:

> 60   μετρίωι γε cυμπέπλεγμαι ῥήτορι.
> τί γὰρ μετεδίδουν;

I've come to grips with a fair old orator. Why ever did I offer him a share?

[1] See J. H. Quincey, *JHS* 86 (1966), 156. Compare for a similar problem concerning asides and particles the treatment of Eur. *I.A.* 655 above (p. 50).

[2] For which see above, p. 34.

[3] Lloyd-Jones makes all of 476–80 an aside.

Smicrines takes no notice of this, but asks whether the two of them are prepared to abide by his decision. It looks, then, as if the lines are to be regarded as an aside, although nothing hangs on whether the other characters hear them or not. There is some indication perhaps in the text that Smicrines has not heard them. When he starts the contest he turns to Daos and says:

> cὺ πρότερος ὁ cιωπῶν λέγε.

> You speak first, the silent one.

ὁ cιωπῶν might confirm that Smicrines has up to now heard nothing from Daos, although one might refer it merely to 62 where, in saying πάντωc, Syriscus replies for both of them. If 60b–1a is an aside, it hovers between being an eavesdropping or a 'conversational' one. Smicrines is aware of Daos' presence, but is occupied in conversation with Syriscus (cf. the situation in Men. *Sic.* 144 f.) and it is thus easier for what Daos says to escape him.

With regard to the end of the scene, it is mistaken, I believe, to regard as asides the series of woeful complaints uttered by Daos after Smicrines has declared him the loser (182b–4, 185b–6, 187a, 189b–90a, 191a, and 193b).[1] He is giving vent to his emotions aloud. His complaints meet with no response from either Smicrines or Syriscus, not because they do not hear them but because they are unsympathetic to his cause. All he meets with is the insistence that he give up his treasure. Once he has done so and Smicrines has departed, Syriscus deigns to comment on one of his expressions of woe (196–7).

Men. *Her.*

Little is clear about 55 ff., either about the speakers' intentions or about who is speaking.[2] The most probable assumption is that

---

[1] οὐκ ἂν ᾠόμην attributed in the papyrus to Syriscus must be given to Daos. Wilamowitz's parallels, especially Plut. *tranq. an.* 474e (add *CGF* 257. 18) are enough to refute Grassi (*A & R* 6 [1961] 146) and Arnott (*CQ* n.s. 18 (1968), 227) who argue that the words belong to Smicrines. The words are exactly appropriate to Daos' situation (they explain his previous utterance αἰcχρά γ᾽ ἃ πέπονθα). Smicrines exits in silence (G. Jachmann, *Hermes* 57 (1922), 113).

[2] For discussions, see Del Corno, Ulbricht, op. cit., pp. 27 ff., A. W. Gomme, *CR* 61 (1947), 32, Webster, *Studies in Menander*, pp. 33 ff., and Sandbach in Gomme–Sandbach, p. 394.

there are two speakers, Myrrhine and Laches, and that during the course of the scene the story of Myrrhine's past comes out and Laches is revealed as the father of her children. Unfortunately it is far from clear how much Laches already knows or suspects and what is his attitude to Myrrhine during the course of the dialogue. What concerns us is the exclamation ἱδρώc, ἀπορία lit. 'sweat, no way out' in 72a which may be an aside comment by Myrrhine on the threat expressed in 71 by Laches.[1] Her comment, if it is hers, is ignored by Laches.

Men. *Per.*

In the scene of banter between Moschion and the slave Daos, where the self-confident slave suggests various rewards for himself if the situation he has described measures up to his description, Moschion speaks of him in the third person at 88 οὑτοcὶ φερόμενος ἡ[μ]ῖν (the sense and restoration is uncertain). Editors have tended to regard this remark as an aside. This may be the case, but it is just as likely that what we have here is the kind of third-person address we have encountered so often already.[2]

Men. *Sic.*

Theron comments at 360b on his interlocutor Cichesias ἀγαθὸς ἄνθρωπος cφόδρα, 'the man's very good'. This is probably the same phenomenon as was discussed in the previous note.

Anon. *CGF* 257 (P. Sorb. 72r).

Greeted affectionately by the newly entered Niceratus, Phaedimus does not reply but continues his deliberations (τί χρὴ

---

[1] Koerte and Sandbach may be right, however, in assuming that Laches turned away after speaking these words and said ἱδρώc, ἀπορία to himself before continuing. ἐc κόρακαc in 70a (cf. Men. *Dysc.* 112a) may be a similar sort of comment and, since it is not normally a woman's imprecation, adds weight to the suggestion that Laches is the speaker of the asides here.

[2] See above, pp. 72 and 129. ἡμῖν, however, does suggest that the audience is being brought into the conversation. J. C. B. Lowe has shown that the comment is more likely to follow a suggestion by Moschion than one from Daos. The dicolon after κράτιcτον marks change of addressee rather than change of speaker (*BICS* 20 (1973), 99). If Moschion has put forward the suggestion about running a mill, it is more probable that he is speaking aside here.

νυνὶ ποιεῖν; 'What is one to do now?' 27) in a soliloquy which spreads over another two lines before the papyrus breaks off. It is clear that he is not addressing Niceratus because of 25 ff., the words he utters before Niceratus is aware of his presence—he is there debating how he should approach the friend whom the ensuing dialogue shows he suspects of having done him a grievous wrong. It remains in question, however, whether we are to regard τί χρὴ νυνὶ ποιεῖν . . . as an aside. Even though not formally addressed to his friend, the words may not have been deliberately concealed from him and, since the papyrus breaks off, we cannot be sure that Niceratus did not take up Phaedimus' remarks.

There remain two cases where I am sure it is wrong to speak of asides.

Men. *Asp.*

> 93 Cμ. εἶτ' ἐντυχεῖν βουλήcομαί τι Δᾶέ cοι
>   κατὰ cχολήν· νυνὶ δὲ καὐτόc μοι δοκῶ
>   εἴcω παριέναι cκεψάμενοc τίν' ἂν τρόπον
>   τούτοιc προcενεχθείη τιc ἡμερώτατα.

Smicrines Then I want to have a talk with you Daos, when you have time. Meanwhile I think I too will go in once I have considered what would be the most humane way of approaching them.

Alongside 93 in the right-hand margin is written ηcυχη. This is obviously misplaced.[1] The person who wrote the word[2] must have intended it to refer to νυνὶ δέ . . .: 93–4a is addressed to Daos. The comment is mistaken in any case.[3] νυνὶ δὲ καὐτόc μοι δοκῶ is certainly soliloquy and not intended for Daos' ears even though the words Smicrines uses when taken at their face value

---

[1] So D. Del Corno, *ZPE* 6 (1970), 214.

[2] One should not assume it was part of the tradition. 'Anything in the margin of a papyrus must be regarded as only ancillary to the text', Lowe, *BICS* 9 (1962), 36. The same *marginale* is found later in the play (re *Asp.* 467) where it is obviously correct. For ἡcυχῆι compare Heliod. *Aeth.* iii. 11. 1 ἡcυχῆι πρόc με εἰπεῖν. On words meaning 'aside' in Greek see above, p. 18.

[3] Unless ἡcυχῆι meant not simply *sotto voce* but could also be used to denote monologue as distinct from dialogue.

look perfectly innocent.[1] There is no need to assume, however, that *by convention* Daos does not hear them. The conversation between Daos and Smicrines is already over. Daos at 91 announced his intention of going into Chaerestratus' house with his entourage. He may have stayed to hear 93–4a, but by the time Smicrines speaks 94b–6 he will have turned to go and, at some point while Smicrines is speaking, will be out of sight as well as out of earshot. One would not call this effect an aside.[2] The person who wrote ἡϲυχῆι in the margin failed to visualise what happened on stage at the end of this scene in much the same way as the scholiast on Soph. *Ant.* mistook the staging of an analogous scene.[3]

Men. *Mis.* 269

οἰήϲεωϲ πωϲ ταῦτα θαυμάϲαιμι δ᾽ ἄν

. . . notion.? How should I be surprised at this?

In the papyrus this line, or rather a part of it, is attributed not to Thrasonides, but to the slave Getas the first three letters of whose name are written above πωϲ. There is also a dicolon following οἰήϲεωϲ. There are strong arguments against accepting this attribution.[4] It is more plausible to believe that the line belongs *in toto* to Thrasonides and that Getas has no speaking part in this scene. The mistaken attribution of a line to a character who had appeared and spoken earlier (Getas left at 237 to fetch Thrasonides—that was his last utterance) occurs at Men. *Dysc.* 214, where Pyrrhias, who had left the stage at 144 and did not return, is wrongly given something to say in the Bodmer

---

[1] τούτοιϲ of course means 'them'. See Del Corno (retracting his previous view) *ZPE* 8 (1971) 302 and Gaiser, *Grazer Beiträge* 1 (1973), 114, n. 9.

[2] See above, p. 34.

[3] See above, p. 71.

[4] The strongest is the difficulty in making sense of πῶϲ ταῦτα θαυμάϲαιμι δ᾽ ἄν; or πῶϲ; ταῦτα θαυμάϲαιμι δ᾽ ἄν. It seems better to follow Webster and Sandbach in taking πωϲ as an enclitic. An additional argument against the attribution in the papyrus is that it demands four actors with speaking roles for this scene (see Sandbach, *PCPhS* n.s. 13 (1967), 44, n. 1), Crateia and Demeas exiting together to be followed without noticeable break by two new actors, Thrasonides and Getas. The only parallel for this in New Comedy does not stand up to scrutiny (see above, p. 120 n. 3).

papyrus. In both cases these incorrect interpretations have worked their way into the tradition and may have influenced the system of paragraphi and dicola by which the parts were distributed in their respective plays. The paragraphus under *Dysc.* 214 must have arisen in this way. The dicolon in *Dysc.* 214, however, which is (as distinct from the marginal indication of the speaker's name) to be regarded as part of the paradosis admits of two explanations. Either it came into the text because some reader decided that Pyrrhias should have something to say or else it is there, correctly, to indicate a change of addressee when Sostratus moves to self-apostrophe. Similarly the dicolon in *Mis.* 269 *may* have come about because of a reader's decision to give Getas something to say. On the other hand it may represent some kind of punctuation. The person who wrote the marginale which Turner (in an addendum in *P. Oxy.*, vol. xxxiii) interprets as εἰcιόν[τ]ι at least envisaged a plausible piece of staging if Getas was present, an address to the retreating back of Thrasonides.

8. Conventional Entrances

WE have noted a form of entrance speech where the newly entered character fails at first to notice that there are other people on stage. We found such a speech to have had its origins in Aeschylean tragedy and to have become a stock-in-trade of the later Euripides.[1] There was, however, in Aristophanes except for paratragedy only one entrance strictly analogous to this tragic type of speech and that occurred at Ar. *Plut.* 332 ff.[2] When we turn to New Comedy it is easy to find examples of this recurring pattern of stage-action (easy, that is, if one includes for the purpose the plays of Plautus and Terence)[3] although the rediscovery of Menander has not brought quite as much of this type of speech in its strictest form as the Roman adaptations of Greek comedy might have led us to expect.[4] The frequency of such conventional entrances in Plautus and Terence and their comparative rarity in Menander can be explained if one accepts the conclusions of Chapter 10 that Plautus and (albeit to a lesser extent) Terence were more stereotyped, repetitive, and 'formulaic' in their handling of conventions than were the Greek dramatists.

I now turn to the examples of what I would call conventional entrances in New Comedy.

At Men. *Dysc.* 153, Cnemon enters a stage already occupied by Sostratus. He soliloquizes angrily without noticing the silent Sostratus until at 167 he sees him lurking in the background and exclaims:

> οἴμοι· πάλιν τις οὑτοcὶ πρὸc ταῖc θύραιc
> ἕcτηκεν ἡμῶν.

Woe is me! Again there is someone here standing at our door.

---

[1] See above, pp. 61 ff., 68 ff.
[2] See above, p. 101.
[3] See the works cited above, p. 68 n. 3.
[4] For a discussion of 'Zutrittsmonologe' in Menander see Blundell, pp. 1 ff.

At Men. *Mis.* 216, Getas comes out of the house talking to himself ἐξῆλθεν ἔξω, 'he's gone out'. He then sees Demeas embracing Crateia, exclaims παῖ, τί τοῦθ'; 'my word, what's this?' before indignantly addressing Demeas.

Niceratus enters (Men. *Sam.* 399) with the sheep he has bought in the agora and expatiates on its qualities. Suddenly he observes that he is not alone:

405   ἀλλ' 'Ηράκλεις, τί τοῦτο; πρόσθε τῶν θυρῶν
       ἔστηκε Χρυσὶς ἥδε κλάουσα; οὐ μὲν οὖν
       ἄλλη.

My god! What's this? Chrysis standing in front of the door here weeping? It's her and no mistake.

Finally in an anonymous comic fragment (*CGF* 257) another Niceratus enters soliloquizing. At l. 22 he notices his friend Phaedimus:[1]

μὴ πολὺ διημάρτηκα τὸν Χαιρέστρατον
εἰς λιμένα πέμψας· ἡμέτερος οὗτος φίλος·
διάδηλός ἐστι . . .

I fear I made a big mistake sending Chaerestratus to the harbour; here is our friend. He is evident(ly) . . .

These passages differ in extent, but they exhibit the same form, the pattern of the Euripidean entrance speech with its two constituents, soliloquy followed by the expression of surprise at finding that one is not alone.[2] Following this there are several directions the dialogue may take. The speaker may for instance address the other person immediately or he may do as Cnemon does in our first example and continue to soliloquize.

---

[1] The attribution accepted here, which is that adopted in Sandbach's *Menandri Reliquiae Selectae* and in *CGF*, makes much the best sense of this much disputed passage (Sandbach expresses doubt now about whether to print it, in Gomme–Sandbach, p. 734). The paragraphi under 22 and 23 and the dicolon following πέμψας are ignored, but we may note that the paragraphus under 23 had already been deleted by the copyist himself. ἡμέτερος οὗτος φίλος explains *in asyndeto* Niceratus' assertion that it was a mistake to send Chaerestratus to the harbour, an assertion that must mark the moment he sees Phaedimus.

[2] In Euripides this would be expressed by ἔα (τί χρῆμα;). One may compare what the porter in Plat. *Prot.* 315b says when reacting to new arrivals ἔα . . . coφισταί τινες. New Comedy uses different means to express this surprised reaction; ἔα was obviously no longer part of everyday usage as a cry of surprise when Menander was writing.

The examples adduced above conform as it were to the basic pattern. The poet may build variations around it, variations that may make it seem less stereotyped, less conventional. He may omit the cry of surprise or the comment making it clear to the audience that the speaker has seen that there are others present on stage. Daos for example at Men. *Georg.* 35 ff. soliloquizes for four lines before noticing Myrrhine and Philinna who had retreated when he entered (Men. *Georg.* 33). He then instructs one of the slaves he has with him to take the provisions into the house and at this point must turn round and see the ladies since he immediately addresses Myrrhine (the ὦ in 41 may indicate surprise). Menander has here dispensed with the conventional intimation to the audience that Daos has seen the others on stage.

Alternatively, the poet may cause the monologue of the entering speaker to be interrupted and thus turn the speaker's attention to the people on stage. Examples of this are provided by Men. *Dysc.* 775 ff. where Callippides notices his son *after* a short conversation between Sostratus and Gorgias, Men. *Epitr.* 207–11 where Onesimus overhearing Syriscus exclaims τί ταῦτα; (what's this?), Men. *Sam.* 657 where Moschion ends Parmeno's monologue by calling to him, and *CGF* 257, 75 ff. where Chaerestratus hears part of a conversation between Niceratus and Phaedimus and exclaims τίc οὗτοc; 'who is this?'.[1]

The type of entrance speech we are discussing, whether unadorned or varied in some way, is a stock means the poet had at his disposal for starting a new scene, analogous to other such devices as the entrance of two characters in conversation or the entrance of a character speaking back into his house. Such devices would be accepted by the audience without qualm because of their familiarity. What concerns us here is the *extent* to which the convention was or might be exploited, the length of time a speaker is allowed to remain on stage unaware of the presence of others.[2] Also of interest is the amount of indication of

---

[1] See below, p. 142; cf. also Men. *Sam.* 429 ff.

[2] On the question of why the new entrant does not immediately see the person on stage—there are often reasons implicit such as the fact that the character is speaking to the audience or has not turned round after coming out of the stage-house—see Blundell, p. 5.

the speaker's intentions when he does become aware of the presence of others that the dramatist felt necessary to put into the text for the benefit of the audience and perhaps also of the reader. This latter will be dealt with in the following chapter in connection with the conventional phraseology appropriate to other situations.[1]

As regards the first topic, we may note that the examples of stereotyped entrance speeches adduced above are brief in comparison with other scenes in New Comedy where characters are allowed to remain self-absorbed—the longest and most akin to the kind of entrance monologues found so frequently in Roman Comedy being Men. *Dysc.* 153 ff. It is surely much less conventional for a character to soliloquize in the presence of someone who is silent than for a character not only to fail to observe the comment of an eavesdropper, but not even to notice the entrance of a new character who converses with the eavesdropper. This latter is the case with Smicrines in the first scene of *Epitrepontes.*[2] It is possible in a case like this to regard the character's self-absorption as indicative of a character trait, showing that Smicrines is something of a fool or at least at this point is not in proper control of his faculties.[3] Smicrines, however, is not the only character in Menander to behave in this way. Later in the same play we find two characters simultaneously so absorbed in their own thoughts that neither is immediately aware of the presence of the other.

After Onesimus has spoken a monologue (Men. *Epitr.* 243–53), Habrotonon comes out of the house at first talking back into it (Men. *Epitr.* 254–5a). Onesimus is too deep in thought to notice her and she, likewise failing to notice him, starts to soliloquize (Men. *Epitr.* 255b).[4] This soliloquy which extends to 265a is

---

[1] See below, pp. 152 f.

[2] Such lack of verisimilitude is taken to extreme lengths by Plautus, e.g. in the scene where Calidorus and Pseudolus eavesdrop on Ballio (Plaut. *Pseud.* 133 ff., especially 201–9) or in the scene where Philolaches eavesdrops on Philematium and Scapha (Plaut. *Most.* 160–284).

[3] See below, p. 173.

[4] It is at this point that one would expect the person entering from the house to notice the person on stage. The former *turns round* having ceased to address the people within and *sees* the latter.

interrupted (259b–60) by a further thought from Onesimus, still unaware of Habrotonon's presence. After Habrotonon's soliloquy Onesimus continues his deliberations (265b πῶς ἄν . . . ἱκετεύω)[1] and is only interrupted by the entrance of Syriscus (266). Syriscus and Onesimus converse until the former leaves at 287. Neither of them sees Habrotonon. Only after Syriscus' exit does Onesimus, who has been on stage now for upwards of thirty lines, become aware of Habrotonon and this awareness is brought about only because she approaches him and asks him a question.[2]

At this point we may digress regarding a point which will be taken up again later.[3] It is notable that the moment when Habrotonon becomes aware of Onesimus' presence—obviously this will occur almost directly after Syriscus' entrance[4]—is not signalled in the text. When this occurs, she must make it clear to the audience by means of a gesture.[5] A piece of stage action like this shows how careful we must be in visualizing a Menandrean play in performance. Often the poet is inexplicit about the action on stage where the Roman adapters of New Comedy (and for all we know Menander's rivals) would have been quite explicit. One might have expected an aside from Habrotonon at this point to make it quite clear to the audience that she was intending to eavesdrop. It only becomes clear to the *reader* that she has been eavesdropping when he hears her question at 295. An even more striking instance of a stage action which becomes clear to the

[1] It seems to me highly unlikely that these words are addressed to Habrotonon: οὖν surely excludes this; cf. Ter. *Eun.* 1006.

[2] See Blundell, p. 5. Gomme, *Essays in Greek History and Literature* (Oxford, 1937), p. 255, seems to me to underestimate the extent of the use of convention in this scene. A parallel for the interlacing of monologues is provided by Plaut. *Merc.* 830 ff.

[3] See below, pp. 147, 168, 175.

[4] l. 295 shows that she has been listening to this conversation.

[5] Wilamowitz's instinct is surely correct here: 'bei der Erwähnung der Tauropolien (275) muss Habrotonon für die Zuschauer wahrnehmbar aufhorchen und weiter durch stummes Spiel ihre Teilnahme kenntlich machen.' See also V. E. Hiatt, *Eavesdropping in Roman Comedy* (Chicago, 1946), p. 26. This passage is relevant to the question put by Handley in *Ménandre*, p. 179. (See also H.-D. Blume *Menanders Samia*, p. 167, n. 12, who warns against expecting a realistic staging in such a case—I believe that the *Epitr.* passage is evidence against the view he takes of *Sam.* 451.) In a way two separate stage actions are taking place simultaneously (contrast what was said above, p. 27). The article by E. T. Merrill entitled 'Simultaneous Action in Roman Comedy' (*CPh* 11 (1916), 340–1) is unilluminating.

reader in retrospect occurs in a play which Plautus adapted from a Menandrean original. Melainis at Plaut. *Cist.* 637 hands over to her slave Halisca a chest (*cistella*) and tells her to knock on the door of the house on stage. Before the order can be carried out,[1] Alcesimarchus rushes out of his house brandishing a sword. Selenium appeals for help (643) to Melainis and Halisca. After all the actors have left the stage, we read on and find that the *cistella* once in Halisca's hands is now on the ground opposite Phanostrata's door. The newly-entered Lampadio comes upon it at 655. While he and Phanostrata are examining it, Halisca returns to look for it. She now explains that she has lost it:

> 675 quamne in manibus tenui atque accepi hic ante aedis
> cistellam, ubi ea sit nescio, nisi ut opinor
> loca haec circiter mi excidit.

That chest I had in my hands here before the house, I don't know where it is, except that I think it fell out somewhere around here.

By now it is obvious to the reader what happened in the preceding scene. When Alcesimarchus made his violent entry, Halisca was holding the *cistella*. At some point during the scene she relinquished it, either dropping it in fright or putting it down when asked to come to Selenium's aid at 643.[2]

I suspect that, on this occasion at least, Plautus is in essentials faithful to his original (he has obviously tampered with the form and length of Halisca's re-entrance speech—it is a *canticum*). As in the *Epitrepontes* scene, so here in *Synaristosae* Menander has left just enough evidence for the reader to work out the stage action. He hesitates to spoil a lively stage action by inserting explanatory comments which an audience would not need and which would be of service only to the reader. Here it would have been possible

---

[1] This is surely the case. Webster believes that Halisca does succeed in knocking on the door (*Studies in Menander*, p. 96) and that, when Phanostrata enters, it is in answer to Halisca's knocking. He adduces as a parallel for 'delayed response to a knock on the door' Men. *Per.* 68–70, but we do not know how long it took Doris there to obtain a reply (the papyrus ends while she is still trying to attract the attention of the doorkeeper). I suspect that almost immediately after 70 the door was answered. The twenty-line delay in *Cistellaria* envisaged by Webster is quite inconceivable.

[2] 'Halisca verliert im Tumult das Kästchen', Ludwig, *Ménandre*, p. 57.

for Halisca to have been told to put down the *cistella* when she was asked to come to Selenium's aid at 643.

To return to our topic, it is not just old men, slaves, and hetaerae who are overcome by such protracted self-absorption on stage. Although he enters at *Epitr.* 588, it is not until 614[1] that Charisius observes that his slave Onesimus is present. The reverse of this situation between master and slave occurs in *Samia*. Parmeno delivers a monologue (Men. *Sam.* 641–57) unaware of the presence of his master, Moschion, who has to attract his attention. These cases and others like them, however, are much less striking than what happens in *Epitr.* 243 ff. In them the person who has not been noticed had withdrawn when the new character entered.

Perhaps the most striking example of self-absorption on stage occurs in *Misumenus*.[2] Getas bursts out of Thrasonides' house (284) so amazed by what he has seen taking place inside that he fails completely to observe Clinias. Not only does he not see him, as is the case with the monologue speakers mentioned in the previous paragraph, but he does not *hear* a series of questions Clinias puts to him (286–7a, 311a, 312, and probably 289b, 290b). Instead he gives the audience a vivid report of what he has just witnessed, stomping around the stage pursued by a bewildered and increasingly exasperated Clinias (συμπεριπατήϲω 'I'll walk around with him' in 296 entitles us to envisage the scene thus). It takes more than forty lines for the latter to 'get through' to the slave.

This is a farcical scene and the behaviour of the characters is exaggerated to a degree that recalls Plautus. No doubt it was not untypical (there are affinities with Ter. *Phorm.* 840 ff.); the excited slave with a story to tell is a stock figure of New Comedy.[3] One expects that the poets when writing such scenes were inclined to 'send up' the convention[4] and that audiences familiar with the character of them 'felt that the normal criteria

---

[1] See the excursus at the end of this chapter.

[2] See Blundell, pp. 6, 21.

[3] We are more used to him as the bringer of good tidings. On the affinities of the *Mis.* scene and Men. *Asp.* 399 ff. see below, p. 175.

[4] 'πόθεν πάρεϲτι; if correctly restored, would be an ironic joke on the convention of prolonged unawareness', Blundell, p. 21.

of realistic presentation did not apply'.[1] Another scene where the behaviour of a character is similarly exaggerated is the soliloquy of Strobilus in the so-called 'Strobilus'-comedy.[2] We break into his speech *in mediis rebus* and so cannot tell how long he has been speaking. The second speaker, who one might guess has been on stage for some time,[3] can be heard commenting in surprise on his behaviour ὦ Ἡράκλεις, τί ποτ᾽ ἐcτὶ τὸ γεγενη-μένον; 'My god! Whatever has happened?' Strobilus continues, however, for another four lines. Then the other person calls him by name, but, as was the case with Clinias and Getas in *Misumenus*, obtains no response. After a second, more extended attempt to attract his attention, Strobilus remarks τίc κέκληκέ με; 'Who has called me?' and after some confusion at last becomes aware of who is addressing him:

357   ἐγώ :: cὺ δ᾽ εἶ τίc; ὦ κράτιcτε τῶν θεῶν,
         ὡc εἰc καλόν c᾽ ἑόρακα.

I did. :: And who are you? Greatest of the gods! How glad I am to see you!

Such exaggerated and extravagant use of the conventions of entrance speeches comes two a penny in Plautus.[4] One cannot believe that they were all that frequent in the plays he was adapting. It is easier to assume that they tended to be reserved for certain stock scenes where the audience expected the over-playing of conventional remarks.

This is a view expressed many years ago by Fraenkel.[5] It has gained strength from the discovery of part of the original of

---

[1] This is Handley's phrase (*Ménandre*, p. 23). He discusses this possibility with regard to both farcical and paratragic scenes.

[2] *CGF* 244. 348 ff.

[3] Obviously we cannot be certain of the attribution and inscenation here. I assume that the first two lines are part of an entrance monologue by Strobilus (it is possible, however, that someone else is speaking and that 351 marks his entrance) and that τί ποτ᾽ ἐcτὶ τὸ γεγενημένον; is the comment (cf. in a similar situation Men. *Asp.* 403) of someone who happens to be on stage when he enters, the same man as tries later to attract the attention of Strobilus. νῦν οἶδ᾽ ἀκριβῶc κτλ. would make a good enough entrance-speech, but if it was we would have something less conventional than the scene I have described, less like the *Mis.* scene.

[4] *EP*, pp. 211 ff.

[5] See the previous note.

Plautus' *Bacchides*, the *Dis Exapaton* of Menander. The meeting there between Sostratus (Mnesilochus in Plautus) and Moschus (Pistoclerus) is effected in an extremely simple and natural way in Menander. Moschus comes out unannounced wondering where on earth his friend is. He sees him immediately and without further ado addresses him and receives an acknowledgement. Contrast the way in which the two friends meet in Plautus. For various reasons Plautus has altered the sequence of entrances,[1] but that does not affect the point at issue. What interests us is the way in which they come into contact. Pistoclerus overhears Mnesilochus' entrance monologue. There follows an elaborately symmetrical two line duet before the two of them come together:

534   *Pi.* estne hic meus sodalis? *Mn.* estne hic hostis quem aspicio
         meus?
      Pi. certe is est. *Mn.* is est. adibo contra et contollam gradum.
      Pi. salvos sis, Mnesiloche. *Mn.* salve.

   Pi. Is this my friend? *Mn.* Is this my enemy I see?
   Pi. Yes it is. *Mn.* It is. I shall approach and move near.
   Pi. I hope you are well, Mnesilochus. *Mn.* Greetings.

Only the beginning of 536 represents anything that is in the Greek: χαῖρε, Cώcτρατε :: καὶ cύ, 'Greetings, Sostratus. :: And to you.'
     Plautus did not invent the kind of by-play found in Plaut. *Bacch.* 534 f. The basic pattern and the stock phrases were to be found in his originals (more on this below in Chapter 11). Plautus' originality in this case lies in his use of such conventional phrases and patterns of action where they are inappropriate; the Menandrean naturalness is destroyed by the elaboration Plautus has introduced. It may be that other poets of New Comedy had more in common with Plautus than Menander in the degree of naturalism they sought to attain. The meeting of Niceratus and Phaedimus in the anonymous Ghoran-comedy (*CGF* 257) looks on the surface to have been much closer to the encounter in *Bacchides* than that in *Dis Exapaton*. It looks as if first one character notes the presence of another and then the second deliberates

---

[1] See E. W. Handley, *Menander and Plautus: a study in comparison* (London, Inaugural Lecture, 1968), pp. 14 f.

for at least three lines before the first man addresses him.[1] Still, the deliberation of Phaedimus here has dramatic point and there is nothing to match the empty bombast and repetition of *Bacch.* 534–5. One would do well not to make too much of a fragment that cannot be restored with certainty and which in any case might come from a Menandrean play,[2] but it is worth noting that the kind of retardation of the action we find in it has no precise parallel as yet in Menander. When Menander makes concessions to convention it is in the length of time he allows characters to spend on stage in ignorance of the presence of others and also in the conventional treatment of certain stock farcical scenes. His conventionality is a conventionality of action. It is conventionality of speech of the kind found in *Bacch.* 534 f.— actors explaining their actions and movements to the audience— that seems more unnatural.

[1] See above, p. 136 n. 1.
[2] See Sandbach in Gomme–Sandbach, p. 730, and the discussion below, pp. 182 f.

Onesimus' movements at Men. *Epitr.* 587–612

I ADDUCED above (p. 141) Charisius' monologue (*Epitr.* 588–612) as a case where an actor remained on stage for a long time unaware of another's presence. In doing so, I took it for granted that Onesimus remains on stage at 587 and is present throughout Charisius' speech, his timorous reaction to his master's vehemence at 612b–614a drawing his master's attention to him[1] and provoking the question οὗτος ἐπακροώμενος | ἔστηκας ἱερόσυλέ μου; 'You rogue, have you been standing listening to me?'. Not everyone takes this view of the scene. Koerte and Wilamowitz (*Schiedsgericht*, pp. 99, 101) both assume that Onesimus leaves the stage at 587 having heard the door of Chaerestratus' house opening, and expecting and fearing his master's entrance, rushes into the nearest available refuge, Charisius' house. Later he returns along with Habrotonon (612) and is speaking to her when Charisius first notices him. Sandbach in Gomme–Sandbach argues against his fellow commentator that this is the case.[2]

There are two[3] points which seem to me to make this inscenation

---

[1] There has been a tendency to take the last words of Charisius' speech τί c' αὖ βλέπω 'γώ; as the first indication that he is aware of Onesimus' presence (this would convert 612b–4a into a genuine aside rather than an overheard exclamation). Though αὖ would have a point addressed to Onesimus (cf. 243 ff.), it has much more point addressed in imagination to Smicrines. It is also a much more natural piece of staging for Charisius to be interrupted by a comment from Onesimus, to turn round and address him for the first time with οὗτος than for Charisius suddenly and for no apparent reason to terminate his soliloquy because he has seen Onesimus (οὗτος would be odd following cε: cf. above, p. 20, on Eur. *Alc.* 773). See also Sandbach ad loc.

[2] Others who support this view include G. Jachmann, *Plautinisches und attisches* (*Problemata*, Berlin, 3), 1931, p. 76, n. 1, R. Graf, *Szenische Untersuchungen zu Menander* (Diss. Giessen, 1914), p. 54, and B. Denzler, *Der Monolog bei Terenz* (Zürich, 1968), p. 35, n. 105. *Contra* H. W. Prescott, *CPh* 37 (1942) 21, n. 56, J. Straus, *Terenz und Menander, Beitrag zu einer Stilvergleichung* (Diss. Bern, Zürich, 1955), p. 59, n. 1, E. Grassi, *A&R* 6 (1961), 146, and Del Corno.

[3] Sandbach in Gomme–Sandbach disposes of a point made by Gomme that if Onesimus had been inside with Habrotonon he would have heard that she had met Pamphila and would no longer be anxious. Onesimus has plenty to be anxious about and in any case he does not trust Habrotonon (N.B. 387 ff.).

much less probable than the one I assumed to be the case above.
First Charisius' surprised τίϲ εἶ ϲύ; in 622 marks his first reaction to
the presence of Habrotonon. The previous line must be her first
utterance in the scene. Charisius is perfectly aware who Habrotonon
is (after all he hired her). His words here must express surprise at
being interrupted by someone whose presence he has not observed.
Now while it is equally possible for someone to react in such a way
when interrupted by someone who has in fact been on stage unnoticed
for some time (cf. Men. *Per.* 397, *CGF* 244. 357) and for someone to
react like this when interrupted by someone who has just entered, the
former situation would produce a remarkable effect here. On Wilamowitz's assumption, Onesimus and Habrotonon come out *together* at 612
and the words which attract Charisius' attention are addressed to her.[1]
Yet when Charisius turns round he sees only Onesimus. Either we
must assume that Habrotonon manages to remain 'in the background'
somehow concealed from Charisius—Sandbach suggests that Onesimus comes forward (perhaps obscuring Habrotonon?) when
Charisius addresses him—or else that 612b–14a is addressed into the
door and Habrotonon is not yet on stage when Charisius turns round.

   A second point seems to me to confirm that the problem of staging
above was created by commentators and not by Menander. We lose a
good joke if we make Onesimus leave the stage at 587. When asked by
his angry master (N.B. ἱερόϲυλε) whether he has been eavesdropping,
the frightened slave does what any slave would do, he produces a
vehement and totally false denial:

> μὰ τοὺϲ θεούϲ,
> ἀλλ' ἀρτίωϲ ἐξῆλθον.

> I swear I've just come out.

Only the audience knows the truth and may now laugh at his falsehood.[2] If this were a true statement, if Onesimus had just emerged

---

[1] γύναι seems the most likely supplement in 613 (Peter Brown allows me to
mention here his tentative suggestion [Τύχη], but it need not imply Habrotonon's
physical presence. Onesimus, who has earlier expressed doubts about Habrotonon's
good faith (387 ff.), may be begging her in her absence not to desert him now that
things have reached the point of crisis (for ἐγκαταλίπηιϲ cf. Men. *Mis.* 306 and
CGF 255. 4).

[2] A similar sort of effect is achieved although in a more prolonged manner at
Men. *Per.* 82 ff. where the audience will recall what they had seen at the close of
the previous act and will realise how little Daos' account squares with the facts and
laugh at the way he is claiming credit where none is owed.

from the house, why should so much attention be drawn to it here?
Why should Charisius be represented as groundlessly suspicious?

Again we may note how Menander refuses to retard a vivid piece of
stage action by introducing an explicit indication of the actor's movements which would make it clear to the *reader* what was going on on
stage.[1] He might easily have added after 587 one of the words or
phrases that indicate that a speaker is going to move into the background and eavesdrop. Instead he avoids a conventional phrase and
an anti-climax: as he withdraws, Onesimus makes a desperate prayer
to Zeus.[2]

[1] See p. 139.
[2] Admittedly Ζεῦ cῶτερ, εἴπερ ἐcτὶ δυνατόν, cῶιζέ με would make a good exit
line (cf. *Epitr.* 379–80), but contrast what happens after Men. *Asp.* 213–15 and
Dysc. 208–11.

9. Conventions in New Comedy— some conclusions

HAVING collected the asides and conventional entrances in Menander and the anonymous comic fragments, we may now say something about the continuity between Old and New Comedy and about the debt New Comedy owes to tragedy. The conventions of New Comedy regarding self-absorption on stage have clearly more in common with Euripidean tragedy than with Aristophanic comedy. With asides too one can parallel from Euripides most of the phenomena found in Menander. Emotional exclamation was by far the most common form of aside in tragedy.[1] It is amply attested in New Comedy; e.g. Men. *Dysc.* 191b–3a, 201b–3a, *Mis.* 210f. Even the most conventional type of aside, the one where an actor announces his intentions or deliberates rationally, is easier to parallel from tragedy than Old Comedy.[2]

How far the connections between New Comedy and tragedy are merely coincidental is questionable. There are, as has been noted,[3] other devices in tragedy which seem to foreshadow typical features of New Comedy—the prologue deity in Euripides, the noise of the stage-door opening and disturbing the characters on stage, perhaps even the announcement of the first entrance of the chorus where the speaker gives out his intention to withdraw (Eur. *Phoen.* 196 ∼ Men. *Dysc.* 230 ff.). No doubt it is possible to exaggerate the connections between tragedy and New Comedy, but surely in regard to form and to convention there is much that New Comedy has borrowed from the former genre. This is probably to be explained in two ways. First we may point to the traditional character of Greek literary composition, secondly to the demands made by the type of plot that prevailed in New

---

[1] See above, p. 57.   [2] See above, p. 66.   [3] See above, p. 85.

Comedy.[1] Originality was not a high priority for Greek poets and in any genre successors tended both naturally and by custom to look back to distinguished predecessors for succour and inspiration. The founding fathers of New Comedy, or shall we say rather those fourth-century poets who began to write the kind of play whose features we would be most likely to associate with New Comedy, would naturally look back to the comedy of their predecessors. The type of plot these new dramatists chose to use, however, demanded a clarity and formality in the shaping of the dialogue that could not be found in Old Comedy. Generally speaking the dialogue in iambic scenes in Old Comedy is much less stereotyped than that of New Comedy and there are indeed occasions when it seems much more natural.[2] The formal parts, the parts with a recognisable structure, come in the lyric and epirrhematic scenes. Having chosen to write plays with complicated intrigues and having excluded the chorus from the action of the play, the poet of New Comedy would find little in Old Comedy to help him as regards the structure and form of the dialogue and in the manipulation of exits and entrances, that is to say in the composition of scenes. It would be natural for him to turn, just as occasionally his predecessors had done,[3] to the other genre and particularly to the dramatist who was regarded as a master of structure and clarity of exposition, Euripides. There dialogue was formal and its parts clearly divided. It provided a pattern for development.[4]

It would be mistaken, however, to think that every aspect of Old Comedy was submerged by the transformation that took

[1] See the discussion by Dover in *Fifty Years (and twelve) of Classical Scholarship*, pp. 149 f. Note particularly his statement 'many Tragic features of New Comedy which at first sight appear independent are probably to be interpreted as necessary consequences of the new type of plot.'

[2] See above, p. 95.

[3] See above (p. 98), where it was suggested that some asides in Aristophanes may owe something to Euripidean asides.

[4] Any such description *in nuce* of the development of a literary technique is bound to be crude and unqualified. Obviously the development of New Comedy was gradual and, when discussing it, it may be misleading to speak in terms of conscious choice by the dramatists who were responsible for it. It would certainly be wrong to suppose that *Menander*, ignoring all the comedy that preceded him, went directly back to Euripides to derive thence his technique.

place in the character of comedy in the fourth century. As we shall see, audience address remains lively in New Comedy. The eavesdropping aside too has no tragic analogy. The parallels for the beginning of *Epitrepontes* as we have it are scenes in *Pax* and *Ranae*. Similarly the technique by which long narratives (as distinct from narrative in monologues) tend to be broken up by comments of surprise, disgust or derision by the person to whom they are ostensibly addressed is a feature of Old Comedy rather than of tragedy. Here we see a survival of the kind of 'aside' which Schaffner called 'bomolochic'. The narrative of the 'democratic man' in *Sicyonius* (Men. *Sic.* 176–271) is quite exceptional in Menander. There the speaker is not interrupted despite the length of his speech. One may contrast another 'serious narrative seriously told' Men. *Asp.* 23–82 where Smicrines interrupts Daos at least five times. The form of the *Sicyonius* speech is tragic: it is modelled, in form at least, on the Euripidean messenger speech and of course it takes as its starting point one particularly famous speech. What effect it had on an audience and why Menander chose to cast it in such a form must remain a matter for speculation.[1] What can be agreed is that it represents something special and that its presence in the corpus of New Comedy serves to show all the more clearly what was the norm as regards the treatment of long narrative speeches.

Several times, in discussing individual passages, stress has been laid on the naturalness of Menander both as regards his handling of the aside-convention and in his tendency to avoid the kind of conventional phraseology which makes the stage action easier for the reader to visualize but which is for the most part unnecessary when the play is in performance. Some general points may be made about these aspects of Menander's technique here.

It should be obvious from the number of examples of asides given under either category (pp. 106 ff., 124 ff.) that of the two

---

[1] See Sandbach, *Ménandre*, pp. 129 ff., and H. Lloyd-Jones, *GRBS* 13 (1972), 194, n. 42. Menander was probably influenced in the choice of this form by consideration of the splendid opportunities for ὑπόκρισις it would give the actor who delivered it (cf. Quint. *Inst.* XI. 3. 91). Not that such opportunities are exclusive to the tragic messenger speech (cf. Men. *Mis.* 284 ff.), but perhaps they are given greater scope.

types of aside I distinguished above, the eavesdropping aside,
where the person who comments aside has as yet not been observed by others on stage, and the aside in conversation, where
the speaker who delivers the aside has up till then been talking to
someone else on stage, the first type is by far the more common in
Menander. This is not likely to be merely an accident of trans-
mission. In terms of 'stage life' at any rate, the first type is much
more natural than the second. In the first type it is to be expected
that the characters are further apart on stage and if we accept
that one has not yet seen the other, we might as well accept that
he does not hear him either. We shall see in the following chapter
an attempt made in Roman drama to motivate and explain in
terms of reality the second type—an attempt which almo:t
certainly derives from Greek drama.[1] It is perhaps significant
that we have as yet no examples of the technique in Menander.
He may have felt that apologizing for the technique was merely
more likely to draw attention to it.

Secondly we must note the length of asides in New Comedy.
Obviously the longer the aside, the less natural the effect. We
note that present evidence tends to support Fraenkel's contention
that in contrast to the asides in Plautus, the asides of New
Comedy were of no great length.[2] Look at the examples:[3] Men.
Asp. 467b, two words; Men. *Dysc.* 168b, half a line; 171a, two
words; 191b–3a one trimeter and parts of another two, the total
not amounting to two whole trimeters; 194b, one iambic metron;
201b–3a, just over two lines; 212b–13a, parts of two lines; 214
κατὰ τρόπον τί; 431b–2a (almost two lines); 435a (three words);
777–9a, about three lines but the words may in any case be

<hr/>

[1] See below, p. 157.

[2] 'perciò quei poeti che fecero largo uso di codeste interruzioni come di una
forma fissa, ebbero tanto tatto da limitarsi ad una frase buttata giú di passaggio (ac-
compagnata, quando l'interruzione è dialogica, da una replica altrettanto con-
cisa), lunga, diciamo, non piú di uno o due versí; essi conservarono sempre [an
exaggeration, N.B. Men. *Asp.* 467b] a queste interruzioni il carattere di esclama-
zioni esplosive e cariche di affetto, oppure di rapidi commenti, ed evitarono in
questo punto le tirate troppo lunghe. Cosí è sempre in Menandro ... sicché
possiamo dedurne che questa limitazione doveva essere generalmente accettata
nella tecnica della Commedia Nuova' (*EP*, p. 204). On the length of Plautine asides
see also G. W. Williams, *Hermes* 84 (1956), 440, n. 2.

[3] I leave out the more doubtful instances.

overheard;[1] *Epitr.* 5b–7a, a line and a half; 11b–12, a line plus
one word; 14b–18 (at least), practically five lines; 433b–4a, three
words; 536–7a, over a line and a half; 540, over half a line;
Carch. 9–10, at least two lines; *Mis.* 210–11a, a line plus one word;
289b, no more than half a line; 296; 300–1; 311a, half a line;
324a, two words; *Per.* 62–4a two and a half lines; 177b–8, a line
plus a word; 181b–2a, parts of two lines amounting to more than
one line; 353–4; 357; 362–3; *Sam.* 375, more than half a line;
383b, practically a line; 386, 387b, two words; 454a, almost a
complete line; 456a, the same; 457–8a, almost two lines; *Sic.*
144b–5, almost two lines; *Fab. Inc.* 23 ff., at least four lines; *CGF*
244.350; *CGF* 257. 24b–6a.

Men. *Epitr.* 14 ff.—a soliloquy followed by a conversation,
both elements quite unobserved by Smicrines—which amounts
to at least five lines is probably the longest aside passage in
Menander.[2] It was suggested above that its length may have been
intended to contribute to the characterization of Smicrines.
However that may be, one would think that an aside in conversation of this length would be much less easy to accept.[3]

Thirdly there is the question of 'stage directional' phrases.
Expressions like προϲιτέον, ἐπανάγω, θορυβήϲω, μεταϲτῶμεν, ὑπαποϲτήϲομαι, πορεύομαι, ἐγὼ δ᾽ ἀναμείναϲ᾽ ὅ τι λέγουϲ᾽ ἀ[κροάϲομαι
in the mouth of actors are not perhaps to modern taste (obviously some may offend more than others: few would feel that
'I'm off now' πορεύομαι sounded as conventional as 'I shall withdraw a little' ὑπαποϲτήϲομαι). Why put them in at all? We have
seen cases where Menander omits stage directional phrases and
where the reader was able to work out the stage action without
them. Yet all the phrases mentioned above occur in Menander
and if we join them to the other repeated formulae suitable for
other occasions, such as someone on stage hearing the house-door
being opened, they would appear to belie the notion that Menan-

---

[1] See above, p. 137.

[2] Blundell notes (p. 64) that Men. *Dysc.* 557–62 is the longest turning away
from a dialogue partner in Menander. He rightly avoids the term aside in describing it.

[3] I do not think *Fab. Inc.* 23 ff. particularly unnatural although on my definition
it is an aside in conversation.

der is a natural author and to give the impression that New
Comedy was a highly conventional genre. This is, with certain
qualifications, not entirely misleading. Such phrases are indeed
a mannerism, a convenient set of formulae on which the poet may
fall back in certain typical situations and in this respect as com-
pared with Old Comedy, New Comedy certainly is conventional
and stereotyped.[1] One ought, however, to take into account the
extent and frequency of the use of such words in New Comedy
and also the dramatic situations in which they occur. Consideration of the Roman comedians in the chapter that follows will
highlight the restraint shown by Menander in the use of conventional phrases; in general it may be said that Plautus and to
a lesser, but not all that significantly lesser, extent Terence
explain far more than Menander ever does and that the impression they leave is of an almost Homeric delight in certain
more or less fixed formulae (also the phrases they use tend to a
greater length than anything in Greek New Comedy, but this is
in no small part due to the natural long-windedness of early
Latin).[2]

It is unfortunate that we cannot at this moment be certain
about the practice of Menander's contemporaries in regard to
such conventional phrases and decide whether the thicker
texture of Plautus and Terence is solely a reflection of the difference between Greek and Roman comedy and not of that between
Plautus, Terence, some other Greek poets, and Menander. I
think it unlikely that there was any significant difference between
Menander and his contemporaries. One might guess that 'conventional' utterances were prominent in the earlier stages of New
Comedy and were used with greater restraint as the genre
developed. One should recall that there may be practitioners of
varying competence or predilection at any stage of the development of any art form and the topic is one that with the present
state of evidence does not repay speculation.[3]

---

[1] Conventional phrases are much harder to find in Old Comedy: note ἐπανα-
χωρήcω Ar. *Eccl.* 28 (cf. also Ar. *Pax* 234 f.).   [2] See below, p. 180.
[3] Comparison between Menander and some of the fragments of New Comedy,
however, does tend to reveal originality and economy as against conventionality
and inordinate length. See Handley's *Dyskolos*, pp. 199 f.

10. Roman Comedy

i

THERE remains a large body of evidence for the conventions of New Comedy which up to now I have virtually ignored, the plays of the Roman adapters Plautus and Terence. It is proposed now to investigate the degree to which these plays supplement our knowledge of Greek aside-conventions and further exemplify phenomena which are less well attested in Greek plays. Obviously the Roman plays need to be used with caution as evidence for the practice of the Greek theatre; the age is long past when it was possible to regard them as more or less literal reproductions of Greek plays. Even so in what follows questions of composition and of the relationship of the Roman play to its original have for the most part been ignored. Rather I have selected motifs and recurring situations, paying particular attention to similarities of phrasing, in Plautus and Terence in the hope that this will lead us back to recurring motifs and situations of the Greek plays. I assume that the technique of Plautus and Terence with regard to the conventions we are discussing is a shared one and that even in cases where they may be altering the context of their originals and composing without the aid of a Greek model they will resort to situations and techniques which they have acquired from familiarity with Greek New Comedy. There are indeed occasions in Plautus and less frequently Terence when the action unfolds in a manner quite unlike anything one could conceive of on the Greek stage,[1] but in such cases one would not speak of the Roman dramatist 'inventing' a different set of conventions. It

---

[1] Both dramatists tend to leave characters unoccupied and unnoticed on stage in a way and, in the case of Plautus, for a length of time that is alien to the practice of the Greek stage; for example, Theoropides in Plaut. *Most.* 684–784 and Pamphilus in Ter. *Andr.* 301 ff. (it is no accident that both these passages are for other reasons thought to show considerable deviations from their Greek models).

would be truer to say that he was misusing or abusing the Greek technique.[1]

If a motif hitherto unattested in Greek New Comedy is frequently to be found in Plautus, we may suspect that it is in fact Greek in origin. If it is also to be found in Terence, suspicion hardens into virtual certainty. We must always remember how much New Comedy was available to Plautus and Terence and how little, comparatively speaking, is available to us. A glance at known titles is salutary. Any day a papyrus is liable to come to light revealing as Greek in origin a conventional situation or motif that was known to us only through the medium of Roman Comedy.[2] A passage in an anonymous comic fragment provides a good example of this kind of occurrence (*CGF* 242. 11 ff. = P. Ant. 55 col. ii. 6 ff.):

> ἀλλ' εἰ ταῦτα [c]αυτ[ῶ]ι cυμφέρειν
> ἡγεῖ, πέραινε· τί γὰρ ἂν ἀντιλέγοιμί coι;
> εἶέν· μόνος δὴ γενόμενος νυ[νί, Δ]ρόμων
> λογιcμὸν ὧν μέλλειc διοικε[ῖν πραγ]μάτων
> cαυτῶ[ι] δόc.

13 suppl. Williams

But if you think this is to your advantage, go ahead; why should I contradict you? Well then! Now that you're alone, Dromon, take account of the affairs you intend to manage.

As Thomas Williams remarks,[3] this formula of transition from dialogue to soliloquy introduced by the self-apostrophe 'you stand (are) alone' is found here for the first time in Greek Comedy.[4] Arguing from the formally analogous passages Plaut. *Pseud.* 394 ff., *Epid.* 80 ff., and *Trin.* 717 ff., Theiler had long ago asserted that this must be a Greek convention.[5] These Plautine

---

[1] See Fraenkel, *EP*, pp. 380 ff. for an assessment of Plautus' creative capability.

[2] Cf. what Arnott says of the recently discovered *Aspis* and *Samia* in *CR*, n.s. 20 (1970), 186: they are 'new evidence for the folly of *argumenta ex silentio* for what Menander couldn't do.'

[3] *RhM* 105 (1962), 194 f.

[4] Cf. the transition from dialogue to (first-person) monologue at Theocr. 2. 64 νῦν δὴ μώνα ἐοῖcα πόθεν τὸν ἔρωτα δακρύcω;

[5] In *Hermes* 73 (1938), 288 (= *Untersuchungen zur antiken Literatur*, p. 384). He went too far, however, in claiming that the motif was specifically Menandrean.

examples were all he had to go on: there were in this case no
Terentian examples.

Let us now turn to Roman Comedy and examine some typical
situations therein which are at present unattested or ill-attested
in Greek Comedy.[1]

ii

The first conventional motif has its origins in the equivocal
treatment of the aside in stage convention.[2] Thoughts that would
not in real life be expressed aloud are often in dramatic dialogue
treated as if they had been. When two people are conversing on
stage and one of them speaks aside, there are two ways of continuing the dialogue. The aside can simply be ignored and, if the
dramatist treats it in terms of real life, be regarded as an unspoken
thought. Attention may be drawn to this by having the actor who
has failed, for example, to get a reply from the aside-speaker comment on the *silence* of his dialogue partner (cf. Plaut. *Most.* 660,
Ter. *Andr.* 498); for him the aside signifies a silence, a failure to
reply to his question.[3] Alternatively, however, the speaker in
whose presence the aside was delivered may draw attention to
a different aspect of his interlocutor's behaviour, perhaps even
intimating that he has heard him say something but failed to
make out what that something was. In this case the aside is
treated as something that has been expressed aloud.[4] The device
is employed with some frequency in Plautus and Terence.

In the following examples the speaker is reacting to an aside
from his dialogue partner: Plaut. *Aul.* 190, 'quid tu solus tecum
loquere?', 549, 'quid tu te solus e senatu sevocas?'; Plaut. *Most.*

---

[1] The article of P. W. Harsh, 'Certain features of technique found in both
Greek and Roman Drama', *AJPh* 58 (1937), 282–93, despite its title says nothing
about the topics which will be discussed here.

[2] See Legrand, p. 416, and Sprague, p. 69.

[3] See Barbieri, pp. 41 f. A possible Greek example of this is to be found at Eur.
I.A. 1140 (see above, p. 55). For an extreme example of the aside being treated as
silent thought see Sen. *Ag.* 126 where we learn that Clytaemnestra's opening speech
has been delivered in the presence of the nurse who has heard none of it.

[4] See Legrand, p. 417, and G. E. Duckworth, *The Nature of Roman Comedy*
(Princeton, 1952), p. 112, who illustrates this approach with reference to Plaut.
Men. 478 and *Merc.* 707.

512, 'quid tute tecum loquere?', 551, 'quid tute tecum?'; Plaut. *Trin.* 567, 'quid tecum, Stasime?'; Plaut. *Truc.* 357, 'quo te avortisti?'; Ter. *Haut.* 200, 'quid tute tecum?'. Two of these passages (Plaut. *Aul.* 549, *Truc.* 357) do not necessarily imply that the speaker has *heard* but failed to understand the aside. All, however, present the same basic pattern, giving as it were a *post eventum* stage direction for the delivery of the aside—the speaker has turned away from his partner. The stereotyped phraseology is striking—quid tute tecum loquere? 'Why are you talking to yourself?' being as it were the theme upon which the poet writes variations.[1]

From the frequency of the motif and from the fact that it occurs in both Plautus and Terence, one might guess that it was to be found in Greek New Comedy. It has been argued that we have something similar in Men. *Sam.* 456, but this is not certain[2] and in any case the idea of 'talking to oneself' or withdrawing is not expressed in that passage. Looking for a Greek equivalent for 'quid tute tecum?' one thinks of something like τί . . . κατὰ μόνας ϲαυτῶι λαλεῖϲ;[3]

The motif can be traced back, however, to tragedy, to the famous scene[4] in Euripides' *Hecuba* where Hecuba speaks aside in the presence of Agamemnon who, while aware that she is making some kind of utterance, admits that he cannot make out what she is saying (Eur. *Hec.* 739 f.). One may be justified in deriving from Herondas, a writer noted for his exploitation of the themes and topics of comedy,[5] evidence for the existence of the motif in New

---

[1] Plautus, fr. 153 Lindsay (32 Leo), 'quid murmurillas tecum et te discrucias?' probably comes from a similar context. Cf. also Plaut. *Cas.* 267, 'quid friguttis?'.

[2] See above, p. 126 and 126 n. 3. Sandbach (followed by Blundell, p. 15, n. 23) takes it in this way but I would prefer as suggested in the footnote above, to take τί φήιϲ; as the surprised question 'what *are* you saying?'; cf. Men. *Dysc.* 563 (note also quid ais? Ter. *Eun.* 654).

[3] I am not of course suggesting that Menander, fr. 722 (*CGF* 297) (if it is Menander), represents a comment on an aside. It may in fact be the beginning of a play (cf. Plaut. *Pseud.* 1 ff.), although Shackleton Bailey's restoration (based on Cic. *ad Att.* xiii 42. 1) ⟨cὺ δὲ δή⟩ . . . makes this less likely than would Wilamowitz's ⟨τρόφιμε⟩ (although cf. Men. fr. 161 on which see Fraenkel, *Beobachtungen zu Aristophanes*, p. 103). [4] See above, pp. 13 ff.

[5] Although it is perfectly natural and realistic in its context (see above, p. 60), Hdas. 1. 47–8 may be borrowed from a situation in New Comedy like Plaut. *Mil.* 955, *Most.* 472, *Stich.* 102, *Trin.* 146.

Comedy. In the seventh mime, after Cerdo has uttered aside a three-line prayer, one of the women to whom he hopes to sell his wares asks:

> 77   τί τονθορύζεις (cf. Plaut. fr. 153) κοὐκ ἐλευθέρηι γλάccηι
> τὸν τῖμον ὄcτιc ἐcτὶν ἐξεδίφηcαc;

Why do you mumble and not seek out of your mind the price openly, whatever it may be?

A situation related to the one where a speaker asks his partner 'quid tute tecum?' occurs when instead of asking the aside-speaker directly, the dialogue partner himself comments aside: Plaut. *Amph.* 954, 'mirum quid *solus secum* secreto ille agat'; Plaut. *Aul.* 52, 'at ut scelesta *sola secum* murmurat'; Plaut. *Merc.* 379, 'quid illuc est quod a me *solus* se in consilium *sevocat*?'; Plaut. *Pseud.* 615, 'quid illic *solus secum* loquitur?'. Once more the phraseology is strikingly stereotyped. On this occasion, as well as having no Greek examples, we have nothing from Terence that may be set beside Plautus.

iii

Moving away from the aside (though some of the passages to be taken into consideration do contain asides) and returning to a topic that was discussed in Chapter 8, the situation where a new entrant coming on to the stage fails to notice the presence of others on stage, we may note a typical situation that occurs after a monologue by the new entrant or after two actors have entered in conversation. After such an entrance there are several directions the dialogue may take.[1] One of them requires our attention here. The transition from monologue (or conversation if there are two actors entering) to dialogue with the others on stage is sometimes effected by the actor who has heard some or all of the entrance speech making a comment which in turn is heard by the person entering who then comments in surprise at finding himself not to

---

[1] See particularly Fraenkel, *EP*, p. 211, and, for a Terentian 'Gesprächseröff-nung', W. Ludwig, *Philologus* 103 (1959), 14 f. Plautus is particularly fond of the 'double aside'. Each party becomes aware of the other's presence, but deliberates aside before addressing the other.

be alone. This is extremely common in Roman Comedy.[1] Here
are some comments by newly entered actors who have just heard
the person on stage making a comment: Plaut. *Bacch.* 773, 'quis
loquitur prope?'; Plaut. *Capt.* 133, 'quis hic loquitur?'; Plaut.
Mil. 276, 'quis hic est?'; Plaut. *Pseud.* 445, 'quis hic loquitur?';
Plaut. *Stich.* 330, 'quisnam hic loquitur tam prope nos?'; Ter.
Andr. 267, 'quis hic loquitur?'; Ter. *Andr.* 783 (this passage is a
piece of 'play acting',[2] but it exploits the same convention), 'quis
hic loquitur?'; Ter. *Haut.* 517, 'quis hic loquitur?'; Ter. *Phorm.*
739, 'quis hic loquitur?'; Ter. *Eun.* 86, 'quis hic loquitur?'

Again we encounter a stereotyped situation which is demonstrably widespread in Roman Comedy. Again we find that it is
given voice in a stereotyped expression, the most common form
being 'who is speaking here?'.[3] One may contrast the way Daos
in Men. *Georg.* comes into contact with the two people who occupy
the stage when he enters.[4]

Until recently we had no exact parallels in Greek Comedy.
Now, however, we appear to have some parallels both for the
situation and for the phrases 'quis hic est?' and 'quis hic loquitur?'.[5] In an anonymous fragment of New Comedy, *CGF* 282.
14 ff., a young man is interrupted by his slave and comments
with surprise on being interrupted:

> σφόδρ' ἂν δοκῇ . [
> τίς ἐστιν ὁ λαλῶν[
> τρόφιμε, τί ποιεῖς . . .

---

[1] Some of the material here can be found in W. Koch, *De personarum comicarum introductione* (Diss. Breslau), pp. 69 ff.

[2] See below, p. 174.

[3] Perhaps Turpilius 212R is a variation used in an analogous situation: set quis est qui interrumpit? On a formula that sometimes follows 'quis hic loquitur?', 'hic quidem est', see H. D. Jocelyn, *Ennius, Entretiens Fondation Hardt* 17, pp. 64 ff.

[4] See above, p. 137.

[5] There are two occasions in Old Comedy when a character comments on an eavesdropper's remark, Ar. *Thesm.* 51 and 58 (τίς ὁ φωνήσας;); τίς ἐστιν οὗτος; occurs at Men. *Per.* 397. There, however, somewhat exceptionally the person exclaiming has not noticed the *entrance* of the person interrupting (τίς οὗτος; occurs at Men. *Dysc.* 913 where Sicon has been pretending to be unaware of Cnemon's presence). τίς οὑτοσί; is the reaction of someone wakened from sleep at Heliod. 8. 12. 4 (cf. Eur. *Hec.* 501). Cf. also τίνος φώνημα; in Soph. *Phil.* 1295–6 and τίς ἀνήρ; in 976. In both cases the speaker is startled by the words of a new entrant.

One cannot be completely certain of the attribution here. In this papyrus a change of speaker is indicated by a paragraphus and by spacing within the line. There is no paragraphus under l. 13 so that it is by conjecture that the first editor gives l. 14 to the slave. This may be correct, but it is possible that the paragraphus under l. 14 indicates change of speaker within the line. If that is the case, the slave will have delivered only half a line before his master exclaimed τίς ἐστιν ὁ λαλῶν; 'who is this speaking?'. The first editor thinks it possible that l. 15 marks the entrance of a new speaker, but the examples of the use of 'quis hic loquitur?' in Roman Comedy suggest that the slave has been eavesdropping on an entrance monologue (lines 10–14 could well come from such a speech) by his master. τίς ἐστιν ὁ λαλῶν; is a comment by the master on the remark the slave makes at the end of the monologue, a surprised reaction on the part of the young man who thought he was alone.[1] I would guess that τίς ἐστιν ὁ λαλῶν; occurred frequently and gave birth to the Latin 'quis hic loquitur?'.

A second example of this type of situation has become clearer to us now that we have an improved text of the anonymous Ghoran fragment (CGF 257).[2] Chaerestratus' entrance monologue (73 ff.) is interrupted by a comment (what it was we cannot restore for sure) from one of the people on stage. He hears this and exclaims τίς οὗτος; 'Who is this?' (cf. Plaut. Mil. 276) before turning round and seeing Phaedimus and Niceratus (CGF 257. 76).

Recent discoveries enable us to provide Greek parallels for another related typical scene and for its stereotyped phraseology. This occurs in a situation much the same as the one we have just mentioned. What distinguishes it is that, whereas in the one situation the interrupted speaker exclaims with surprise after the

---

[1] The question τί ποιεῖς; might be thought more appropriate as an address to a person who has been present for some time than to someone who has just entered (cf., however, Men. Sam. 452).

[2] The essential point is that we should follow the papyrus in marking a change of speaker after δεῦρο in 69; the colon following the word (cf. line 24 where there is a colon after ἐστί) and the scriptio plena show that this was the intention of the person who wrote the papyrus.

interruption, in the other the speaker interrupted turns round immediately and recognizes the interruptor without any comment of surprise like 'Who's that?'. At Ter. *Phorm.* 848, Geta bursts in (as a 'running slave') and after some by-play starts conversing with Antipho. He does not observe that Phormio is also present until Phormio breaks in and asks him a question. Thereupon (858) Geta exclaims 'oh tu quoque aderas, Phormio', 'Ah! So you were here too, Phormio.' Similarly at Ter. *Hec.* 340 Sostrata when addressed by Parmeno whom she has not as yet observed exclaims 'ehem?'[1] Parmeno tun hic eras?' ('Ah! So you were here, Parmeno') and at Ter. *Ad.* 901 Aeschinus is asked a question by his father whom he has not yet seen and exclaims 'ehem pater mi, tu hic eras' ('Ah! You were here, father'). These passages[2] have now a parallel in the beginning of act one of *Samia*. There Chrysis observes Moschion and Parmenon entering and tells us she will remain and hear what they have to say (Men. *Sam.* 58–60). They enter conversing and do not observe her. She listens to their conversation until 69 when she interrupts with the words τί βοᾶις, δύσμορε;, 'Why are you shouting, you wretch?'. At this Parmenon exclaims[3] καὶ Χρυσὶς ἦν ἐνταῦθα, 'Chrysis was here too.' The resemblance between this and the phraseology of *Phorm.* 858, *Eun.* 86, and *Hec.* 340 is striking, but those Latin passages have in fact their closest parallel in a tragic line. The messenger who comes to tell Menelaus of the disappearance of Helen suddenly sees the real Helen and exclaims (Eur. *Hel.* 616) ὦ χαῖρε Λήδας θύγατερ, ἐνθάδ' ἦcθ' ἄρα, 'Greetings, daughter of Leda, so you were *here*.' Perhaps the poets of New Comedy took up this phrase and it hardened into a formula.[4]

---

[1] For *ehem* in such a context see G. Luck, *Über einige Interjektionen der lateinischen Umgangssprache: kritische Beiträge zu Plautus und Terenz* (Heidelberg, 1964), pp. 70 ff.

[2] Cf. also Plaut. *Truc.* 719: 'amabo, hicin tu eras?' In Ter. *Eun.* 86 the two formulae 'quis hic loquitur?' and 'tun hic eras?' are combined. Daos in Men. *Georg.* 42 explains to Myrrhine after he has greeted her and she has returned his greeting, οὔ cε καθεώρων (cf. Ter. *Andr.* 183 'erus est neque provideram').

[3] It would be mistaken to call this an aside.

[4] For the discovery of the original of another of the 'conventional formulae inherited by the *palliatae* from New Comedy' (Men. *Sam.* 405 ff. ∼ Lucian *Tim.* 54 ∼ e.g. Ter. *Eun.* 848) see J. C. B. Lowe, *BICS* 20 (1973), 98.

iv

Next we turn to a type of situation that depends on a convention whereby it is possible for there to be two separate actions
taking place on stage simultaneously. That X can be on stage
concurrently with Y and unaware of Y's presence or that they can
be mutually unaware of each other's presence is an established
convention of the Greek stage. When an actor enters an already
occupied stage, he is in comedy usually represented as at first
unaware of the presence of the other people on stage. On some
occasions they are represented as unaware of him and the two
actors or groups of actors proceed in mutual unawareness for
some time. A clear instance of this last contingency was discussed
above (pp. 139 f.) in connection with Men. *Epitr.* 254 ff. where
Onesimus does not observe Habrotonon's entrance and likewise
she does not at first see him. Perhaps the interlacing of the monologues of Onesimus and Habrotonon is meant to suggest that
they are speaking (or thinking) at the same time. At any rate
there are certainly two separate actions taking place simultaneously. The effect though in no sense realistic puts less strain
on the audience's belief than some of the passages we will discuss
below because it is carefully motivated: the two characters are
represented as too occupied in their own thoughts to notice each
other.

Another type of double action is frequently found in Roman
Comedy. This is the situation where, when there are three people
on stage, two of them converse apart from the third.[1] I do not in
this instance mean the situation which occurs when an eavesdropper listens to and comments on the conversation taking
place between two other actors (like Moschion at Men. *Per.*
348 ff.) or its converse, two people commenting aside to each
other while they eavesdrop on the soliloquy of a third[2] (like
Habrotonon and Chaerestratus at Men. *Epitr.* 16 ff.). What I am
referring to is the situation where A, B, and C meet and begin

---

[1] See Legrand, p. 416.
[2] Duckworth, op. cit., p. 113, calls this a 'double aside'. I would prefer to keep
the term confined to such occasions as Plaut. *Most.* 571 and Ter. *Eun.* 274. [See J. C. B.
Lowe, *Phoenix* 39 (1985), 10 n. 11]

a conversation during the course of which A withdraws for consultation with B, leaving or trying to leave C out of earshot. It is easy to find examples of this in Roman Comedy and, as with the phenomena we noticed in previous sections, it is easy to find a recurrent stereotyped phraseology used to describe it.

At Plaut. *Men.* 822 the old man, on receiving a surprising answer from the person he supposes to be his son-in-law, turns to his daughter and says: 'concede huc, mea filia'[1] ('Come this way, my daughter'). He speaks to her for a couple of lines and returns to address Menaechmus at 825. Similarly later in the play, Messenio calls one of the Menaechmi to speak with him apart from the other: 'te volo igitur, huc concede' ('I want *you*. Come this way'), (1086). After this consultation he returns and addresses the other (1095).

At Plaut. *Most.* 575 ff. Tranio tries to converse with the money-lender apart from Theoropides. He says to him 'concede huc' and in the following line warns him not to raise his voice. After thirty-four lines of conversation, Theoropides is given something to say. Suspicious of Tranio, he comments:

> 609 calidum hoc est: etsi procul abest urit male.
>
> this affair is warm; even from afar it scorches me,

an indication that the conversation is taking place at some distance from him on stage. The question he asks in the following line (610) shows that he has overheard some of the conversation.[2]

At Plaut. *Pers.* 605 ff. the people on stage are the pimp Dordalus, Toxilus, who has been with Dordalus for some time softening him up for the deception that is about to take place, Sagaristio, and the girl Sagaristio has brought with him to help effect the deception. Toxilus, acting as Dordalus' agent, requests that the girl be handed over to him. Sagaristio complies, saying to the girl: 'i sane ac morem illi [sc. Dordalo] gere.' He tells the

---

[1] The passages in Lodge, s.v. 'concede', ii. 4, suggest that Fleckeisen's solution is to be preferred to Müller's 'tu concede huc' (cf. however, Ter. *Eun.* 1068).

[2] This scene differs from the others in that the speaker who is excluded from the conversation, Theoropides, never actually meets or converses with one of the people in the conversation, the money-lender.

pimp to interrogate her. At this point Toxilus slips in some last minute instructions aside to the girl and she replies aside. Toxilus then turns to Dordalus and tells him to withdraw— 'concede istuc'—as he will fetch the girl. Summoning the girl he again converses aside from Dordalus, addressing one line (610)[1] to her. After this he leads the girl over to Dordalus as he had promised.

At Plaut. *Trin.* 515 ff. Stasimus, the slave of the young spendthrift Lesbonicus, has been attempting to dissuade his master from giving away a farm, his last remaining piece of property, as his sister's dowry. Listening to Lesbonicus persisting in his offer despite the generous gesture of his prospective father-in-law Philto who is prepared to waive any dowry, Stasimus decides on a plan which will ensure that the property is not given away. Accordingly he summons Philto: 'Philto, te volo. huc concede' ('Philto, I want you. Come this way'). Philto agrees and the two move apart from Lesbonicus so that Stasimus can give Philto some fictitious information about the farm, calculated to deter him from accepting it even as a gift. The conversation lasts until 562 when they return to Lesbonicus: 'redeo ad te, Lesbonice' ('I'm coming back to you, Lesbonicus'). During it Lesbonicus stands idly by except for an aside at 527–8.[2]

---

[1] l. 610 which is only in the Ambrosianus was ejected by J. H. Gray, *CR* 14 (1900), 24: '. . . an intolerable repetition. All that it contains has been already said, and said better and more fully, in the previous asides between Toxilus and the girl.' One may agree that the line is repetitious without believing it to be an interpolation. To take it out only brings difficulties. Without 610 the promise 'ego illam adducam' is followed directly by the instruction 'sequere me' and the assurance given to Dordalus 'adduco hanc'. What then is the point of having Dordalus withdraw? Surely the request is there to enable Toxilus to say something aside to the girl. With the excision of 610 all he says to her is 'sequere me'. If actors are at work here providing an alternative version of the scene (as Gray suggests), then it would make better sense to take out 609–11. The whole section, however, looks as if it has been greatly expanded by Plautus (what the scene was like in the Greek original is problematical since in the Plautine scene there are four speaking parts). Note that in 606 we hear Sagaristio saying to Dordalus 'exquire quidvis' and following the asides and seemingly pointless repetition of instructions we hear Dordalus again being told (this time by Toxilus) 'exquire'. One might suggest that in the original the interrogation began at 606 and that Plautus has added an extra set of instructions. The repetition might be less pointless if, ignoring the manuscript attribution in 606, we give the whole line to Sagaristio. The girl would then receive instruction from both her mentors.

[2] This scene will be discussed in more detail below.

At Ter. *Eun.* 706 Phaedria draws the eunuch Dorus aside and away from Pythias in order to elicit the truth from him, the truth which he does not wish revealed before her. The conversation lasts for two lines.[1] Later in the same play when Gnatho wishes to lay all his cards on the table in his consultations with Phaedria and Chaerea, he dismisses his patron Thraso: (1068) 'tu concede paulum istuc, Thraso' ('You withdraw a little that way, Thraso'). The three of them confer and when a satisfactory arrangement is reached, Gnatho calls back Thraso (1088).

In view of the examples collected here,[2] it is surprising to find Jachmann asserting: 'Dass eine Unterhaltung so [as Plaut. *Trin.* 515 ff.] geführt wird, dass ein auf der Bühne Anwesender sie nicht hören soll, kommt überhaupt äusserst selten vor: kein Wunder also dass sich eine feste Typik der Gestaltung dafür nicht herausgebildet hat.'[3] There surely does exist a basic pattern for such scenes and a stereotyped phraseology to describe them. If this is not a 'Typik', what is?

Some of the Plautine conversations aside are of considerable length and we may well feel on occasions that the convention is being abused. A great deal depends, however, on the character of the scene where such a conversation occurs and upon the character of the person excluded from the conversation. If like Thraso in *Eunuchus* he is a natural gull[4] there is less reason for the

---

[1] The line in which Phaedria effects the manœuvre raises textual problems (I do not discuss here the merits of the various ways of restoring metre to the line) 'concede istuc †paululum: audin? etiam nunc paululum; sat est.' Since 'concede istuc' is a formula of dismissal (cf. Ter. *Eun.* 1068), since it must be addressed to Dorus (the peremptory 'audin?' rules out any possibility that Phaedria is addressing Pythias) and because Phaedria converses with Dorus directly after uttering it, Dziatzko wanted to read 'concede istim huc' (or 'concede istinc'). This is unnecessary. When three people are on stage together and one of them wishes to converse with another apart from the third, there are two methods of achieving this. He may move away from the person he does not wish to hear him and instruct his companion to follow him. Alternatively he may tell the person whom he wishes to address to withdraw and then follow himself. The second method is, as far as we know, employed only here, but it produces a perfectly acceptable piece of stage action.

[2] Cf. also Plaut. *Rud.* 1403 ff.   [3] *Plautinisches und Attisches*, p. 231.

[4] Actors are not dummies and a competent actor would be able perhaps to get through such scenes without appearing unnatural (cf. Jachmann, op. cit., p. 232). Of course an over-zealous or a selfish actor might 'upstage' the people on whom the audience's attention ought to be focused.

dramatist to feel it necessary to keep such conversations down to a moderate length. Does an audience feel uneasy at seeing the actor excluded from the conversation loitering on stage with nothing to say for a long period? This depends on the dramatic situation and the characters involved, but one should bear in mind that an audience generally attends to that which the dramatist means them to and that, in the scenes that have been discussed above, the spotlight is as it were concentrated upon the persons conversing and not upon the person left out. These scenes are easier to accept than some in Plautus in which there has been no proper formula of withdrawal and the presence of the third party consequently seems quite pointless.[1]

The *Trinummus* scene described in brief above has provoked a good deal of argument regarding Plautus' handling of this convention and much speculation as to what Philemon's practice may have been. It repays closer attention since it well illustrates the kind of problems that confront us when we try to discover the Greek conventions that underlie Plautus.

At 512 Stasimus pleads with his master *not* to give away the farm. Nevertheless during the course of a forty-five line[2] aside-conversation between Stasimus and Philto, we hear the following remark by Lesbonicus, guessing at the content of that conversation:

> 527 consuadet homini, credo. etsi scelestus est,
> at mi infidelis non est.

He is trying to persuade the man, I believe. Even if he is a rascal, he is still loyal to me.

This is quite at odds with what has gone before. How can Lesbonicus believe that Stasimus has undergone such a change of heart that he is now pleading with Philto to *accept* the farm? The explanations that have been offered to account for this glaring inconsistency reflect the approaches to Plautus favoured in the pre- and post-Fraenkelian eras of Plautine scholarship. At one time the lines were regarded as an actor's interpolation and

---

[1] See above, p. 154 n. 1.
[2] Of these 538–55 are certainly Plautine. See Fraenkel, *EP*, pp. 121 f.

accordingly deleted. More recently they have been regarded as
the work of Plautus and part of a much larger scheme. Jahn[1] put
forward the radical thesis that the Stasimus–Philto conclave was
not originally an aside conversation, but was taken by Plautus
from its context in a later scene in Philemon's *Thesaurus* and
inserted here, having been reworked after the pattern of a scene
like Ter. *Eun.* V. 9.[2] An aside was given to Lesbonicus because
otherwise his long silence might seem awkward; Plautus when
he composed the scene forgot to integrate the aside properly into
the preceding action. Jachmann has adequately refuted Jahn's
hypothesis,[3] but the problem of 527–8 remains. It is hard to believe that they stood in a similar context in the Philemon play in
the form in which we have them. If, however, they are a Plautine
addition, why have they been added? Surely not for the reason
suggested by Jahn. To judge by scenes like *Amph.* II. 2, *Bacch.*
IV. 9, and *Most.* 684 ff., it would not have disturbed Plautus to
leave an actor on stage for a long time with nothing to say.

Perhaps speculation on this point is idle, but one might suggest
that Plautus has added the remarks of Lesbonicus in order to
introduce a comic motif he found in other Greek plays and
regarded as particularly appealing. This motif consists of the man
who is excluded from an aside conversation believing that one of
the parties in it is acting in his interests and on his behalf when
this is far from being the case (this is the position of Thraso in
Ter. *Eun.* V. 9 and of Pyrgopolynices for much of the second part of
Plautus' *Miles*). A comment aside affirming this belief during the
conversation makes him appear even more ridiculous and the
audience laughs all the more at his credulity. If we believe that
he inserted Lesbonicus' aside here for that purpose, we must also
believe that Plautus cared little if at all for consistency of motivation or characterization—there is nothing before or after
527–8 which would justify Lesbonicus' credulity here—during

---

[1] G. Jahn, *Hermes* 60 (1925), 33–49.

[2] Unfortunately the provenance of the *Eun.* scene is hotly disputed (note that
there are four speaking parts within it). If Jahn believed it to derive from the *Colax*,
he missed an additional argument since we know from Ter. *Eun.* 25 that Plautus
adapted that play.

[3] Op. cit., pp. 230 ff.

the course of a single scene if he could raise a laugh by introducing a motif foreign to that scene. Few nowadays would find
that difficult to believe.

So much for the aside-conversation in Roman Comedy. Perhaps the ultimate ancestor of the motif is to be found in Eur. *Ion*
1520–1 where Ion attempts to converse with Creusa apart from
his attendants.[1] Fortunately we now possess a Menandrean
scene closely related to the type found in Roman Comedy. At the
beginning of the fourth act of *Samia*, Niceratus and Moschion
meet and are in conversation when Demeas comes out of his
house speaking back into it. His entrance is so abrupt that it
interrupts Niceratus in mid-sentence (Men. *Sam.* 439). After
completing his remarks to the people inside the house, Demeas
turns and addresses Apollo Agyieus (444 ff.) making further
reference to his present situation. He is clearly self-absorbed and
has not as yet noticed Niceratus and Moschion when Niceratus
suggests to Moschion that he approach his father:

451 cὺ πρότερος, Μοcχίων, πρόcελθέ μου.

You approach him first, Moschion.

There is nothing in the text to show the point at which Niceratus
and Moschion register Demeas' presence.[2] It seems most likely
that the two of them are to be thought of as having been in
conversation while Demeas is speaking and that 451 expresses
aloud the upshot of that conversation.[3] Niceratus despatches
Moschion to negotiate with his father and Demeas first becomes
aware of Moschion's presence when addressed by him.[4]

Demeas and Moschion now hold a conversation while Niceratus stands in the background. One must remember that all
three characters in this scene harbour delusions about the
situation in hand. Demeas thinks Moschion is the father of
Chrysis' baby and wishes this to be kept dark in case a scandalized

---

[1] See above, p. 59. Cf. also Ar. *Av.* 1647, δεῦρ' ὡc ἔμ' ἀποχώρηcον, ἵνα τί cοι
φράcω.

[2] Cf. above, p. 129.

[3] See Handley, *Ménandre*, pp. 178–9.

[4] ποῖα, Μοcχίων; is probably meant to suggest that he has just become aware of
Moschion's presence. It is not clear when he is first supposed to see Niceratus.

Niceratus may not allow Moschion to marry his daughter. Moschion, who does not know that Demeas believes this of him, thinks that Chrysis has been ejected simply because she has kept the child. Niceratus believes the same as Moschion. As a consequence both of them find Demeas' behaviour out of character, particularly since earlier he had seemed reconciled to bringing up the child. Of the three only Moschion knows the truth about the child's origins.

The ensuing conversation between Moschion and Demeas proceeds as one might expect on a path of mutual misunderstanding, with Demeas at one point (461) appealing to the audience (or to the world in general)[1] to witness the iniquity of Moschion's conduct and at another (463) Niceratus coming in to back up Moschion. We reach a crisis at 464. Moschion suggests that Niceratus fetch Chrysis out of his house so that they may all hear the truth. Demeas, terrified that the truth (or rather what he believes to be the truth) will out as a result, after an impassioned plea,[2] hints to Moschion that he knows all ($\pi\acute{a}\nu\tau$' $o\mathit{i}\delta a$). In front of Niceratus, who has clearly made no move since he joined the conversation at 463, this is all he can safely say.[3] When Moschion fails to take the hint, but persists in his demand that Chrysis be reinstated, Demeas becomes angry. His words reveal that he is no longer in control of himself; before a more alert listener than Niceratus what he says in 467–8 and 469–70 might have aroused suspicions much earlier than in fact they do. The outright demand from Moschion, 'I want Chrysis present at my wedding', almost drives him to distraction. Moschion, finding this latest outburst quite incomprehensible, asks for an explanation. There is nothing for it now but to be completely frank. Demeas attempts to tell Moschion what he knows without Niceratus hearing. Accordingly he summons Moschion away from Niceratus and closer to him with the words $\delta\epsilon\hat{v}\rho o$ $\delta\acute{\eta}$, 'this way' (476). The explanation which he now gives serves only to create further misunderstanding.

---

[1] See below, p. 191 n. 2.

[2] For the emotional chiasmus $Mo\sigma\chi\acute{\iota}\omega\nu$ $\check{\epsilon}a$ μ' $\check{\epsilon}a$ $\mu\epsilon$ $Mo\sigma\chi\acute{\iota}\omega\nu$ compare Men. *Per.* 256.

[3] For a somewhat similar situation (one actor forced by the presence of a third to give hints to the person with whom he is conversing) cf. Ter. *Phorm.* 805 ff.

When he tells Moschion that he has heard the story from Parmenon, Moschion assumes that he has heard the whole truth, that is to say that he knows the child is Plangon's (not Chrysis') and that Moschion is the father. He still cannot understand why Demeas' wrath should fall on Chrysis—the blame is his entirely and even so Demeas' anger seems a little excessive in the circumstances. What he did was not so very terrible. Others had done it before. Such arguments are not likely to soften Demeas' anger. Now his passion gets the better of his desire to keep the whole affair secret. 'Before witnesses',[1] he asks, 'I ask whose is the child?' He no longer cares whether or not Niceratus knows. 'Tell Niceratus', he challenges Moschion. When Moschion not unreasonably demurs, Niceratus enters the conversation (492). He has guessed 'the true state of affairs' and angrily accuses Moschion of impiety and unfilial conduct.

The scene we have just described contains in 476 ff. a Greek parallel for the scenes in Roman Comedy where characters withdraw and converse apart from a third character. It also contains a Greek equivalent for 'concede huc' in δεῦρο δή. In this case the attempt to hold a conversation aside fails because one of the parties gives it up. Nevertheless the scene is enough to prove, if proof were needed, that aside-conversations of this kind were a developed convention of New Comedy. It is interesting to compare the scene with Plaut. *Trin.* II. 4. In Plautus the conversation aside is not properly prepared for and the behaviour of the party excluded from it, Lesbonicus, psychologically improbable. He has several times told his slave to shut up, yet now he allows him forty lines of conversation aside without interrupting him when in all probability the slave is arguing against what the master wants. Not all of this is, I think, attributable to Plautus. In Menander, all is neat and natural. Moschion is delegated by Niceratus to plead with Demeas. Hence Niceratus need not adhere too closely to the conversation. Add to this the indications given earlier in the play (and later reinforced by 588 ff.) that Niceratus is slow on the uptake and somewhat naïve (106 ff.) and his behaviour in this scene is easy to account for. It takes him a long time to put

---

[1] τῶν παρόντων (488) means, I believe, the audience.

two and two together. The attempt by Demeas to converse apart
from him may contribute to the budding of his suspicions, but if
it does they are very slow in coming to fruition.

V

Another typical situation of Roman Comedy occurs when a
character fakes a monologue, that is to say pretends to be unaware of the presence of another party on stage and affects to be
speaking for himself alone. The information thus imparted is
intended to deceive and mislead the listener.[1]

Plaut. *Mil.* IV. 2 is full of this device. Milphidippa comes on
stage primed by Palaestrio to help mislead the soldier about the
'matrona' who is allegedly pining for him. Her entrance is
elaborately prepared for (985-9). Pyrgopolynices and Palaestrio
withdraw in order to eavesdrop ('concede huc clanculum').
When Milphidippa arrives, she at first speaks genuinely aside,
reminding the audience that in the scene which follows she will
be pretending not to notice the soldier. The audience had
received prior warning that she would come (in the plotting
scene of III. 3) and might have been expected to have guessed
how she would behave without this reminder. Her aside is
followed by an instruction to Palaestrio from Pyrgopolynices—
'tace . . . subauscultemus',[2] 'keep quiet . . . let us listen to her'.
This is extraordinarily unnatural. Palaestrio has said nothing
since 990. Pyrgopolynices must be referring to that remark when
he says 'tace', but since then we have had a two-line aside from
Milphidippa. It is obvious that 993 would be much better placed
directly after 990 and one might guess that the aside 991-2
breaks up the context of the Greek original. Such a guess gains
support from the Plautine pun in 991.[3]

---

[1] Hiatt, *Eavesdropping in Roman Comedy*, p. 29, n. 10, notes this phenomenon and
argues that 'the considerable amount of this type of scene in both Plautus and
Terence lends support to the assumption that it is Greek Technique and not
original with Roman dramatists.' It is not so much the quantity of examples as
that the scenes display a striking similarity of pattern that matters.

[2] For the motif of the eavesdropper telling his fellow eavesdropper to keep quiet
compare Plaut. *Pseud.* 206-7, *Poen.* 1187-91. It goes back to Ar. *Thesm.* 45 and
Ran. 339.   [3] See Fraenkel, *EP*, pp. 7 ff.

Milphidippa now begins her play-acting:

994 numquis hic prope adest qui rem alienam potius curet quam
 suam?
qui aucupet me quid agam, qui de vesperi vivat suo?

Is there anyone there more concerned with other people's business
than his own to spy on what I am doing, a man who dines off his
own food?

Here she puts into words her behaviour as it is described by
Palaestrio at 990. She goes on to say that she is afraid someone
may see her as she goes to meet the man her mistress adores, the
charming and handsome Pyrgopolynices. There follows a conversation aside between the two eavesdroppers (999b–1009).
This, like other such aside conversations in Plautus, is of inordinate length.[1] Here, however, the length may be excused
since the audience knows that Milphidippa is well aware of the
presence of eavesdroppers, but there is good reason for thinking
that Plautus has enlarged on what was in the original: we may
note the Plautine joke in 1000–1 and the Plautine identification
in 1006. The upshot of the conversation is that Palaestrio is
despatched to approach the maid on behalf of the soldier. This is
the cue for Milphidippa to continue her monologue. At 1011
Palaestrio breaks in and addresses her. She affects surprise, using
the conventional language appropriate to such a situation: 'quem
ego hic audivi?'[2] Conversation begins between the two of them
with Palaestrio hinting at the presence of the soldier and Milphidippa still affecting not to have seen him. Palaestrio now
returns to the soldier to report back ('iam ad te redeo', 1020) and
presently back to Milphidippa ('redeo ad te', 1025). The second
conversation with Milphidippa is genuinely aside. In it Palaestrio
gives her some last-minute instructions before returning at 1031
once more to give the soldier a false report of his dealings with
Milphidippa. The soldier gives permission for her to approach
and this particular piece of by-play ends.

This is a farcical scene (it is more or less repeated with a
slightly different cast later in the play). We may well believe

[1] See above, p. 151 n. 2.   [2] See above, p. 159.

that Plautus has thickened its texture and heightened its farce,[1] but its framework probably derives from the Greek original. One should note that the soldier is throughout the play depicted as a narcissistic fool, an easy prey for such a deception. The farce is enhanced by the way in which Milphidippa makes use of the stock lines appropriate to conventional situations in Comedy. Only a besotted mind could be taken in by them.[2]

Equally farcical, but unlike the *Miles* scene in that it in no way advances the action, is Plaut. *Persa* 81–9. The parasite Saturio observes Toxilus entering but does not hear his first words. In them Toxilus tells us he has a plan for deceiving the pimp. In 83 he sees the parasite and tells us (84) that he will affect not to have seen him ('simulabo quasi non videam'). Then he raises his voice and starts to fake an address back into the house (the sort of thing an actor would say when he really was entering). Saturio makes several comments aside on Toxilus' speech, a speech of course largely concerned with and relevant to Saturio's métier. At length Toxilus deigns to hear one of these asides and, using appropriate conventional language,[3] says: (99) 'prope me hic nescioquis loquitur', ('Someone or other is speaking near me'), which leads to a meeting between the actors.

Pythias gets her revenge on Parmeno (Ter. *Eun.* 942 ff.) by faking an entrance monologue. She enters during a monologue of Parmeno[4] and resolves in an aside to pay him back for what he has done:

---

[1] By guying the conventions—see below, p. 180.

[2] Cf. the way the avaricious Smicrines is taken in during the farcical scene Men. *Asp.* 399 ff. The general statement made in that play in connection with the projected deception of Smicrines (326 f.) would apply equally well to Pyrgopolynices:

ὃ βούλεται γὰρ μόνον ὁρῶν καὶ προςδοκῶν
ἀλόγιςτος ἔςται τῆς ἀληθείας κριτής.

[3] See above, p. 159.

[4] Exactly when is debatable and far-reaching conclusions about the composition of *Eunuchus* have been drawn from the lack of clarity here. Arnott, *RhM* 108 (1965), 37 ff., considers it possible that Pythias has been listening to Parmeno behind Thais' door. As an alternative explanation he suggests that 'istis dictis' is to be referred to Parmeno's role in the play and not to what he has just said. I am sure that the context rules out the second suggestion and am fairly certain that if the audience was meant to assume that Pythias had been listening behind the door, there would have been some reference to it in the text.

941 ego pol te pro istis dictis et factis, scelus,
ulciscar, ut ne impune in nos inluseris.

I'll avenge those words and deeds, you rascal, so that you won't
mock us and get away with it.

Henceforward she is 'putting on an act':

pro deum fidem, facinus foedum! infelicem adulescentulum!

Ye gods! What a terrible thing! The poor young man!

Hearing her Parmeno exclaims 'What is it?' and, when she continues, decides to approach her (947). The way is now open for
her to tell him a story which will get him into trouble with his
master.

It is not only monologues that are faked. In Ter. *Phorm.* 348 ff.
Phormio stages a little play for the benefit of the newly arrived
Demipho. He at first converses aside (genuinely) with Geta
('iam ego hunc agitabo'). Then the two of them, having
decided on their plan of action and pretending not to have
seen Demipho, start to simulate a quarrel. Demipho listens
for a while with mounting anger. At 373 he calls on Geta
who affects not to hear him. He has to call again before he
gets an answer from him. Geta pretends a surprised reaction—
'quis homo est? ehem . . .' (cf. Parmeno's faked reaction at
Ter. *Eun.* 976).

Another such piece of play-acting is to be found at Ter. *Andr.*
744 ff. One of the parties involved, Mysis, however, does not
understand what her partner is trying to do and her bewilderment ensures that she gives a more authentic performance. Davus
sometimes gives her advice in genuine asides, at one point
instructing her to speak up for the benefit of the person for whom
the deception is being staged: 'dic clare', 754.[1] Throughout the
scene the third party, Chremes, believing himself unobserved,
comments aside. When Davus wants the play to end he chooses to
hear one of these asides and, as other characters have done, uses

[1] For this motif cf. in another dissimulation scene (Plaut. *Mil.* 1220) 'ne parce
vocem ut audiat.' For the reverse situation, a speaker in an aside conversation
trying to keep his partner's voice down, see Soph. *Phil.* 574 and Plaut. *Most.* 576.

the appropriate conventional language to indicate that he is aware of the other person's presence:

783   quis hic loquitur? o Chremes per tempus advenis.

Who is speaking here? Chremes, you've arrived at the right time.

Such dissimulation scenes[1] have their antecedents in Greek tragedy, particularly in the exciting scene in Sophocles' *Electra* where the reunion of Orestes and Electra is unexpectedly interrupted and Electra immediately 'puts on an act' so that the newcomer may not guess at the truth.[2] The nearest analogy in New Comedy is a scene which has some formal analogies to Pythias' dissimulation in *Eunuchus*, Men. *Asp.* 399 ff. Here Daos pretends that Chaerestratus is at death's door in order to deceive Smicrines. The audience has been prepared for such a performance by the plotting scene that occurred immediately before (particularly by 364 ff.). Daos begins to play a part with the first words he utters in the third act:

399   ὦ δαίμονες, φοβερόν γε νὴ τὸν Ἥλιον

Gods! It is a fearful thing, by the sun . . .

There is in this case no conventional aside to make it clear that he has seen Smicrines and is about to play a part (cf. Ter. *Eun.* 941 f.).[3] Possibly he makes it clear to the audience by some gesture immediately he enters that he has seen Smicrines. There are reasons for doubting this, however. Daos' entrance should be sudden—he should burst out of the house shouting.

One might initially raise realistic objections to such a staging. If Daos simply bursts out of Chaerestratus' house exclaiming that a disaster has befallen it, is there not a risk that he will rush on to an empty street and that his words will fall on empty air? One might attempt to counter this by saying that his shouting is calculated to bring Smicrines out to see what is happening on the street, but I doubt whether we are supposed to apply realistic

---

[1] Cf. also Plaut. *Pseud.* 960 ff.

[2] See above, p. 81. Those who take a different view of Soph. *Phil.* 574 f. from the one expressed there may take it as a parallel for these dissimulation scenes.

[3] With which cf. Ter. *Eun.* 461 and *Phorm.* 892.

standards here. It is more economical dramatically to have
Smicrines on stage when Daos rushes out than to have him
come out after Daos' entrance. We are not supposed to wonder
how Daos knows to choose his moment so well.[1] Analogies with
other scenes suggest that this is the case. This is a type-scene—the
audience know that they are not expected to apply real-life
standards to it.[2] It has affinities with the scene in *Misumenus*
described above (p. 141). The only real difference between the
scenes in fact is that Daos is shamming and Getas is in earnest.
We have seen in Roman Comedy how actors who are shamming
unawareness of other people on stage and 'acting' use the conventional language appropriate to the type of scene they are
acting. Daos in his speech uses the same kind of language to start
his speech and behaves in the same way as does Getas in *Misumenus*. In that play Getas bursts out of the house—there is a
warning that the door is opening from the man who happens to be
on stage at the time[3]—with an exclamation resembling that used
by Daos in *Aspis* (note that both speakers use the strong oath νὴ
τὸν Ἥλιον)

> ὦ Ζεῦ πολυτίμητ', ὠμότητος ἐκτόπου
> ἀμφοῖν ἀπανθρώπου τε, νὴ τὸν Ἥλιον.

O Zeus, what remarkably savage and inhuman behaviour on the
part of both of them, by the sun!

After that he wanders around the stage completely self-absorbed
and quite failing to communicate with Clinias. In *Aspis*, Daos
rushes round the stage (N.B. 410) reciting tragic lines appropriate
to the situation and taking no note of Smicrines.

---

[1] The entrance of Pardalisca at Plaut. *Cas.* 621 is similar. She too bursts on to
the stage and puts on an act for those who are on it. How does she know that there
is anyone there? As in *Asp.* there is no indication to the audience that she is going
to put on an act (we only learn that she is doing this at 685). This raises problems
in connection with the composition of *Casina* since there is no apparent preparation
(589 f. might be considered preparation of a sort) in the play for her behaviour
here. Has Plautus omitted a plotting scene? See Leo, *PF*, p. 208, n. 1, for the
problems of the plot in this play.

[2] See W. S. Anderson, *Phoenix* 24 (1970), 229 ff., who collects the parallels from
Roman Comedy.

[3] Perhaps the absence of such an announcement in the *Aspis* is meant to suggest
the suddenness of Daos' irruption on stage.

The behaviour of Smicrines in this scene is at first like that of
Parmeno in the *Eunuchus*-scene. After Daos' first outburst, he
exclaims: (403) τί ποτε βούλεται; 'whatever does he mean?' (cf.
'quid est?', Ter. *Eun.* 944).[1] Unfortunately the top of a column is
missing in the papyrus after 403 and we cannot as a result be sure
what Smicrines did next or whether Daos at this stage let the
audience know that he had seen him. I would guess that 410 is
Smicrines' first attempt to address Daos rather than an exasperated exclamation after another failure to make contact. He does,
after all, call him by name (contrast 414 and Men. *Mis.* 312) and
not simply use an abusive adjective. Perhaps this interpretation
gains support from the beginning of 406. There is a paragraphus
under this line so that in all probability it was spoken by Smicrines.[2] It looks as if Smicrines is commenting aside on Daos'
behaviour, saying something like μαίνεται ἄνθρωπος.[3] After a
couple more frustrated comments by Smicrines (414, 415),
Daos ends his 'gnomology' by addressing Smicrines directly.
There is no feigned surprise at discovering his presence as in the
Roman scenes. The scene is farcical, but the humour arises more
from the exaggerated behaviour of Daos and his quotation of lines
from tragedy than from exploitation and guying of conventional
formulae.

vi

These typical situations of Roman Comedy[4] have provided us
with further evidence of what was possible on the Greek stage. It

---

[1] Such short questions are a regular feature of the type of scene where a new
person comes on stage and fails to notice that he is not alone. W. Milch, *Hermes* 85
(1957), 159 f., collects the Terentian examples—they almost certainly derive from
the Greek originals—and goes on to show how Plautus extends and elaborates the
convention by producing schematic double line comments whose purpose is to
incorporate jokes.

[2] See also Sandbach in Gomme–Sandbach, p. 742.

[3] ὑπ.[tempts me to suggest ὑπαποστήσομαι. Smicrines decides not to approach
Daos, but to listen in. In that case, however, he would change his mind rather
quickly since he is addressing Daos again four lines later.

[4] One interesting situation for which we have as yet no parallel in Greek drama
occurs at Plaut. *Amph.* 197 where a speaker decides to rehearse a narrative and is
overheard by an eavesdropper. S. Sudhaus, *Der Aufbau der plautinischen Cantica*
(Leipzig, 1909), p. 43, n. 1, suggested that this situation (the rehearsal of a speech)

would be comforting to suppose that a comparative study of the conventions of Menander, Plautus, and Terence would provide a new key with which to solve the many vexed questions of composition connected with Roman Comedy. I fear that this is an over-optimistic hope, but such a comparison may at least be of some help. At any rate the kinds of topics that have been chosen for comparison here, although the prime purpose of the selection has been to discover some typical situations of Greek Comedy, are of some assistance in assessing the respective styles of the Greek and Roman comic poets.

The typical scenes handled above show how stereotyped and repetitive in their treatment of recurring topics the Roman dramatists were. This becomes obvious when, as in the case of Men. *Asp.* 399 ff. or Men. *Sam.* 449 ff., we are able to set beside the Roman scenes a Menandrean treatment of the same motif. The Greek dramatist handles such scenes naturally; the Roman draws attention to the conventions for example by over-using such formulaic phrases as 'quis hic loquitur?' or 'quid tute tecum?'[1] One might argue that such a judgement ought to be backed up by statistics or that impressions are misleading since we have so much more Roman Comedy in a well-preserved state

had a Greek analogue in Epicharmus fr. 99, where he thought Odysseus alone on stage was rehearsing a speech. The discovery of the commentary on Epicharmus contained in P. Oxy. 2429 (see *CGF* 84) though, as is often the case with papyri, not removing any of the obscurities of this fragment has shown that this view of the scene is mistaken. Page (*Greek Literary Papyri*, p. 247—he is followed by Blume, *Menanders Samia*, p. 31, n. 54) takes the second Didot-rhesis as a rehearsal speech, but ἄνδρες in l. 3 is obviously the theatre audience and not some imagined assembly. The rehearsal scene at the beginning of Ar. *Eccl.* is essentially something different.

[1] On this tendency of Roman dramatists, particularly Terence, see Gomme, *Essays in Greek History and Literature*, pp. 254 ff. I do not think he is justified in using Ter. *Eun.* 549–50 as an example. He believes that the scene began in Menander with 550 and that 549 is Terentian and awkward. But it is only the presence of Antipho that makes the line look contrived and, if we are to believe Donatus (which *pace* Fraenkel I do), Antipho was not present in the Menandrean scene. I believe that the Menander scene did begin with something approximating to 549. The new entrant 'Chaerea' looks round first to see whether he is alone (cf. ἐρημία μέν ἐστι . . . directly preceding audience-address in the second Didot-rhesis). Then he turns to the audience to explain why he is so overjoyed (552–4). Terence's known avoidance of direct audience address, or at least direct acknowledgement of their presence (Euanthius III. 8, Leo, *PF*, p. 112, n. 3, H. Haffter, *MH* 10 (1953), 18) may have contributed to his decision to recast the monologue into dialogue.

than we have Greek New Comedy. I do not think we are yet in a position to assemble comparative statistics that would have much significance, but one can surely confirm one's impressions by pointing to passages like Plaut. *Aul.* 190, 549 and asking whether it is possible to believe that Menander (or whoever wrote the original of the *Aulularia*) would have repeated the same formula in the same play.[1] Or else we may point to Plaut. *Most.* 512, 551 and ask whether Philemon would have done likewise within the space of forty lines. They may have done so, but there is nothing so far in Greek New Comedy to make it very likely that they did.

The evidence we have provided for formulaic phrases to describe the situations we have been discussing in this chapter and the contrast we have remarked upon between the liberal use of them in the Roman dramatists and their comparative rarity in Greek comedy leads us back to a topic that was touched upon in the previous chapter. There it was remarked that in Greek comedy formulae to indicate speakers' intentions and movements were comparatively rare.

Plautus of course is noted for his lack of verisimilitude in manipulating dialogue conventions: Fraenkel has given ample evidence in the seventh chapter of *Elementi plautini*.[2] Terence too is replete with formal phrases not all of which were present, we may guess, in his Greek originals.[3] It is this frequency of stereotyped phrases contrasted with their sparsity in what we have of Greek comedy that enables us to describe Menander as 'natural' and to

---

[1] Repetition of the sort found in *Aul.* seems to me different from the kind of verbal echo found in Menander where there is a deliberate comic effect in having different people react in the same way when for example roles are reversed. It is I suppose conceivable that Menander might have repeated for such an effect some of the formulae I have been discussing.

[2] Cf. also Jachmann, *Plautinisches und Attisches*, p. 208.

[3] Contrast e.g. the single Menandrean 'decision to approach'-phrase προϲιτέον at Men. *Sam.* 383 with the many such occasions where using different expressions (see McGlynn, svv. *accedo, adeo, adgredior, cesso*) Terentian characters inform us of their intentions to approach others on stage: *Andr.* 845, 974, *Haut.* 179, 426, 757, *Eun.* 269, 461, 557, 650, 850, 947, 1006, *Phorm.* 252, 285, 609, *Hec.* 429, 622, 731, 855, *Ad.* 309, 460. Perhaps more significant than numbers is a single line like Ter. *Eun.* 461 where Terence feels compelled to *tell* the audience that his actor will be dissimulating:

'adibo atque adsimulabo quasi nunc exeam.'

Cf. too Ter. *Phorm.* 892 and *Ad.* 639–40.

feel that in regard to these conventions Roman comedy is somewhat ponderous.[1] In the case of Plautus the heaviness is in part
a function of the metrical patterns he chooses—he incorporates
more extended versions of stereotyped phrases to suit long lines
or cantica[2]—and in part a function of a delight displayed by all
early Latin writers and exemplified most clearly in the Roman
adaptations of Greek tragedy[3] in pleonasm and bombast. On
many occasions conventional lines whether elaborated on or not
would provide fine opportunities for 'sending up' the conventions.
The kind of hamming found in the two deception scenes in
Miles provides a good example of this. One cannot always,
however, ascribe the duplications, verbosity, and labouring of
formulae in the Roman dramatists to an attempt to send up the
conventions they had inherited. The conventions were the bricks
with which the play was put together and the length at which
they verbalize about them is simply something that came naturally to them. I do not think for instance that there is any particularly humorous effect to be found in Plaut. *Bacch.* 534 ff. (on
which see above, p. 143) apart from the inherent comedy of the
situation in which the two young men find themselves. Compare
too the way in which another typical scene is handled by
Menander and by Plautus. At Men. *Mis.* 216 Getas comes out of
the house with the words ἐξῆλθεν ἔξω, sees Demeas and Crateia
embracing, exclaims παῖ, τί τοῦτο;, and immediately addresses
Demeas αὐτή τί coι; (see above, p. 136). All this takes up one
line only. How different is the entrance (in trochaic septenarii) of
Antamoenides in a similar situation at Plaut. *Poen.* 1294: just
over a line explaining his arrival where Getas took two words, six
lines of surprised exclamation when he sees what is going on on
stage where Getas took three words, then a decision about what

---

[1] Cf. Handley, *Menander and Plautus: a study in comparison*, 17.

[2] See H. Haffter, *Altlateinische Dichtersprache* (*Problemata* 10) (Berlin, 1934),
passim, and particularly on the various Plautine periphrases for 'quis hic loquitur?',
p. 48.

[3] The locus classicus is Accius 592R,

'egredere, exi, ecfer te, elimina urbe',

which may be translating any one of the four short commands to leave occurring
in the corresponding scene of Eur. *Phoen.* (cf. also Accius 583R ~ Eur. *Phoen.* 4).

action to take as regards the girl, followed by a generalization and finally, when the metre reverts to senarii, a decision to approach and the question to the people on stage.[1] The difference in tone and effect between two passages handling essentially the same material and sharing what is basically the same framework could scarcely be greater.[2] Apart from the most obvious difference, that of length, there is a significant detail which makes the Menander seem so much more natural than the Plautus: in the former there is nothing corresponding to the announcement of the decision to approach, nothing to match 'adire certum est' (1304). One wonders if there was such a statement (cf. προσιτέον in Men. *Sam.* 383) in the Greek original of *Poenulus*. It is with regard to questions like these that the lack of Greek material to set beside Menander seems particularly frustrating.

The impressions we have been setting out of the contrast between Roman and Greek comedy are, it should be stressed,[3] impressions of a contrast between Roman comedy and Menander. If only we had sizeable fragments of what we knew for certain to be Philemon, Diphilus, or Alexis! Strip away the Plautine padding and jokes from the *Poenulus* scene and we have a quite conceivable sequence of events for the Greek stage—monologue, surprised comment on what is going on on stage, and decision to approach the people on stage.[4] This last item could well have been present in the Greek. If it was, it would make us compare the scene from Alexis' *Carchedonius* unfavourably with this scene in Menander's *Misumenus* since here, as so often elsewhere,[5] Menander has chosen to omit the conventional phrase and, by doing so, rendered his character's behaviour much more psychologically acceptable than that of the soldier in *Poenulus*. Angry and surprised people do not deliberate so carefully about their movements. Unfortunately the evidence does not exist to

[1] Menander does give Getas the chance to describe the stage scene and to express his indignation—there is in the Greek some equivalent to Plaut. *Poen.* 1298–1304—but this comes much more naturally *after* the address to the man on stage.

[2] There is no better way of seeing the difference than in setting the three Greek utterances at their appropriate places in the margin of one's text of Plautus.

[3] See above, p. 153.

[4] See above, p. 135.

[5] See above, p. 139.

enable us to compare Menander with his contemporaries. It should be borne in mind, however, that other exponents of the genre may have treated such scenes differently from Menander and their plays may have displayed more formal resemblances to those of the Roman dramatists than Menander's do.

Even with Menander, we are scarcely on sure ground. We still possess only a small portion of his work and we can scarcely be certain that that portion is typical. We now know that he sometimes composed scenes of broad comedy like that at the end of *Dyscolus* and we also know that his plays contain a considerable amount of audience address. Neither of these considerations played all that great a part in estimations of him when knowledge was based almost exclusively on the plays in the Cairo codex (even though there were signs of both therein). There are *some* highly conventional phrases and scenes in the Menander we now possess[1] and we may well find more. It is therefore inadvisable to use as an argument against Menandrean authorship of an anonymous comic fragment the presence for instance of an over-conventional (or what seems to a modern reader over-conventional) entrance speech or 'stage directional' phrase. We should not be as confident as Koerte was in 1908 arguing against Menandrean authorship of the Ghoran fragment (*CGF* 257).[2] He took exception (as did Legrand, p. 540) to the entrance of Chaerestratus in that play:

> 67   οὐχ ὠιχόμην εἰς λιμένα· ἀπαντήσας με γὰρ
> σύμπλους ἀνέστρεψέν τις εἰπὼν ὅτι . . .

I did not go to the harbour. For a fellow voyager met me and turned me back saying . . .

He could find nothing like it in Menander and contrasted it unfavourably with Men. *Georg.* 35 ff. where Daos' entrance speech is directed at the mute slave Syrus. Chaerestratus has no motive for saying what he does here: his words are only for the spectators.

---

[1] See above, p. 152. The artificiality is often a function of a stock or farcical scene.

[2] *Hermes* 43 (1908), 55. His linguistic arguments against Menandrean authorship are demolished by Sandbach in Gomme–Sandbach, p. 730.

Describing this as 'ganz die konventionelle Art des Beiseite-sprechens',[1] the kind of thing found so frequently in Plautus and Terence, Koerte attributed the play to some later poet of New Comedy. 'Was ein Meister erfand und mit beweisster Feinheit verwertete, ist von den Nachfolgern gedankenlos benutzt; aus dem Stil wird die Manier.'

This argument betrays two misconceptions. First it is mistaken to regard Menander as the inventor of the conventions of New Comedy:[2] as we have seen, Menander was a man writing within a long and developing tradition that owed much to the types of drama that had preceded it. He did not invent his conventions. It would be much more convincing to suppose that he transfigured them. Hence it is not a convincing argument for the priority of Menander to the author of this fragment to argue that this is a bald use of a conventional motif. It might indeed be thought more probable, given that entrance monologues in comedy developed from those of Euripidean tragedy, that the stereotyped and unadorned entrance monologue of the type found here was at first the predominant form, in other words that its presence here argues for pre-Menandrean authorship.

Fortunately speculation of this kind is unnecessary, since Koerte is also mistaken in the second part of his argument. Menander does not avoid entrance monologues which have no naturalistic apology at the beginning and whose content is more or less undiluted narrative for the benefit of the spectators. Men. *Dysc.* 259 ff. is an exact parallel for what we have here. Koerte's mistake perhaps is due in part to his confused description of Chaerestratus' speech as an aside. It makes no real difference with this type of speech whether the speaker comes on to an already occupied stage (as here and in the *Dysc.* passage) or on to an

---

[1] 'Beiseite' is not apt. Chaerestratus does not at this stage know that he is not alone (cf. above, p. 61 n. 3). Barbieri rightly criticizes Koerte here (p. 4, n. 3).

[2] Koerte repeats this view in *RE*, s.v. 'Komödie', 1267—'aber den Anstoss zur Ausbildung der neuen K-Stils müssen wir, dem antiken Urteil folgend, Menander zuschreiben, und so erscheint es geratenes den Anfang der νέα erst rund 320 einzusetzen.' Just because Aristophanes was *the* poet of Old Comedy, that does not mean that we should assume that he gave the genre the form that we recognize as typical of it.

empty stage. Koerte, if he had recognized this, might have noticed the similarities of this passage to the entrance of Onesimus at Men. *Epitr.* 243 ff. which contains a similar reference back which can only be for the audience's benefit. The technique may be highly conventional, but, as we shall see in the chapter that follows, it is thoroughly Menandrean.[1]

[1] See below, pp. 195 ff.

11. Audience Address in New Comedy

i

ON the modern stage at least audience address is not simply a matter of direct mention of the presence of the audience in the second or third person. When, for example, an actor has to speak alone on stage, the director of the play has a choice of instructions to give him.[1] He may tell the actor to direct his speech at the audience as though he were conversing with them. Alternatively, he may tell him to attempt to create the impression of a man expressing his thoughts aloud and, as far as possible, to affect not to be aware of the presence of an audience. In such cases it is the bearing and manner of the actor that makes all the difference. Actor and director may, if they wish, ride roughshod over what was the writer's intention, converting the most matter-of-fact narrative into a reverie or turning the most reflective of soliloquies into a confidence shared between actor and audience. If such a choice faces the modern director, we may well hesitate before committing the ancient producer to any one approach towards the direction of monologues and soliloquies or before trusting our instincts with regard to what is 'flat' narrative and what is reflection or the expression of emotion.

[1] e.g. in Chekhov's short farce, *The Bear*. The two leading characters in the play, both when alone on stage and when in each other's company, soliloquize about their own feelings and discuss the other actor's behaviour. I have seen productions in which these monologues are treated as speeches quite openly directed at the audience. In other productions, however, neither actor gave any hint of being aware of the presence of an audience. Each approach was effective enough. There is indeed a third possibility. The actor may alternate between the two extremes, sometimes communing with the audience, sometimes talking to himself. I strongly suspect that this is how Old Comedy was played. On the difficulty of telling apart the two types of soliloquy see also Sprague, p. 63.

These considerations must be borne in mind when in section v of this chapter an attempt will be made to classify monologues primarily in Menander in connection with audience address. First, however, we may take account of those passages in New Comedy where the actor makes it quite explicit that he is addressing the audience. It is obvious at a glance that New Comedy has inherited from Old Comedy the possibility of direct communication with the audience.

Audience address is frequently to be found in places which are strictly speaking outside the drama, the prologue and the end of the play (for a collection of such passages in the latter place see Austin on *Misumenus* 464 ff.). There are in the prologues several unambiguous references to the audience addressed either by ἄνδρες 'gentlemen' or θεαταί 'spectators' or by means of second person plural verbs:[1] Alexis fr. 108. 1–2[2] ὑμεῖc ... εἴδετε ('you have seen' with reference to a character who must have appeared before the prologue), Philemon fr. 91. 8 ὑμῖν (the divinity Aer is speaking), Men. *Asp.* 113 f. μεμαθήκατε ... ('you have learned', the divinity Tyche is speaking), Men. *Dysc.* (Pan speaking) 1 νομίζετε 'imagine', 46 ὄψεcθ' ἐὰν βούληcθε. βουλήθητε δέ ('you will see the details if you wish, but do wish'), Men. *Per.* 7 f. (the divinity Agnoia speaking) ἣν ... εἴδετε ὑμεῖc ('whom you have seen' as in the Alexis passage), 47 εἰ τοῦτ' ἐδυcχέρανέ τιc [sc. ὑμῶν] ('if anyone of you took this ill'), 50 f. ἔρρωcθε ... θεαταί ('goodbye, spectators'), Men. *Phasma* 19 'perhaps you (ποθεῖτε) still want to know this', Men. *Sam.* 5 (Moschion speaking) ὑμῖν, 33 -ηcθε, Men. *Sic.* 23–4 = Men. *Dysc.* 45–6, ? Menander *Pap. Didot* II (p. 330 in Sandbach's *OCT*)[3] 13 ἄνδρες 14 ὑμᾶc, second person plural

[1] On audience address in 'Middle' Comedy see above, p. 102 n. 1.

[2] On the date of the play from which this fragment comes see above, p. 104 n. 3.

[3] It is much disputed whether this is a fragment of a prologue. The case against is argued by G. Rambelli, *SFIC* 19 (1942), 15–43 (he is followed by Del Corno) and Gomme, *CQ* n.s. 10 (1960), 108–9. The case for, which seems to me the more plausible one, can be found in Th. Williams, *RhM* 105 (1962), 204, and more extensively in K. Gaiser, *Gymnasium* 75 (1968), 193. The notion first entertained by Kock and argued by R. Herzog, *Philologus* 89 (1934), 194 (so also M. van der Valk, *AC* 37 (1968), 486, n. 27) that the passage is imitated at the beginning of Lucian's *Nigrinus* is mistaken and even if it were correct would tell us nothing about the position of the fragment in the play from which it comes. The fragment of Plautus'

verb in 4, Men. fr. 13 (*Adelphi*)[1] 2 ὦ coφώτατοι 'o people most
wise',[2] Men. fr. 396[3] ὑμῶν, ἄνδρες γλυκύτατοι 'sweetest gentlemen',
CGF 252 (certainly a god at 14, possibly, but not certainly,
Dionysus; see Austin on 15) 12 ὑμᾶc 28 τιc ἂν φήcειεν [sc. ὑμῶν]
'one of you might say' (cf. Men. *Phasma* 19).

The prologue speaker, then, converses freely with the audience.
Five of the speakers are certainly gods. Three (the one in Alexis
fr. 108, Moschion in *Samia*, and the speaker of (Men.) the second
Didot rhesis) human. The speaker of fr. 396 is more likely to have
been human than divine and the same holds good for the speaker
of Men. fr. 13. We have no information about the speakers of the
prologues of *Sicyonius* and *Phasma*. The kind of information they
impart and the way they impart it, however, strongly suggest
that they too were gods.[4]

We may note that the human prologue speaker whose speech is
best preserved, Moschion in *Samia*,[5] although addressing the

---

Artemo 'nunc mihi licet quidvis loqui: nemo hic adest superstes' may come from
a similar context.

[1] It is suggested by Gaiser, apud O. Rieth, *Die Kunst Menanders in der Adelphen des
Terenz* (Hildesheim, 1964), pp. 139 f., that this is from a prologue.

[2] Remarking on the coφία of the spectators is an age old practice of comic poets.
See Meineke, *Fragmenta Comicorum Graecorum* II. 192 f. (on Cratinus fr. 323 Kock).

[3] On this see Th. Williams, *Hermes* 91 (1963), 305.

[4] Wilamowitz insisted (*Schiedsgericht*, p. 143, n. 1) against Sudhaus that the
speaker in *Phasma* was a god. Of the three modern editors only Sandbach follows
him. Two points are surely conclusive on present evidence. The speaker is better
informed about τὰ ὑποκείμενα than any of the mortals who might have spoken as
the prologue ought to be. Secondly the question τουτὶ γὰρ ἔτι ποθεῖτ' ἴcωc; suits
a deity rather than a character in the play (cf. Philyllius fr. 8, Heniochus fr. 5,
CGF 215. 1, *CGF* 252. 28, and probably Men. *Asp.* 99–100: imagining the spectator's thoughts is obviously a *topos* of the New Comedy prologue speech, but there
is no certain example of it in the mouth of a character in the play speaking a prologue). Koerte objected to the direct speech in the first part of the narrative and in
particular to πρὸc τῶν θεῶν in 6. If Turner is right (*GRBS* 10 (1969), 232) in revers-
ing the order in which we read the leaves of the St. Petersburg parchment, these
words do not belong to the prologue in any case (see, *contra* Turner, Sandbach in
Gomme–Sandbach, p. 676), but the objection is misconceived. The *Sicyonius* prologue speaker who is surely a god (see Sandbach ibid., p. 636) also reports direct
speech. If a deity could say βέλτιcτε, θάρρει I do not see that it is beneath another
one to say πρὸc τῶν θεῶν (μὰ τὸν Δία in the mouth of Rhea in *CGF* 215. 12 is of
course different. There is deliberate incongruity in putting the oath into the
goddess's mouth and this is in any case from a different kind of play. I am not
sure of the nuance of νὴ Δία in *CGF* 252. 13).

[5] It is unfortunate that we do not have the end of his speech. One would like
to know for certain that there was no appeal to the audience for a fair hearing.

audience directly, does not at any stage abandon the pretence that he is Moschion and reveal to us that he is in fact an actor playing Moschion (he does not for instance address the spectators as θεαταί like Agnoia in *Periciromene*).[1] Nor does he reveal anything that it would be unreasonable to expect the character he is playing to know. This is in contrast to the technique of many prologue speeches in Roman Comedy. For example in the 'postponed' prologue of Plaut. *Mil.*, Palaestrio, as well as including a formal appeal to the spectators to give the play a fair hearing comparable to those found in Men. *Dysc.*, *Per.*, and *Sic.* (Plaut. *Mil.* 79 ff.), reveals information about the plot and makes predictions that he is (as a character) in no position to reveal at this stage of the proceedings.[2] He has become for the moment 'the prologue', a purveyor of information and not a character in the play. There are indeed several such Plautine prologues, spoken by persons who do not identify themselves as deities or as characters having a part in the play.[3] Terence continues this tradition. His prologue not only does not appear in the play (or rather, since he is an actor, does not reveal what role he is to play), but does not even tell us the plot; instead he acts as the poet's mouthpiece in literary controversy. It has been suggested that the use of an impersonal 'prologue' must have had a Greek antecedent.[4] The fragments of New Comedy do not support this suggestion and the only evidence for it is largely inference from ancient literary critical writings. The famous

---

[1] The speaker of the second Didot rhesis does mention the θέατρον but the effect is a more subtle one than mere rupture of the illusion. The speaker is still in character. In his spiritual awakening he sees all the elements of Athenian life in a new light, including the spectators in the theatre.

[2] See G. W. Williams, *Hermes* 86 (1958), 101 f. and 101, n. 2. Charinus in *Mercator* is like Moschion even though he does refer to comedy in 3–4.

[3] *Asin.*, *Capt.*, *Men.*, *Poen.*, *Truc.* Some, but scarcely all, of these are post-Plautine.

[4] This has been urged particularly by Leo, *PF* pp. 224 ff. (also Legrand, pp. 495 ff. and Süss, *RhM* 65 (1910) 448 ff.). Wilamowitz (*Schiedsgericht*, pp. 144 f.), attacking Leo, rightly stresses the implications of *CGF* 252 where ?Dionysus 'polemisiert gegen die ausführlichen Götterprologe und zugleich die blutlosen Schemen, die in ihnen als Götter auftreten'. This fragment establishes that expository prologues spoken by deities were typical of New Comedy. Possibly such prologues contained references to rival poets and general discussions about literature as this one does. That does not amount to saying, however, that New Comedy has 'a prologue' rather than a prologue deity.

prologue[1] of Antiphanes' *Poiesis* (fr. 191) points at first sight in both directions. On the one hand, its content is similar to what we might expect to find in the parabasis of an Old Comedy and to the treatment of literary topics found in the prologues of Roman Comedy. Also the speaker admits that he is an actor in a way that is unexampled in the prologues of New Comedy: the professional 'we' in 17 makes this clear.[2] On the other hand, what he says about the speakers of comic prologues is extremely strong evidence against the notion that impersonal, extra-dramatic speakers were at the time of writing the norm in comedy:

20   ἂν ἕν τι τούτων παραλίπηι
        Χρέμης τις ἢ Φείδων τις, ἐκκυρίττεται.

If a Chremes or a Pheidon omits any one of these details, he is hissed off the stage.

It is the typical comic *character*, the Chremes or the Pheidon,[3] who begins the play and tells the audience the plot.

---

[1] We cannot be absolutely certain that this is a prologue, but that must remain by far the most likely assumption. Casaubon attributed the fragment to Aristophanes, but that is excluded by the typical comic names at the end of the fragment. These are, as Meineke, p. 339, saw, suggestive of Middle and New Comedy. The fact that Chremes is the name of an Aristophanic character is of no relevance. What matters is that the type of comedy under discussion in the fragment is one in which there are typical recurring names. What clinches it that the fragment is not Aristophanic is the recurrence of the names conjoined (with Φειδύλος for Φείδων) in Alciphron 4. 2 (see K. Gatzert, *de nova comoedia quaestiones onomatologicae*, Diss. Giessen, 1913, p. 20). One imagines that the fragment continued, as does CGF 252, when finished with literary polemic, with the exposition of the plot (O. Bianco RCCM 3 (1961), 91, brings no convincing arguments against its being a prologue). One would dearly like to know what a play called Ποίησις was about: it is hard to associate it with a typical New Comedy plot. It is possible that the prologue deity was herself Ποίησις and gave her name to the play just as did the prologue speaker of Menander's *Heros*. It might be objected to this that Κωμωιδία (as in Edmonds) is a more natural name for this speaker—N.B. ἡμῖν)(the tragedians in 17. Possibly, however, the deity introduced herself as Poiesis and was speaking out of character when she said ἡμῖν 'we the people who have to do with comedy' rather than 'I, the goddess of comedy'.

[2] On this see below, p. 199 n. 1.

[3] The mention of mortal prologue speakers only should not be used as evidence that the most common type of prologue speaker in fourth-century comedy was mortal. (Incidentally Antiphanes fr. 168 is almost certainly an expository speech of one of the characters.) The speaker of this prologue is concerned to stress the *differences* between tragedy and comedy. Hence it is much more effective to mention here typical comic characters than prologue deities. Prologue deities are at home

ii

It is not merely in the extra-dramatic prologue and epilogue that the actor of New Comedy retains the right the old comic actor had of conversing freely with the audience. In trying to locate audience address within the action of a play, we are hampered by a consideration that was mentioned earlier.[1] In a fragmentary play remarks addressed to a plurality may give the appearance of audience address, but in fact be explicable in other ways. In the case of Menander and the poets who are demonstrably writing New Comedy, the presence of ἄνδρες in the text is generally clinching, but there may have been occasions when a plurality of people on stage was so addressed.[2] In the case of earlier fourth century poets, however, poets like Alexis whose career spans Middle and New Comedy, we cannot always be sure that ἄνδρες does not represent an address of a chorus that still had some role to play in the action of the play[3] and was able to converse with the characters.[4]

The following passages seem to me certainly to contain address of the audience within the play: Men. *Dysc.* 194 (ἄνδρες;[5]

in both tragedy and comedy: Chremes and Pheidon belong only to comedy (Horace twice uses Chremes when characterizing New Comedy, *Ars Poetica* 94 and *Sat.* 1. 10. 40). For the use of type-names to characterize the genre cf. τοὺς Καρίωνας καὶ Ξανθίας ὑποκρινόμενος (Aeschines 2. 157, speaking of the comic actor Satyrus).

[1] See above, p. 102 n. 1.
[2] Any suggestion that ἄνδρες in New Comedy is an address to the chorus is refuted by a passage like Men. *Dysc.* 194 where it occurs before their first entry.
[3] ἄνδρες in *CGF* 239. 18, 26 is usually taken to be an address of the chorus (which is thought to be speaking in 24 f.), but Austin rightly points out that we cannot be sure that this play is either by Alexis or from 'Middle' Comedy. Hence it is possible that we have here another *allocutio spectatorum*. [But see *ZPE* 36 (1979, 37.]
[4] Uncertainty therefore surrounds the identity of the ἄνδρες mentioned in passages like Eubulus fr. 30, the beginning of a speech by a man who has had a good meal, Anaxandrides fr. 6. 3 where a man explains the reference of lines from Timotheus, Alexis fr. 231 (this is missing from Jacobi's index, s.v. ἀνήρ) the beginning of a speech by a man looking forward to a wedding feast, and Nicostratus fr. 8 (II. 221, although this may well be the man who was second in the Dionysia of 311 (I.G. ii² 2323a) and not the son of Aristophanes—see Webster, *CQ* n.s. 2 (1952), 22, n. 1, and Koerte, *RE*, s.v. Komödie, 1257) part of a cook's speech, or by ἄνδρες Ἑλλήνων ἄκροι in Alexis fr. 62, an appeal not to envy the new method of distributing unguents used abroad. I suspect that most of these are addressed to the audience. τινας ὑμῶν at Antiphanes fr. 190. 12 is surely a reference to the audience.
[5] On the text here see above, p. 109 n. 2.

Sostratus eavesdropping on Cnemon's daughter), *Dysc.* 482 ff. (second person plural verb in 484;[1] Cnemon alone on stage), *Dysc.* 657 ff. (ἄνδρες in 659; Sicon turns from abusing the people inside the shrine), *Dysc.* 666 (ἄνδρες; Sostratus' first word on entering), *Epitr.* 565 ff. (ἄνδρες in 567; Onesimus alone on stage), *Sam.* 216 ff. (second person plural verb; Demeas alone on stage), *Sam.* 267 ff. (ἄνδρες and ὑμᾶς in 269; same speech), *Sam.* 327 ff. (ἄνδρες in 329; Demeas alone on stage), *Sam.* 447 (ἄνδρες; Demeas believing himself alone on stage),[2] *Sam.* 682 ff. (ἄνδρες in 683; Moschion soliloquizing), *Sic.* 405 (ἄνδρες; Moschion soliloquizing), *Men.* fr. 24 (ἄνδρες in 3; a description of the luxury of a house, a slave speaking?),[3] *Men.* fr. 656 (ἄνδρες in 1, the opening of a monologue),[4] Apollodorus fr. 10 (III. 290 Kock) (ἄνδρες in 2; gnomic utterance, possibly the opening of a monologue), Damoxenus fr. 3, III. 353 (ἄνδρες in 9; speech describing a ball game at a symposium), Nicolaus[5] fr. 1, III. 383 (ἄνδρες in 1, second person plural verb in 14, παῖδες in 41; long speech about parasites), Antiphanes[6] fr. 187 (ἄνδρες 1; speech in favour of drinking), Anon. *CGF* 267. 1 (ἄνδρες; no context), Anon. *CGF* 292 (ἄνδρες 25; description of a meal).

iii

So much for passages where explicit reference is made to the audience.[7] One may note that in the majority of instances ἄνδρες

---

[1] See Gomme–Sandbach, p. 210.

[2] See above, p. 168. It is possible in the scene that follows that Demeas once more addresses the audience. Oguse supplements 461 τοῦθ' ὁρᾶ[θ' ὑπερβολή. Blume (*Menanders Samia*, p. 188) takes ἐνθυμεῖσθε in *Sam.* 481 as a cry to the public 'stellt euch das vor!'. See, however, Sandbach ad loc. for what seems to me the more likely interpretation of that passage.

[3] εὐποροῦμεν in 1 suggests this. See below, p. 200. [4] See Fraenkel, *EP*, p. 164.

[5] Possibly this is Nicolaus of Damascus. See C. Habicht, *Gottmenschentum und griechische Städte*² (*Zetemata* 14) (Munich, 1970), p. 175, n. 33.

[6] This cannot be by the Antiphanes who was the pre-eminent poet of Middle Comedy since our chronological information about him makes it impossible that he could have mentioned King Seleucus (l. 4), the title existing only in and after 307 B.C. The author must be Ἀντιφάνης νεώτερος, υἱὸς Παναιτίου. See A. Wilhelm, *Urkunden dramatischer Aufführungen in Athen*, Sonderschriften der österreichischen Archäologischen Institutes in Wien, Bd. 6 (Vienna, 1906), 55 ff.

[7] Miss Dedoussi in her commentary rightly points out that Niceratus' ἰώ 'νθρωποι at *Men. Sam.* 580 is wrongly classified as an *allocutio ad spectatores* in the index to

has an almost exclamatory function, equal practically to 'my word!'. Sostratus is excited at Men. *Dysc.* 194 and 666, Demeas angry in Men. *Sam.* 269. The position after the oath in Men. fr. 656 and the various exclamations of gleeful speakers describing the delights of the symposium in some of the other fragments[1] conspire to show that it is not simply a surrogate for the address of the chorus that might have been found in equivalent situations in Old Comedy; it is there to enliven the narrative.[2] One may note that there is no real equivalent in Roman Comedy.[3]

Second person plurals and references to ἄνδρες are the obvious pointers to audience address; they leave us in no doubt that the speaker who uses them is addressing the audience directly. But a speech may be directed at the audience without there being any specific reference to them contained in it.[4] We are confronted with several alternatives when required to instruct the actor who has to speak, for example, Ar. *Nub.* 627 ff.:

> μὰ τὴν Ἀναπνοὴν μὰ τὸ Χάος μὰ τὸν Ἀέρα,
> οὐκ εἶδον οὕτως ἄνδρ' ἄγροικον οὐδένα . . .

By Breath, by Chaos, by Air, I have never seen such a stupid man!

Is Socrates addressing the chorus? Is he addressing the audience? Is he simply expressing himself aloud? Dover in his commentary opts for the third possibility and one feels certain that he is correct. The angry oath lifts the speech above the level of narrative. Even so the lines do have a narrative function. They are not there merely to show Socrates' exasperation. They tell us

---

Koerte–Thierfelder. It is a Notruf directed at anyone who might be about (cf. e.g. ἰὼ πόλις Soph. *O.C.* 833). Apollodorus fr. 5 which begins ὦ πάντες ἄνθρωποι is also something different. See Bain, *CQ* n.s. 25 (1975), 20. [Cf. *ZPE* 44 (1981), 169 ff.]

[1] Cf. too the fragments quoted from Middle Comedy above, p. 190 n. 4.

[2] Cf. the emotively placed ἄνδρες in Lysias 1. 23 Ἐρατοσθένης, ὦ ἄνδρες, εἰσέρχεται and see Fraenkel, *SBAW* 1965, *passim*.

[3] On audience address in Roman Comedy see W. Kraus *WS* 52 (1934), 66 ff. The equivalent would be *spectatores*, but none of the Plautine instances except possibly Plaut. *Cist.* 678 seems to me to have quite the same nuance as ἄνδρες. It is significant that we have θεαταί only once in Menander and that (Men. *Per.* 51) spoken by a deity in an appeal to the audience to give the play a fair hearing. R. Crahay and M. Delcourt, *AIPhO* xxi (1952) (= *Mélanges Grégoire* IV), 86, stress the distinction between θεαταί and ἄνδρες. (Possibly *populares*, Ter. *Eun.* 1031, *Ad.* 155, echoes an original ἄνδρες.)

[4] Cf. above, p. 185.

that Strepsiades is a poor pupil who forgets everything he is taught. The scene which follows in which Strepsiades demonstrates the truth of his teacher's statement would follow rather abruptly if we did not have this little introduction to it. Strepsiades may not have looked particularly clever up to now, but the audience is not to know what course the play will take. They might have expected Socrates to have succeeded with his instruction. Since what Socrates teaches is in fact absurd, the audience needs guidance before they can appreciate what sort of pupil Strepsiades is supposed to be. They must be given the impression that Strepsiades is slow and stupid when confronted by the subtle teaching of Socrates. The dramatist has to 'put over' information of this kind to the audience. He may disguise what he is doing, as here, by allowing narrative (in this case the information that Strepsiades has not become intelligent since the audience last saw him) to develop out of an utterance in character (in this case an exclamation of disgust). Such a technique became a standard piece of the equipment of a poet of New Comedy. The obvious ancestor[1] is the type of speech found at Eur. *Alc.* where Admetus' servant, on an empty stage, prepares us for the re-entry of Hercules. The slave begins with a general statement which *expresses* his resentment at the behaviour of the guest in his master's house:

> 747 πολλοὺς μὲν ἤδη κἀπὸ παντοίας χθονὸς
> ξένους μολόντας οἶδ' ἐς Ἀδμήτου δόμους
> οἷς δεῖπνα προὔθηκ'· ἀλλὰ τοῦδ' οὔπω ξένου
> κακίον' ἐς τήνδ' ἑστίαν ἐδεξάμην.[2]

I have known many guests from many lands coming to the house of Admetus for whom I have served a meal; but I have never entertained a worse guest than this one.

This is not simply a bald statement of the form 'the stranger is behaving disgracefully'; it is rather the equivalent of 'how disgracefully the stranger is behaving!' After it the speaker moves on to narrative ὃς πρῶτα μέν . . . , 'since he first of all . . .' and when

---

[1] See Leo, p. 37, Fraenkel, *QS*, pp. 48 ff., and *EP*, pp. 158 and 421.

[2] On the form of the opening see Fraenkel, *Glotta* 39 (1960), 1 ff. (= *Kleine Beiträge* I. 505).

his narrative is over, as if it formed proof of a thesis he was trying to argue, he asks himself:

771   ἆρα τὸν ξένον
              cτυγῶ δικαίως;

Surely I am right to hate the stranger?

The poets of New Comedy were confronted with problems of exposition which did not exist for poets of Old Comedy. One obvious method was cut off—a character could no longer address his remarks to an ever-present chorus. On other occasions it might not always be convenient to put over essential information by means of dialogue between actors—the plot might demand for example that only the speaker and the audience should be aware of a particular piece of information. Hence often the monologue was the most effective way of putting the audience in the picture. The schema of Eur. *Alc.* 747 ff. proved highly suitable for such a purpose.

The question must be asked how far such speeches were treated in New Comedy as genuine monologues and how far the speaker of them admitted that he was addressing an audience. It is interesting to note that Men. *Dysc.* 666 displays exactly this type of monologue opening, the type which, in tragedy at least, might be thought of as disguising the transition to narrative by characterizing the speaker and showing him reacting emotionally. Yet as well as this 'ethical' beginning the speaker is given the word, his very first word, ἄνδρεc 'gentlemen'. This suggests that the schema does not necessarily have a disguising function and that a clear-cut distinction between emotional expression on the one hand and direct address of the audience on the other will not hold good. I want now to examine Menander to see if it is possible to find evidence that may enable us to say whether particular monologues or particular parts[1] of monologues are played at the audience when there is no specific indication of this.

---

[1] Even if a speech starts with a direct address of the audience we are not compelled to assume that the rest of it is 'to the audience' any more than a law-court speech is to the jury throughout. Likewise an opening that we regard as not directly addressed to the audience does not exclude the possibility of their being directly addressed later.

iv

One type of monologue which it is hard to regard as anything other than a direct address of the audience is that in which the speaker introduces himself for the first time and tells us his name. Unfortunately we have no Menandrean examples.[1] There are plenty of such speeches in Roman Comedy and enough examples in the comic fragments to show that they were an established feature of fourth-century comedy.[2] The evidence, such as it is, leads one to suspect that such speeches were associated particularly with certain stock characters as for example the parasite; one doubts whether young lovers, their fathers or their girl friends introduced themselves in this way or whether such speeches were used to advance the action or communicate essential detail to the audience.[3] It is rather the monologue delivered by characters already known to the audience that one expects to contain expository material. It often happens that an actor who left the stage with some purpose in mind of which he had apprised the audience before he left returns to the stage soliloquizing. In such a case, the audience expect to learn about the success or the failure of his mission and why he has returned at this particular point. Here, if anywhere, one expects to see the audience addressed directly.[4]

The third act of *Epitrepontes* (and possibly the second too)

---

[1] People do make their first entrances soliloquizing in Menander (e.g. Cnemon and Callippides in *Dysc.* and the old man at *Cith.* 53 ff.—possibly also Charisius in *Epitr.*), but in every case the entrance has been prepared for and there is no need for the speaker to introduce himself.

[2] See Leo, *PF*, p. 106, and Arnott, *GRBS* 9 (1968), 166. Antiphanes fr. 195, 10–11, is an early example of such a speech, the ancestor of what we find in Ter. *Eun.* 232 ff. which presumably derives from Menander's *Colax*.

[3] Peter Brown draws my attention to Chaereas in *Aspis* who first speaks in a monologue (Men. *Asp.* 284 ff.) but things are contrived so that he does not have to introduce himself. One would like to know whether human prologue speakers introduced themselves by name in New Comedy—it is always possible to avoid this by having the speaker divulge his name by reporting what someone else said to or of him.

[4] On such speeches see Leo, p. 45, who traces them back to Middle Comedy and Antiphanes fr. 206, the speech of a man who is returning from market having laid in provisions for a wedding:

ἥκω ('I am back') πολυτελῶc ἀγοράcαc εἰc τοὺc γάμουc.

opens with the entrance of Onesimus. The last time the audience saw him immediately before the act break, he told Syriscus that he would show the ring found with the baby to his master. Now he returns speaking as follows:

243   τὸν δακτύλιον ὥρμηκα πλεῖν ἢ πεντάκις
τῶι δεσπότηι δεῖξαι προσελθών.

More than five times I was on the point of going and showing the ring to my master.

He goes on to explain why he has come on stage and thus ensures that the audience knows that his master has not as yet seen the ring (they probably see he has the ring with him; when he speaks with Syriscus later, he points to it with the word οὑτοcί).[1] His speech contains narrative rather than reflection. There is no opening generalization or exclamation to disguise this. Nor, however, is there any explicit address to the audience. As the speech continues, having become entangled with the speech of the newly entered Habrotonon, he does, I believe, make a direct appeal to the audience:[2]

265   πῶς ἂν οὖν, πρὸς τῶν θεῶν
πῶc ἄν, ἱκετεύω;

How might I? How might I? I beg you, tell me.

The beginning of Smicrines' re-entrance monologue (*Epitr.* 407 ff.) is in a fragmentary state of preservation. It looks, however, as if it began with a general statement which was backed up by some explanation.[3] After this there probably followed a narrative in which Smicrines explained his movements since last the audience saw him and the reason for his returning now. This is suggested by εὐθύς in 410 which recalls εὐθὺc γάρ beginning a similar kind of narrative in *Dysc.* 525.

---

[1] Possibly, however, he produces it from his ἱμάτιον as he delivers the line.

[2] We have examples of the motif, the actor asking the audience for help and advice, in Roman Comedy: Plaut. *Aul.* 713 ff., *Cist.* 678 ff. (for ἱκετεύω, cf. 'obsecro', Ter. *Eun.* 1006).

[3] We cannot be certain that Robert was right in inserting here the quotation ἡ πόλις | ὅλη γὰρ ᾄδει τὸ κακόν but it would be highly appropriate in the context (cf. Ter. *Ad.* 92–3). On the phrase see A. W. Bulloch, *CQ* n.s. 20 (1970), 274, n. 5.

We are again forced to speculate as to the manner of Habrotonon's re-entrance at 533.[1] The papyrus resumes while she is speaking, but it does not seem likely that she has been speaking long since Pamphila is on stage and has failed to notice her. Can we be certain her speech is a monologue and not an address back into the house from which she emerged? It might seem more reasonable to say 'I will go out' to people inside as one is going out than to say it to oneself or the audience once one is out. However, if she is speaking back into the house, whom can she be addressing? Since the banqueters dispersed at 407 ff., the only people likely to be left in the house are Charisius and Onesimus.[2] It would be surprising if Habrotonon were addressing the former and the description of Charisius' movements given by Onesimus soon afterwards (571 ff.) would appear to exclude the possibility that Onesimus was being addressed by Habrotonon here. It seems to me more likely that she is speaking for the benefit of the audience, explaining to them why she has appeared and why she brings the baby with her.[3]

At 558 Onesimus enters with an exclamatory utterance:

> ὑπομαίνεθ' οὗτος, νὴ τὸν Ἀπόλλω, μαίνεται,
> μεμάνητ' ἀληθῶc. μαίνεται, νὴ τοὺc θεούc.

He's rather mad, by Apollo, he's mad. He's quite mad. He's mad by the gods!

This leads to explanation and narrative:

> 563   πρὸc ταῖc θύραιc γάρ . . .

For I was at the door . . .

The pattern here is identical to that of the slave's speech in *Alcestis*. There is one element, however, to distinguish it from

---

[1] In Gomme–Sandbach it is suggested (p. 357) that this is in fact an exit line. I disagree because of my view of line 540 on which see above, p. 125.

[2] See Del Corno, p. 175, n. 24. It is just possible that she is addressing Syriscus' wife, of whose movements we hear nothing after she is sent by her husband into Chaerestratus' house at 229. Peter Brown notes that we cannot exclude the possibility that she is addressing 'miscellaneous household slaves'.

[3] Presumably if Habrotonon's presence on stage is accidental and not deliberate we are to suppose that the baby is brought out because Habrotonon believes it will stop crying once outside and in the fresh air. Wilamowitz translates 'Ich bring' das Kindchen etwas an die Luft'.

the tragic speech.[1] After his initial exclamation, Onesimus immediately makes it clear to the audience that he is speaking of his master: τὸν δεσπότην λέγω Χαρίσιον, 'I mean my master, Charisius.' This is surely addressed to the audience. Later in the speech 566 f., he does address the audience quite explicitly. At the end of the monologue too he explains why he has come out at this particular juncture. This again is for the audience.

Sosias' re-entrance speech at *Per.* 52 conveys important information to the audience. Polemon has repented of his violent conduct towards Glycera and is now totally wretched. Sosias has been sent back as a spy. The speech begins on an emotional note:[2]

> ὁ coβαρὸc ἡμῖν ἀρτίωc καὶ πολεμικόc,
> ὁ τὰc γυναῖκαc οὐκ ἐῶν ἔχειν τρίχαc
> κλάει κατακλινείc.

The man who was violent and warlike just now, the man who was preventing women from keeping their hair, is lying down and sobbing.

Further detail follows. This is narrative, but narrative disguised by the emotional colouring of its opening. How far, however, is Sosias communicating directly with the audience from the start? Since one of the possible nuances of ἡμῖν in 52 might give an explicit indication of audience address, the use of the word here must be investigated. There are in fact at least three ways of taking it.

First one might regard it as merely an alternative for the first person singular. This seems unlikely since, although it is not always easy to be sure of the idiom,[3] it seems much too elevated

---

[1] Wilamowitz notes the contrast between the form of Onesimus' monologue and of Charisius' which follows it (*Schiedsgericht*, p. 150): Charisius' speech is a 'real monologue'; Onesimus addresses the audience. Charisius' speech is perhaps most akin to Chaereas' monologue in *Asp.* 284 ff. which is highly emotional and in parts of which the language rises accordingly ('elatioribus verbis', Austin). There is naturally no hint of audience address in it.

[2] It seems certain that this is a re-entrance speech. The audience must know who he is otherwise he would have needed some introduction. It is clear from what Agnoia says in the prologue (8 τοῦ cφοδροῦ | τούτου νεανίcκου) that the audience has already seen his master, Polemon. On the emotional nuance of the repeated article here, see Fraenkel, *Glotta* 41 (1963), 235.

[3] See Wackernagel, *Vorlesungen über Syntax*, I. 98–9 and H. Zilliacus, *Selbst-*

for comedy. We find Aphrodite speaking of herself in the first person plural in the prologue of an unidentified play of New Comedy (*CGF* 339. ii, 5, 12). Possibly this is a deity using the 'royal we'. Alternatively Aphrodite is associating herself with all the people who have to do with the production of a comedy.[1] On other occasions where we have a plural where we might have expected a singular, there is always some special significance. Niceratus' exclamation on observing his friend ἡμέτερος οὗτος φίλος (*CGF* 257. 24)[2] comes after he has already mentioned another friend Chaerestratus. Probably Phaedimus is here mentioned as the friend of both the speaker and Chaerestratus.[3] Later in the same play Phaedimus attacks Niceratus with the words

66   κατηγόρηκέ μοι τὰ πράγματα
ἀλλότριον ἡμῖν ὄντα σε . . .

Events show that you are no longer my friend.

gefühl und Servilität (*Societas Scientiarum Fennica Commentationes Humanarum Litterarum* xviii. 3) (Helsingfors, 1953), pp. 31 f. For ἡμεῖς where we would have expected the singular in the orators see Wyse on Isaeus 7. 37.

[1] As e.g. the prologue deity in Antiphanes fr. 191 may do (see above, p. 189 n. 1). Twice in Ar. *Thesm.*, Agathon speaks of himself in the plural (183, 196). Is this affectation (introducing tragic diction in comedy) or is it the professional 'we' of the craftsman? I suspect a little of both. The same holds good for the pseudo-doctor at Men. *Asp.* 445 (for examples of the professional 'we', see Antiphanes fr. 123. 6, 144. 6 and Nicomachus fr. 1. 3).

[2] On the attribution here see above, p. 136 n. 1.

[3] Perhaps too the three men belong to the same association. One gets the impression that the three men in this play are contemporaries and are all young (a young man could scarcely send an older man on an errand, hence Niceratus is either older than Chaerestratus or a contemporary. φίλος suggests that he is a contemporary of Phaedimus and the fact that Phaedimus can suspect him of being a rival in love surely clinches this). Their names do not exclude this. Niceratus is used both of older men (as in *Samia*) and of younger (see Gatzert, *Quaestiones Onomatologicae*, p. 23). Chaerestratus is likewise an ambiguous name. On the one hand we have the middle-aged man in *Aspis* and on the other the Chaerestratus of Men. *Eun.* (= Terence's Phaedria, see Persius, *Sat.* v. 162) and of *Epitr.* This latter person is not, as some have thought, middle-aged: he is Syriscus' master (231–2) and Syriscus refers to him as his τρόφιμος (201). See Ida Kapp, *Hermes* 47 (1912), 317 ff. whose arguments are not refuted by C. Robert, *Sitzungsberichte der königlich. Preuss. Akademie der Wissenschaften* 1912, 423 n. 1. The points he brings against the identification of Chaerestratus with Syriscus' τρόφιμος are invalid. *Dysc.* 413 shows that there is nothing to rule out connecting a proper name with τρόφιμος; *Asp.* 34 shows that if a man is called τρόφιμος, it need not imply that his father is still alive. See also T. MacCary *TAPhA* 101 (1970), 284 ff.

At first sight this looks a clear case of ἡμῖν = μοι, but there may be something in the plot to explain this use of ἡμῖν—e.g. 'to me and to the girl I love'.[1]

A second possibility is that ἡμῖν does mean 'us' and includes both speaker and audience. This (the interpretation of C. Robert, *Hermes* 44 (1909), 234, and of Capps) has much to be said for it. Both parties, Sosias and the audience, have witnessed or at least heard about Polemon's recent violent behaviour. Sosias means 'the violent man we saw just now'.[2]

The third possibility is that Sosias is regarding himself as the member of a group, the household of Polemon.[3] Slaves frequently use the first person plural when speaking of anything relating to the household to which they belong.[4] It does not seem possible to decide firmly for either the second or third explanation.

Sosias' next entrance is not prefaced by any such lively introduction. When he returns he remarks simply:

164   πάλιν πέπομφε τὴν χλαμύδα φέροντά με
        καὶ τὴν σπάθην ἵν' ἴδω τί ποιεῖ καὶ λέγω
        ἐλθών.

He has sent me back carrying the cloak and the sword so that I may see what she is doing and go back and tell him.

This obviously links with his previous entrance speech: we may regard it as a kind of resumption of a conversation with the audience that was interrupted earlier. The words explain to the audience why they are seeing Sosias again at this point.

Moschion's re-entrance speech (unusual in that the monologue is preceded by a piece of by-play)[5] follows a pattern which

---

[1] 'Personal enemy' (Page) is much too strong a translation of ἀλλότριον ἡμῖν (cf. Men. *Asp.* 189 and Plat. *Euthyphro* 4b5 where the contrast is ἀλλότριος)(οἰκεῖος).

[2] ἡμῖν at Men. *Per.* 88 surely brings in the audience. Cf. Men. fr. 16. 2 ὁ χρηστὸς ἡμῖν μοιχός and Aeschines 3. 73: ὁ γὰρ μισαλέξανδρος καὶ μισοφίλιππος ὑμῖν ['the one you all know about'], οὑτοσὶ ῥήτωρ δὶς ἐπρέσβευσεν εἰς Μακεδονίαν.

[3] Koerte, *RE* v, s.v. 'Menandros', 743, denies that Sosias is a slave (169 is surely against him). Even if he is not, he is still connected with Polemon's household.

[4] e.g. Men. *Sam.* 649 f., *Per.* 180, *Mis.* 236, *Her.* 34, Ar. *Pax* 260, *Vesp.* 1474 f. House owners sometimes speak in this way too (Men. *Sam.* 236, Hdas. 1. 9).

[5] The text is not explicit enough for us to be sure what happens when Moschion enters and what specifically is the point of 276–81. It is odd that Sosias should still be present (281) οὑτοσί—he said he was leaving at 231. Is this another (cf. above, p. 139) instance of Menander refusing to make the stage action clear for the reader by inserting conventional remarks?

is by now familiar. It begins with a general statement containing a comparison 282 ff. which is immediately followed by a narrative designed to illustrate the validity of that generalization: ὡς γὰρ τάχιστ᾽ εἰςῆλθον, 'since, as soon as I entered'.

It is far from certain what he is saying when next we see him at 344–8, but the likelihood is that this is again the type of speech where the actor returning to the stage takes up a topic with which the audience is already familiar, perhaps even continues a previous conversation with the audience. It is tempting in fact to connect this short monologue with the long monologue which began at 282. That monologue began with him asserting that he was the most unhappy of men. When at 300 it is interrupted by the long lacuna, Moschion still has not told us anything to justify his opening generalization. Clearly he is leading up to something important. It is natural to guess that he is going to tell us of some discovery he has made in connection with Glycera. At 348 he seems to be admitting the possibility[1] that she is his sister and his behaviour throughout the recognition scene is hard to explain unless he had previously acquired some clue by which he had reached this position.[2] It could be that this clue was mentioned at the end of the monologue that began at 282. At the time Moschion may have communicated it to the audience with an indication of his own disbelief. Perhaps then he said he was going to think it over. This would make his arrival at this crucial stage (344) somewhat less contrived than if he just happened to come out of his mother's house at this moment. There is no explanation in the rest of the recognition scene of why he appears at this time. If he had earlier said something like ἀλλ᾽ ἐκποδὼν ἄπειμι καὶ βουλεύσομαι 'I'm off to think it over' (Men. *Georg.* 20 ending a monologue), the audience would be prepared for his reappearance at any time.[3]

---

[1] That is if we prefer Koerte's restoration here to that of Wilamowitz.

[2] His asides at 357 and 362 surely argue for this. It is not necessary to assume that he has learned anything *directly* from his mother. He might (like Demeas in *Samia*) have accidentally overheard a conversation that led him to believe that Glycera was his sister.

[3] Cf. the exit of Moschion in Men. *Sam.* 94–5 which prepares for a later entrance monologue (120 ff.). Gomme proposed a different reconstruction of the manner in which Moschion learned about his sister (*CQ* 30 (1936), 68). I do not think his

In *Samia*, we do not have the beginning of Demeas' great third-act monologue, but we can be certain that it too began with a general statement of some kind,[1] a statement which, it is immediately asserted, holds good of this individual, Demeas:

τοιοῦτο γὰρ καὶ τοὐμόν ἐϲτι νῦν.

For this too is my position now.

The narrative to justify this assertion follows at 219 ὡϲ γὰρ τάχιϲτ᾽ εἰϲῆλθον, 'for as soon as I entered'. At the end of his narration, Demeas' anger wells up and significantly as he had done before (216) he turns to the audience to try to curb his suspicions (269 f.).

Niceratus' re-entrance monologue when he returns to the stage bringing a sheep for the wedding feast (399 ff.), save possibly for the deictic pronoun in 399, betrays no overt sign that it is addressed to the audience. It might be played in this way with the speaker's attention so concentrated on the audience that he fails at first to notice Chrysis. Alternatively he is simply self-absorbed.

Although Moschion speaks the prologue and in the course of it addresses the audience directly, neither of his two re-entrance monologues looks as if it is addressed to the audience. His short speech at 428 simply expresses his impatience, as such a sufficient explanation of why the audience sees him again at this point. The lengthy monologue beginning at 616 *narrates* his feelings, but there is nothing in it to suggest a conversation with the audience —at one point indeed (630) he addresses his absent bride to be.[2]

Parmenon's monologue that follows immediately on this speech of Moschion starts with an exclamation and towards the end contains self-apostrophe. At 645, however, he appears to take the audience into his confidence ϲκεψώμεθα (cf. ϲκέψαϲθε in 216 and

---

reasons for rejecting the more usual view (see Ulbricht, pp. 49 ff.) set out above are cogent.

[1] Cf. Austin on 206–9: 'sententia communis narrationi praemissa'. Austin's description of Demeas here as 'valde perturbatus' can only be referred to his inward state. According to his own narrative (262 ff.) he came out of his house quietly and outwardly in control of himself.

[2] Later in the same scene, however, he does address the audience directly (683).

see Blume, *Menanders Samia*, p. 258). The sort of uncertainty that
occurred with Men. *Per.* 52 recurs here. It seems to me just
possible that Parmenon could be saying to *himself* 'let's consider',[1] but more likely that he gives the audience a share of his
deliberations.

At *Dysc.* 259, Sostratus, who left just before the end of the
previous act to fetch Getas, returns and explains why he has
come back alone. This is necessary since his return is contrary to
the audience's expectations: when told earlier that he is off to
fetch the clever slave to help him win the girl, the audience, as
any audience familiar with the plots of New Comedy would,
assumes that there will be some kind of intrigue devised by the
slave to help his young master. Dispensing with any preliminaries,
Sostratus explains his return:

τὸν μὲν Γέταν οὐκ ἔνδον ὄντα κατέλαβον.

I found that Getas was not at home.

This narrative is surely directed at the audience. When later in
the play he returns from his fruitless sojourn in the fields waiting for Cnemon, he begins his monologue with a general
statement:

522   ὅςτιc ἀπορεῖ κακῶν, ἐπὶ Φυλὴν ἐλθέτω
κυνηγετήcων.

Anyone who doesn't have enough trouble should come to Phyle
to hunt,

moving on to narrative at 525: εὐθὺc γάρ . . ., 'for as soon as . . .'.
At the end of his speech (as at the end of Onesimus' speech,
Epitr. 584), we are given the explanation of why he has appeared
at this moment. In his next monologue (666 ff.) we have already
noted that the comparative opening exclamation is combined
with an explicit address of the spectators.[2] As we have come to

---

[1] If with the second person plural or singular we are not always obliged to
assume the physical presence of an addressee (see Fraenkel, *MH* 24 (1967), 190 ff.,
and 25 (1968), 179 f.), we might expect the same to hold good of first person
plurals.

[2] See above, p. 191. Fr. 656, spoken by a young man in love, is an exact parallel.

expect, the generalization is justified by a narrative introduced in the usual way:

670   ὁ Γοργίας γάρ, ὡς τάχιστ' εἰσήλθομεν . . .

Since Gorgias, as soon as we entered . . .

At *Aspis* 149, Smicrines explains why he did not make more precise inquiries about the booty brought back by Daos. There is no explicit reference to the audience in this monologue, but it may well be correct to interpret it as the sharing of a confidence.

Later, at the beginning of the third act, Smicrines enters with an ironical statement: 'Daos was quick to bring me the inventory' (of course he has not brought an inventory at all). This is therefore another example of a re-entrance monologue with an emotional opening. Its purpose is to explain Smicrines' presence (highly convenient at this point)[1] and further to exhibit his πονηρία.

At *Sic.* 361 Dromon says ἡ μὲν τροφίμη 'cτιν ἀcφαλῶc τηρουμένη ('the young mistress is being safely looked after'). Kassel interpreted this as his words after he had ceased ₊to eavesdrop on Cichesias and Theron. It is much more likely that this is the beginning of a re-entrance monologue by Dromon, unaware that he is not alone on stage.[2] There is no indication in the text that he has been present in this scene up to now and his eavesdropping would have little point.[3] What seems more likely and accords well with the phenomena we have been discussing is that the audience is being referred back to the last time it saw Dromon. Perhaps at that point (alternatively Stratophanes may have announced that he had given him this mission without the audience seeing him) he was being given instructions with regard to Philumena. His return at this point—crucial to the action since he is the one who recognises Cichesias—is thus explained

[1] See above, p. 175.
[2] See also Sandbach, *Ménandre*, pp. 117 f. who notes that μέν is more appropriate for someone who is arranging his thoughts for his own or for an audience's benefit than for someone breaking into a conversation. The statement Dromon makes is much too unemotional to be addressed to Cichesias in a situation like this.
[3] This is not perhaps a conclusive argument. See Hiatt, op. cit., on 'pointless eavesdropping'. It would be remarkably cool for this slave to eavesdrop on his long-lost master.

to the audience as he enters. He fails at first to notice the two people occupying the stage just as Sostratus re-entering at *Dysc.* 259 fails to observe Gorgias and Daos (cf. also Niceratus at *CGF* 257. 20 and Chaerestratus at 73).¹

Another possible re-entrance speech is the fine monologue from *Plocium* fr. 333, which Gellius quotes when comparing Caecilius and Menander. The speaker assumes that the audience knows him and is familiar with his circumstances. At first sight it might be thought to begin with a narrative and to move on towards reflection.² This would be to mistake the tone of its opening. Though they contain statements with particular reference, the first two sentences are loaded with emotion. The old man speaks of his wife with bitter irony, referring to her as ἡ 'πίκληρος ἡ καλή, 'the beautiful heiress', and calling her achievement μέγα καὶ περιβόητον, 'great and famous'. Even so the speech might, as we have argued for other monologues that have emotional beginnings, be addressed to the spectators. One pointer one might adduce in favour of this is what the speaker says in l. 9 ϲιωπᾶν βούλομαι τὴν νύκτα, 'I want to keep quiet about the night.' This is not perhaps the kind of thing a person thinking aloud in real life might say, but stage 'thinking aloud' is a different matter from real thinking aloud.³ One hesitates therefore to take this as conclusive evidence for the manner of delivery of this speech.

V

Consideration of these passages⁴ suggests that it is unwise to be dogmatic about the amount of audience address in New Comedy.

¹ It would be interesting to know how the *Sic.* scene continued. I suspect that π]α̣τ̣ε̣ρ in 362 if it is addressed to Cichesias, shows that Dromon has not yet recognised Cichesias. Would a slave address his long-lost master thus? Surely we have a slave addressing an elderly man whom he did not know (e.g. Syriscus to Smicrines at *Epitr.* 55). Possibly, however, Theron is speaking and being respectful towards the older man.

² Interestingly Caecilius in transforming this speech into a *canticum* uses the more obvious monologue scheme, generalization followed by justifying narrative.

³ Flury, op. cit. (p. 113 n. 2), p. 74, oversimplifies when he characterizes the Menandrean passage as mere narrative. See above, p. 185.

⁴ Plaut. *Aul.* 475 provides a good example (one of many) from Roman Comedy.

We have too often to fall back upon instinct and in cases like this people's opinions about what is natural or effective vary greatly.

One can say that Menander's monologues fall broadly into two categories. Some begin 'ethically' with the actor responding ἐν ἤθει to the situation of the play.[1] Others begin factually with an uncoloured statement of information particular to an understanding of the action of the play.[2] The natural inclination which corresponds to the traditional view of the matter would be to regard the latter as directed *ad spectatores* and the former as not. The new Menandrean discoveries, however, show that such clear-cut distinctions no longer apply. We have already noted Men. *Dysc.* 666. One must also mention those occasions where the actors at moments of emotion and stress address the audience. Demeas does so several times in *Samia* (216, 269, 329)[3] and so does Sostratus in *Dyscolus* (194). Emotional outbursts therefore can no longer be taken as a guarantee that the audience is not being addressed.

With the factual type of monologue opening, instinct tells us that the audience is being addressed and, though some reservations (see the comments on the *Plocium* monologue) remain, instinct seems likely to be correct.

One would like to know what kind of distinction, if any, was made in respect of the persons in comedy who were permitted to address the audience[4] or in respect of the extent to which they might address the audience. Are all the characters capable of addressing the audience or only the more important ones? Are 'comic characters' more often given audience address than 'serious' ones? Do, for instance, some characters keep up a running conversation with the audience?[5] Sostratus in *Dysc.* seems to have a kind of rapport with the audience (see above, p. 203) and perhaps the same may be said of Sosias and Moschion in *Per.*, Onesimus in *Epitr.*, and Demeas in *Samia*. Unfortu-

---

[1] Men. *Epitr.* 558, *Per.* 52, 282, *Sam.* 399 f., 488, 616, 641, *Dysc.* 522, fr. 333. Strato, *CGF* 219 conforms to this pattern. See R. Kassel, *ZPE* 14 (1974), 127.

[2] *Epitr.* 243, *Per.* 164, 344, *Dysc.* 259, *Sic.* 361, *CGF* 257. 67 ff.

[3] Probably also 461 and 488.

[4] See Blundell, pp. 75–6.

[5] For the suggestion that such a rapport existed in Roman Comedy see W. Kraus, *WS* 52 (1934), 76.

nately these are the kinds of questions which need the evidence of more complete plays before they can be answered. We are able to plot the movements of Sostratus and check on each occasion whether he is referring back to some previous utterance. The issue with characters in other (less complete) plays is more complicated. What of Getas in *Misumenus*? At one point, commenting on the action he sees before him on stage, he asks (217) οὐκ ἐγὼ 'λεγον;, 'Didn't I say this?' Is he referring back to something he said earlier (to the audience) in a previous monologue: 'Didn't I tell you?'? Is he referring to something he said earlier by way of warning to Thrasonides: 'Didn't I tell him?'? Or, as a third possibility, is οὐκ ἐγὼ 'λεγον; an idiomatic phrase which does not necessarily imply an addressee, a kind of 'Lo and behold.'?[1] I would incline to the first interpretation, but lack of evidence ensures that such a problem remains unsolved.

[1] The same phrase occurs in Cnemon's mouth (*Dysc.* 172). It refers back to what he said earlier in that monologue. I think it unlikely that this is addressed to the audience and would supply there 'to myself' rather than 'to you'. Discussing Ar. *Ach.* 41 οὐκ ἠγόρευον; (cf. Soph. *O.C.* 838 οὐκ ἠγόρευον ταῦτ' ἐγώ;), Dover, *QUCC* 9 (1970), 22, plausibly suggests that it is a stereotyped expression of indignation (ἀγορεύω simplex is an archaism). One might well apply the same approach to οὐκ ἐγὼ 'λεγον;. I suspect, however, that it retains its literal meaning. The phrase is found at Lucian *Tim.* 46 (cf. too Ar. *Av.* 1019 οὐκ ἔλεγον ἐγὼ πάλαι;, which refers back to a threat made at 1012–13). It is possible that 'dixin hoc fore?' (Ter. *Ad.* 83) translates it and that Plaut. *Mil.* 1130 expands it.

12. Play with the Dramatic Illusion

So far in discussing audience address and the dramatic illusion, we have confined ourselves more or less to the downright and obvious, to the direct appeals to the audience made by the actors and choruses of comedy, to the frequent ruptures of the illusion caused by reference to the conditions of the theatre, and most recently to the kind of expository narrative of New Comedy which, if not always easy to detect, is still in breach of the illusion. There are, however, other possibilities open to the dramatist with regard to the illusion besides the observing or the breaking of it.

When in the course of a play, an actor refers to the action of the play or any particular aspect of the play as being 'like a play', then the effect is somewhat special. The illusion is preserved since he does not admit that the activity in which he is at present engaged *is* in reality a play. Nevertheless the illusion does not remain quite intact. The spectators will be well aware that what they are viewing is indeed a play and will consequently realize that the dramatist is, as it were, 'playing with the illusion'. In the case of Elizabethan drama, in particular of Shakespeare, this effect has been studied with great perception by Mrs. Anne Righter in her book, *Shakespeare and the Idea of the Play*.[1]

Is it possible to find anything in Greek Drama resembling the sophisticated effects found in Shakespeare and discussed by Mrs. Righter? Does any actor there make the comparison between life and the play?[2] Does anyone speak of himself as playing a part?[3]

---

[1] London, 1962 (Paperback edn., Harmondsworth, 1967).
[2] To mention only the most famous instance: 'All the world's a stage', *As you like it* II. vii. 139.
[3] 'It is a part that I shall blush in acting' says Coriolanus (*Coriolanus* II. ii. 142–3).

Have we anything resembling the wish of the conspirators in *Julius Caesar* that they may obtain a posterity of their own by having their own 'play' re-enacted in future ages?[1]

Mrs. Righter searches in vain for the comparison of life to a play or for anything that might be termed play with the illusion in fifth-century drama. The absence of such effects she ascribes to the 'ritual' nature of the Greek theatre at the time.[2] Her argument is flimsy and betrays a common misunderstanding of non-professionals with regard to Greek drama and ritual. Nevertheless the absence of such phenomena does require an explanation.

Theatrical imagery would be most surprising in tragedy. The tragedians were for the most part attempting imaginative re-creations of the Homeric world.[3] In that world the stage has no place. No one could deny that there are anachronisms in Greek tragedy, but there is no anachronism so blatant[4] as the attribution of knowledge of the stage and the conditions of the stage to the heroic age. In general it may be said that the tragedians

---

[1] 'How many ages hence shall this our lofty scene be acted over!' exclaims Cassius (*Julius Caesar* III. i. 112–13).

[2] 'Pythagoras [sic! presumably this is a confusion with his famous comparison of life to a panegyris (Iamblichus *VP* 58 and Diogenes Laertius viii. 8)] may have observed to his disciples that human life was like a play, but no character on the ritual stage of Aristophanes, Aeschylus, Sophocles or even Euripides ever did so', p. 60. On the comparison generally and on its frequency in literature see E. Curtius, *European Literature and the Latin Middle Ages* transl. W. R. Trask (London, 1951), pp. 138 ff., M. Kokolakis, *The Dramatic Simile of Life* (Athens, 1960), and L. G. Christian, *Theatrum Mundi—The History of an Idea* (Diss. Harvard, 1969). Stage imagery is especially frequent in writers of the second sophistic and novelists. See E. Rohde, *Der griechische Roman³* (Leipzig, 1914), p. 479, and J. W. H. Walden, *HSCPh* 5 (1894), 1 ff.

[3] See Wilamowitz, *Einleitung in die griechische Tragödie*, p. 119.

[4] For a discussion of anachronisms and the literature on them see Gudeman on Aristotle, *Poetics* 1460a. In many details, such as the use of iron weapons for bronze, and dowries instead of bride-prices (though Homer is not self-consistent in these things: see P. Cauer, *Grundfragen der Homerkritik³* (Leipzig, 1923), pp. 279 ff., 286 ff.) and the notorious use of the non-Homeric *tyrannos* censured often by ancient scholars (see especially Hypothesis II to Soph. *O.T.*), the tragedians are anachronistic and severely reproved in ancient commentaries (as can be seen from Schwartz's index to the Euripides scholia the most frequent criticism made in the scholia is that the poet has disrupted the traditional chronology of heroic legend). Gross anachronisms like the mention of the theatre or the use of theatrical imagery are absent from tragedy (even from a play like Aesch. *Persae* which has a contemporary setting) and one should note the occasions when the dramatist can be seen as alluding to practices and customs alien to the society of his own day (e.g. Aesch. *Ag.* 242 ff., 1382).

were much more sensitive to anachronism than the Elizabethan dramatists were. The costume of Greek tragedy was after all very different from that of everyday fifth-century life in a way that was quite unlike the costume of Elizabethan drama. Shakespeare was prepared to permit a knowledge of billiards to people living in Alexandria in the first century B.C. Though the Greek tragic poet frequently makes reference to his art, he does so obliquely by referring to song and dance, age-old activities which are amply attested in Homer. If panhellenic games are mentioned in tragedy, there are at least games in Homer and the foundation legends of the various games, even if unhistorical, connect them with figures from the heroic age. If some of the archaic cities of tragedy seem to be democratically governed, there is at least a demos and a council of sorts in Homer.[1] In the case of their own city, the poets may have felt that they had especial sanction in treating it as having been a democracy from a very early date. The traditions surrounding Theseus' political activities may not have been of any great antiquity;[2] the dramatists were scarcely likely to have known this.

Similarly with fifth-century comedy, it is no real surprise that we fail to find play with the illusion or comparison of life to a play. In the case of the latter, Old Comedy, it should be remembered, is not by nature a sententious genre. Such general reflection as it contains tends to be borrowed from other genres, in particular from tragedy, and exploited for comic purposes (e.g. Ar. *Ran.* 1475). In the case of the former, the illusion in Old Comedy is too brittle a thing to be played with. The phenomena discussed by Mrs. Righter have point only if the dramatic illusion of the plays in which they occur is a reasonably sustained one. While it is not true that there is no dramatic illusion in Old Comedy,[3] no one would say that it is ever kept up for long.

When we look for ancient parallels for the techniques and

---

[1] See H. Lloyd-Jones, *CQ* n.s. 9 (1959), 94, and *AC* 33 (1964), 358 f.

[2] On Theseus the democrat and his legend generally see H. Herter *RhM* 85 (1936), 177 ff. (especially 182 f.). Thucydides assumes (2. 15. 2) that before Theseus, Attica was inhabited κατὰ πόλεις each of which had πρυτανεῖα and ἄρχοντες. The result of Theseus' συνοικισμός was ἓν βουλευτήριον καὶ πρυτανεῖον.

[3] See above, pp. 3 ff.

motifs in question, we turn most naturally to Plautus. There is a famous passage in *Mostellaria* where the victorious slave Tranio advises the master he has deceived and defeated:

> 1149   si amicus Diphilo aut Philemoni es,
> dicito eis quo pacto tuos te servos ludificaverit:
> optimas frustrationes dederis in comoedias.[1]

If you are a friend of Diphilus or Philemon, tell them how your slave made a fool of you. You will provide them with excellent intrigues for their comedies.

In the classic article which solved the mysteries of 1149,[2] Leo discussed the type of joke involved in the passage, distinguishing it from other passages in Plautus where the illusion is merely broken.[3] There is a clear contrast between this passage and one like Plaut. *Poen.* 597. There one of the actors turns to the spectators to point out that the money he is handling is only stage money. Tranio, however, in our passage does not admit that the deception he has practised is part of a play. His words could have been uttered by a real slave in a real situation. The audience of

---

[1] *in comoedias* R. Kassel, *RhM* 112 (1969), 103; *in comoediis* vulg.

[2] *Hermes* 18 (1883), 558 (= *Ausgewählte kleine Schriften* I. 3). See also Legrand, p. 306.

[3] 'ipse iocus ad id genus pertinet quod, ut dramatis naturae optime convenit, et apud aliarum nationum comicos poetas et apud Plautum haud raro deprehendimus, ut scilicet persona comica de scaenicis rebus, poetis, fabulis, histrionibus loquatur tamquam vitam non fabulam agat' (see also Leo, *PF*, p. 154, n. 1). For a specific allusion to another play see Plaut. *Bacch.* 911 f.

> 'satin est si plura ex me audiet hodie mala
> quam audivit umquam Clinia ex Demetrio?'

where Clinia and Demetrius are surely comic characters—Clinia is a common enough name in New Comedy and there is a play of Alexis entitled *Demetrius* whose fragments do not suggest that it dealt with either of the two famous historical Demetrii and which if, as is likely, it was adapted by Turpilius (W. G. Arnott, *RhM* 102 (1959), 253), is hardly likely to have been a contemporary satire—rather than the historical Demetrius of Phalerum (or Demetrius Poliorcetes) and some otherwise unknown real-life Cleinias as Leo (op. cit., pp. 559 = 4) believed. Gaiser sees in the lines a reference to the Clinia of Ter. *Haut.* (*Philologus* 114 (1970), 82) and assumes that Demetrius was the name in Menander for Terence's Menedemus. Against this we may note: (1) There is no guarantee that Terence retained the name of the young man in Menander. (2) The scolding Clinia got from Menedemus is something referred to in passing in a narrative in *Haut.*; it is not enacted. This seems unlikely to have been enough to have made it proverbial (Gaiser assumes that Terence has greatly truncated his original). I should have thought it more likely that the *Bacchides* reference was to a famous *scene* where a Cleinias confronted a Demetrius.

course are well aware that Tranio is not a real slave, but a comic one, and that they have been watching a play of the kind written by Philemon or Diphilus, perhaps even written by one of them.[1] They are aware in other words that the dramatist is 'playing with' the illusion.

Play with the illusion is a common motif in Plautus.[2] Is it Plautine or does it derive from the originals of his plays? In 1883 with very little comparative material to help him, Leo asserted that a passage like Plaut. *Most.* 1149 ff. *must* derive from the Greek model. He could point to the occurrence of the motif in Caecilius and Terence[3] (we can probably add Turpilius),[4] but adduced no

---

[1] Obviously it would add extra spice to the joke if one of the poets mentioned was the author of the play and, since we know that Philemon wrote a *Phasma*, the one fragment of which might with a certain amount of goodwill be found a context in *Mostellaria*, it is tempting to make the connection. It is, however, equally possible and perhaps *a priori* more likely that a third comic poet is referring to two of his prominent rivals in this way. The *Mostellaria* passage provides sure but not particularly specific evidence for the *date* of the Greek original, a time when Diphilus and Philemon were flourishing competitors. H. Fuchs, *MH* 6 (1949), 106, n. 5, argues that the only reference in the original was to Diphilus and that Plautus has added the reference to the play's author, Philemon (he is followed by Webster, *SLGC*, p. 125). All things are possible and Plautus *may* have done something of the kind (or even added both names), but I do not find it as difficult as Fuchs apparently does to believe that a Greek dramatist might have mentioned himself in this way.

[2] Leo provides plenty of examples: Plaut. *Persa* 465, *Pseud.* 1081, *Trin.* 706 stand out.

[3] Caecilius fr. inc. 3 is very close to the *Mostellaria* passage. The most secure Terentian example is Ter. *Hec.* 865–7: 'neque opus est adeo muttito. placet non fieri hoc itidem ut in comoediis omnia omnes ubi resciscunt.' (N.B. Donatus ad loc.: mire quasi haec comoedia non sit, sed veritas.) This neat device (the intermediary between Ter. *Haut.* 335–6 and Plaut. *Pseud.* 720–1) may have had as its starting-point the formulaic ending which we see in Roman clothing in Ter. *Andr.* 980, Plaut. *Cist.* 782 (see Kraus, op. cit., p. 74 who argues that both derive from Menander). It has been asserted that Apollodorus is here satirizing comic conventions or even that Terence has added a criticism of Greek comedy to his original. There is admittedly an element of satire present, but one ought to recall that it is integral to the plot of *Hecyra* that most of the characters throughout the play are in ignorance of the truth. The slave Parmeno has a particularly bewildering and frustrating time, always acting in ignorance of the real situation and being sent on fool's errands. Other passages in Terence which merit consideration as playing with the illusion by referring to stock topics of the genre are *Andr.* 474–6, 583, *Haut.* 101, *Phorm.* 848.

[4] Turpilius fr. 37R:

> 'at enim ineptus meus mihi est iratus pater,
> quia se talento argenti tetigi *veteri exemplo* amantium'

(cf. *via pervolgata* in Ter. *Haut.* 101).

Greek examples. It seems worth while examining later Greek comedy to find analogous phenomena.

We may eliminate at the start those passages of Greek comedy which allude specifically to tragedy. Mrs. Righter (p. 60) cites Men. *Epitr.* 149 as a parallel for the Plautine passages. There Syriscus says to Smicrines: 'I'm sure τεθέαcαι τραγωιδούc[1]. You understand what I am talking about.' This specific reference in a comedy to another type of drama is quite different from the phenomena we are discussing. Tragedy, its plots, characters, situations and conventions form a natural topic of conversation at Athens at almost any period. Looked at from one point of view, allusions to it in the mouths of characters in comedy are no different from references to the contemporary political scene, to the eccentric behaviour of the denizens of the Academy, or to the iniquitous price of fish. A comparison between a real-life situation and a tragic one comes easily to the mouth of any Athenian.[2] There exists in such references and comparisons no tension between real life and the play. Hence we may leave out of account passages like Men. *Sam.* 589 or Men. fr. 951 (where a character is referred to as θεὸc ἀπὸ μηχανῆc).[3] What we are looking for are references in a comedy to the situations, plots, conventions, and characters of *comedy*.

The examples that may be adduced are few and, as is generally the case with comic fragments, their interpretation is not without difficulty. First there is a passage from Alexis' Κυβερνήτηc (fr. 116), a play of unknown date. The speaker is a parasite and he is

---

[1] This may mean 'you have seen tragic actors' but it is also one of the ways a Greek might say 'you have seen tragedy', τραγωιδοί being used in records generically to describe that part of a festival given over to the performance of tragedy; see H. Richards, *Aristophanes and Others* (London, 1909), pp. 340 ff., and A. W. Pickard-Cambridge, *The Dramatic Festivals of Athens*[2] (Oxford, 1968), p. 127.

[2] Cf. Dem. 21. 149 where Demosthenes describes Meidias' birth as ἀπορρήτουc ὥcπερ ἐν τραγωιδίαι.

[3] Similarly, I do not believe that Amphis fr. 17. 4 contains any play with the illusion—the speaker who is enlarging on the superiority of country over town says

ἄcτυ δὲ θέατρον ἀτυχίαc cαφοῦc γέμον

I do not think that the listener would take this as referring to the comic stage, even though there occur at times situations in comedy which might be described as ἀτυχίαι. Xenarchus fr. 7 in which the speaker mentions poets to contrast them with fishmongers might contain a reference to comic poets but it seems too general to be an example of the phenomenon under discussion.

discussing types of parasite with a person who is probably his patron.[1] He begins:

δύ᾽ ἐcτί, Ναυcίνικε, παραcίτων γένη·
ἓν μὲν τὸ κοινὸν καὶ κεκωμωιδημένον,
οἱ μέλανεc ἡμεῖc· θάτερον ζητῶ γένοc . . .

There are two sorts of parasite, Nausinicus: one the common one, ridiculed in comedy, ones who wear black like us. I am seeking the other sort . . .

The text of this fragment is not securely settled and its interpretation is controversial.[2] It is clear, however, that in it a comic character representing one of the stock types of comedy, the parasite, describes the class to which he belongs as being ridiculed in comedy. He also alludes to the conventional stage costume of the class to which he belongs.[3]

The continuation is obscure and it is far from clear who precisely is meant by the second class of parasite. The speaker seems to suggest that this second class 'plays the part well' (ὑποκρινόμενον εὖ l. 6) of satraps or generals. This may mean that they are in fact satraps and generals and that they flatter kings or tyrants or whoever happens to be their overlord, in which case we would have an allusion to the contemporary Hellenic world and the audience would no doubt be able to supply names.[4] The point

[1] The speaker uses the first person plural (3, 12, 13) which might at first suggest that the person he is addressing was also a parasite, but the plural is probably 'professional' (see above, p. 199 n. 1) rather than sociative. In the final two lines, he asks Nausinicus ἆρά γε διδάcκω; and Nausinicus replies with praise οὐκ ἀcτόχωc but adds that if he praises him further, the parasite will be asking him for a fee. One might take this as implying that the interlocutor is a prospective pupil of the speaker (cf. Ter. Eun. 260 ff. for this idea), but the reply could equally well belong to a person of higher status than the parasite. I am inclined to think it has more point if Nausinicus really is the patron of the first speaker.

[2] See W. G. Arnott, Hermes 93 (1965), 303, who provides a full bibliography. It is hard in l. 3 to see why the speaker should want to 'seek after' (ζητῶ cod.) or 'wish good luck to' (ζήτω Arnott) the second type of parasite. Nor does 'there are two kinds of parasite, on the one hand the ordinary, but I am speaking of the other' (θάτερον δὲ λέγω γένοc Herwerden) seem an acceptable way of speaking. Blaydes's ζηλῶ is psychologically apt, but one expects a sentence of the form 'there are two kinds of parasite, the ordinary and the other (adjective) kind'. To restore this one would have to extract from the second half of 3, δέ elided and an adjective (possibly comparative). But it may well be that the corruption extends over 4–5.

[3] See Pollux, iv. 119.

[4] See Webster, SLGC, p. 48.

would be that such men whom one would not ordinarily regard as parasites (contrast Men. *Col.* 90–1) were no different from the typical parasite in the way by which they made a living. The only difference between the two sorts of men was that these men were more successful. Alternatively the speaker is describing parasites who behave in an arrogant way (by raising their eyebrows etc.) 'as if' they were important people like satraps and generals and saying that these methods make them more successful than the run of the mill parasite. This seems to me less likely since ὑποκρινόμενον εὖ has more point on the first interpretation and 9–10 appears to confirm that the speaker is saying something highly paradoxical.[1]

Despite the uncertainty surrounding this fragment, its effect is clear,[2] a highly piquant piece of play with the comic illusion. Additional piquancy is attained if indeed we have a reference to real-life people acting out a role ὑποκρινόμενον. However that may be, we may safely assert that nothing in the fragment destroys the illusion. Its significance in the history of the technique of comedy was recognised by Thierfelder[3] in an important article which set out to investigate to what degree comic poets showed awareness of their own motifs and themes and how free they were in alluding to them. He could find no other examples in fourth-century comedy.

We find a reference to comic costume in another fragment of Alexis, this time in a play named after a hetaera, *Isostasion*, but again of unknown date.[4] During a description of the way wealthy

[1]   τούτων δ' ἑκατέρου τῶν γενῶν ὁ μὲν τύπος
          τῆc ἐργαcίαc εἶc ἐcτι, κολακείαc ἀγών.
ll. 11–12 too would appear to confirm that this special class of parasite was attendant on kings.

          ὥcπερ ἐπὶ τῶν βίων δὲ τοὺc μὲν ἡ τύχη
          ἡμῶν μεγάλοιc προcένειμε τοὺc δ' ἐλάττοcιν.

[2] Perhaps there is added piquancy if Arnott is correct in suggesting that Alexis was the first to call this comic type 'parasite' (*GRBS* 9 (1968), 161).

[3] *Hermes* 71 (1936), 322.

[4] Webster, *CQ* n.s. 2 (1952), 22, asserts that fr. 97 must refer to the famous dining club alluded to in Athenaeus 614 d–e. Even if it does (and Callimedon/Carabus is the only point of coincidence—a man who was alluded to in early Menander (*Methe*)), this does not compel us to believe that the play was produced before Chaeroneia.

hetaerae dress up their protégées, disguising mutton as lamb (fr. 98), the speaker describes how girls are provided with 'falsies' of the kind the comic actors wear (cτηθί᾽ ἔcτ᾽ αὐταῖcι τούτων ὧν ἔχουc᾽ οἱ κωμικοί, l. 13). The reference to comic actors and the costume they wear when playing females[1] does not, as far as we can tell, contain play with the illusion. The speaker is a man playing a man.[2] Hence we may take it that he is not wearing the costume he describes and it does not appear likely that there are any such 'girls' present while he speaks. The mention of comic costume is simply a vivid detail added to a speech about hetaerae.

A fragment of Demetrius' *Areopagites*[3] does, however, seem relevant to our inquiry:

cύ μου καταφρονεῖc, ὅτι μάγειρόc εἰμ᾽ ἴcωc.[4]
ὅcον δ᾽ ἀπὸ ταύτηc τῆc τέχνηc εἴργαcμ᾽ ἐγὼ
οὐδεὶc ὑποκριτήc ἐcθ᾽ ὅλωc εἰργαcμένοc

You look down on me perhaps because I am a cook. But no actor has ever earned as much as I have earned from this art.

It looks at first sight as if there is some play with the illusion: 'I've earned[5] more money from my profession than any actor has from his.' The cook might, for instance, be acknowledging that his interlocutor is an actor while conveniently suppressing his own real techne. It is difficult otherwise to find a point for the reference to an actor here,[6] unless our passage followed an allusion to some famous actor or to the profession generally. Possibly there was a reference to an actor who was also known as a cook, that is to say who had written a cook-book. If that were the case, one might, as a very long shot, connect this passage with a reference

---

[1] Cf. Lucian *de salt.* 27.

[2] This at least appears probable from the way he refers to the hetaerae in the third person.

[3] fr. 1 (III. 357 Kock). Clearly this is New Comedy. See Meineke, p. 265, and Webster, *SLGC*, p. 107.

[4] The initial trimeter is restored from the introduction to the quotation in Athenaeus by Kock; he may not have been justified in doing so.

[5] *LSJ*, s.v. ἐργάζομαι II. 4.

[6] Sosipater fr. 1 connects cooking with other τέχναι—ἀcτρολογία, ἀρχιτεκτονία, τὰ cτρατηγικά, but the point there is that a cook has to have knowledge of these τέχναι in order to become a good cook (see Legrand, p. 588, n. 1).

in Alexis fr. 135 to an otherwise unknown Simus[1] who, in a double-edged compliment that presages one that was later to be given to the composer Borodin, is described as:

14   ... τῶν μὲν ὑποκριτῶν πολὺ
κράτιστός ἐστιν ὀψοποιός ...
... τῶν δ' ὀψοποιῶν ὑποκριτής.

He is much the best cook among actors and much the best actor among cooks.

This fragment comes from a play entitled *Linus*. The title and the manner in which the fragment is cited in Athenaeus show clearly that it was a mythological spoof of the kind associated particularly with 'Middle' Comedy, but we have no criteria for deciding when the play was first produced,[2] and we cannot be certain when it was that comedians ceased to write plays of that type. Chronology might, however, act as a bar to connecting the Demetrius and Alexis fragments since the former can only have been written in the 290s at the earliest.[3] The man Simus may of course have had a long career and in any case any reference to him in Demetrius may have been posthumous. If there is some reference to him in our fragment, then the passage does not contain play with the illusion since, according to Alexis the man in question was a *tragic* actor (fr. 135. 13 f.).

Clearer testimony to set beside Alexis fr. 116 comes from a source more noted for obscurity than light. The Heidelberg Papyri edited in 1956 by Siegmann[4] contain further fragments of

---

[1] See J. B. O'Connor, *Chapters in the history of actors and acting in Ancient Greece, together with a Prosopographia Histrionum Graecorum* (Diss. Princeton, 1908), no. 438, and *RE* IIIa. 200–1, Simos 2). There is no good reason to identify this man as 'the musician Simos of Magnesia' as Pape–Benseler do.

[2] Webster puts limits on it of 360–340 (*CQ* n.s. 2 (1952), 18) because of the mention of Menecrates. But we do not know: i. how long this man lived; ii. whether the reference to him in Alexis implied that he was still alive; Athenaeus 289 f simply says that Alexis mentioned him (N.B. the past tense reference to him in Ephippus fr. 17). The man became proverbial (on Menecrates see, above all, O. Weinreich *Tübinger Beiträge* 18 (1933) = *Religionsgeschichtliche Studien* (Darmstadt, 1968), pp. 299 ff.); iii. whether Alexis mentioned him in *Linus*, Λίνωι being Meineke's quite arbitrary emendation of Μίνωι in Athenaeus (on the possible plot of a *Minos* see Weinreich pp. 98 f.). We cannot be sure that among Alexis' vast output there was not a *Minos* as well as a *Linus*.

[3] Mention of Lachares (l. 8) makes this certain.

[4] *Literarische griechische Texte der Heidelberger Papyrussammlung* (Heidelberg, 1956).

a play that has come to be known as the Strobilus comedy (*CGF* 244). In one of the better preserved portions (*CGF* 244. 221 ff. = Incerti Auctoris Fabula on p. 337 of Sandbach's *Menander*, 1 ff.), we find a cook (probably called Libys) speaking:

ἐπέρ]χεται δ[ὲ πο]λλάκις, νὴ τοὺς θεούς,
ἐπὰν θεωρῶν τυγχάνω κωμωιδίαν
ὅπου μάγειρός ἐcτιν, ἐλεεῖν τὴν τέχνην
καὶ τὸ γένοc ἡμῶν, εἰ τοιαῦτα κλέπτομεν.

Often pity for our profession and for our tribe comes over me, by the gods, whenever I happen to be watching a comedy where there is a cook, if we steal such things.

The cook is thus complaining of the theatrical treatment of his profession (τέχνην) and of the class of people to which he belongs (γένοc). He goes on to describe in vivid detail what cooks in comedy are habitually depicted as doing. The picture is one of theft and cheating.

For our purposes what is important is the way the cook introduces his topic: ἐπὰν θεωρῶν τυγχάνω κωμωιδίαν,[1] 'If ever I happen to be watching a comedy'. Here we have a cook in a comedy asserting that he goes to see comedies and complaining about the way his fictional *confrères* behave in comedies. The effect is, as Treu was the first to remark,[2] exactly analogous to that of the Plautine passages collected by Leo in connection with Plaut. *Most.* 1149 ff., perhaps the closest parallel being Plaut. *Rud.* 1249 f.[3] The sophisticated play with a particular γένοc of people resembles that of Alexis fr. 116. Neither the Heidelberg poet nor Alexis is content with a straightforward description of a particular comic type.[4] Both achieve their effects by making the

---

[1] I presume that, when Treu states that this is the first appearance of the word κωμωιδία in Middle and New Comedy outside of prologues, he takes the famous Philippides fragment (fr. 25. 7) ταῦτα καταλύει δῆμον, οὐ κωμωιδία as coming from a prologue.

[2] *Philologus* 102 (1958), 230 (see also T. B. L. Webster, *Hellenistic Poetry and Art* (London, 1964), pp. 125–6). Treu incidentally does not mention the parallel provided by Alexis fr. 116.

[3]   'spectavi ego pridem comicos ad istunc modum
             sapientes dicta dicere, atque is plaudier.'

Cf. also Plaut. *Bacch.* 1209.

[4] On the comic treatment of particular γένη see above all Leo, *PF*, p. 131.

speaker who is to talk about a comic type approach his subject from the standpoint of real life, as a person who is familiar with comedy and capable of appreciating that stage types are hackneyed and conventional (Alexis' τὸ κοινὸν καὶ κεκωμωιδημένον corresponds to πολλάκις, ἐπὰν θεωρῶν τυγχάνω κωμωιδίαν in our play).

Alexis fr. 116 and the Heidelberg fragment are sufficient evidence[1] to show that play with the illusion of the kind discussed by Leo was indeed a feature of fourth-century comedy and that Leo's instincts were correct when he assumed that a Greek motif underlay Plaut. *Most.* 1149 ff.[2] Perhaps with Thierfelder we may detect in Old Comedy the origins of such a motif. The opening of Aristophanes' *Frogs* (especially Ar. *Ran.* 16 f.) might well bring it to mind. There, however, the joke is more direct. Xanthias, I believe, though such distinctions are not easy to draw, acknowledges the presence of an audience when he speaks line two:

ἐφ' οἷς ἀεὶ γελῶσιν οἱ θεώμενοι

The kind of thing at which the spectators always laugh.

I find it hard to take it as referring generally to audiences rather than to the people in the audience (as at Ar. *Ran.* 1475 'the ones who come every year and are here today'). Passages like this, however, probably provided a starting-point for fourth-century dramatists who wished to allude in their plays to what was typical in comedy. The refinement they introduced was not to

---

[1] Other passages which might be taken to be relevant to our inquiry prove too ambiguous and obscure for anything to be made of them. Philemon fr. 143, a general statement saying that a stupid listener is a nuisance because he blames the speaker rather than himself when he does not understand, might be a theatrical reference, but need not necessarily be (see Crahay–Delcourt, p. 87, n. 1, against Lejay, *Plaute*, p. 8). The listener is referred to as καθήμενος, but the theatre was not the only place where people sat to listen (cf. Aristophanes fr. 7. 3 Dem.). Even if this has a theatrical reference, it is more likely to have come from a prologue (Legrand, pp. 507, 512) where the illusion did not obtain. θεάτρωι occurs in Amphis fr. 14 where it refers to the audience of a dithyrambic contest. Alexis fr. 41, an instruction to women about where they should sit in the theatre, is completely obscure, as is κύβηλις ἀγωνιστρία in Anaxippus fr. 6. 6. Eubulus fr. 136 is nearer to what we are looking for, the speaker announces he is going to deliver a messenger-speech. Cf. also the list of comic themes in Antiphanes fr. 239.

[2] This does not of course entitle us to assume that on every occasion the motif occurs in Plautus, Plautus is faithfully reproducing his Greek model. He sometimes uses it in passages that are clearly his own invention, Plaut. *Bacch.* 215, 649–50.

drop the dramatic pretence, not, for the moment, to acknowledge that such comments were in fact being spoken by actors participating in a play.

What, however, of the poet of New Comedy who is *consensu omnium* the most refined and subtle? Does Menander demonstrate any such play with the illusion? If he does so in that part of his work which has survived, he has done so in a manner which is by no means obvious (unless of course, as is quite possible, the Strobilus comedy is in fact Menandrean).[1] Menander, however, is not an obvious writer and this encourages me to offer in conclusion a passage where he *may* be alluding to typical plot situations of New Comedy. This is speculation of the rankest sort and those who accept the tenor of this chapter up to now are not required to believe what follows.[2]

In *Aspis* one of the incidental consequences of the report brought home from Caria by Daos of the death of Cleostratus is the inconvenience it causes the cook hired to supervise the wedding feast of Cleostratus' sister, a wedding feast that obviously will not now take place. At 216 we see this cook coming out of Chaerestratus' house and hear him complaining:

> ἂν καὶ λάβω ποτ' ἔργον, ἢ τέθνηκέ τις,
> εἶτ' ἀποτρέχειν δεῖ μισθὸν οὐκ ἔχοντά με,
> ἢ τέτοκε τῶν ἔνδον κυοῦσά τις λάθραι,
> εἶτ' οὐκέτι θύους' ἐξαπίνης, ἀλλ' οἴχομαι
> ἀπιὼν ἐγώ· τῆς δυσποτμίας.

If I ever *do* get a job, either someone has died and I've got to run off without my pay, or one of the girls has given birth after a secret

---

[1] For speculation on this see J.-M. Jacques, *Le Dyskolos*, p. 55, n. 3, and Austin, *CGF*, p. 252.

[2] Of other possible theatrical references in Menander, I do not think that τρίτα λέγει in Men. *Theophorumene* fr. 1. 17 has any special significance. The speaker is not κακοήθης and the metaphor was common (we also meet τὰ δεύτερα in fr. 418). In its context it would hardly remind the audience that the speaker was an actor. Possibly, however, fr. 690

> δεδράμηκά σοι
> δρόμον τοιοῦτον οἷον οὐδεὶς πώποτε

where the speaker is clearly a *servus currens* (H. Lloyd-Jones, *Emerita* 34 (1966), 147, suggests that here we have a slave Dromo punning on his own name) is relevant. Did the speaker continue 'as no slave in comedy has ever run'?

pregnancy and all of a sudden they are no longer sacrificing and I've had it. O my wretched luck!

Two kinds of disaster deprive him of his pay. It is the first that has apparently occurred here. The report of Cleostratus' death is the operative reason for the cook's departure. We will allow the cook some degree of exaggeration because of his disappointment, but we must acknowledge that such an occurrence cannot have been all that common a reason for postponing a wedding. The second contingency does not apply here and one cannot and should not entertain the notion that the cook is unconsciously revealing an element of the play that has been concealed from us because the play as we have it is incomplete. No one has given birth secretly in this play and no one will. If one had or were about to, Tyche in the prologue would have told us. Now, in real life, just as people die, so do unmarried girls become pregnant. Perhaps such secret pregnancies which bring temporary calamities to their relations and cause the postponement of marriages and the attendant discomfiture of cooks occur more commonly in the theatre of Lycurgus on festive days than elsewhere in Athens. What I suggest is that, in addition to the humorous exaggeration which so effectively characterizes the cook, these lines have a special point. This second cause of frustration is mentioned by the cook because it contains a typical theme of New Comedy: wedding preparations are disrupted at a late date because of the discovery of the bride's pregnancy (or indeed of the pregnancy of any girl in some way connected with the bride or groom's families). Such a disruption leads to the temporary frustration of cooks in comedy and also to the expression thereat of their grievances, frustration and complaint,[1] both being characteristic functions of the cook in comedy. Here our cook is speaking with an additional voice. He is the character of this particular play, but he is at the same time 'I, the comic cook, the character who appears year in year out in plays put on by various comic poets'. It so happens that there is no play extant with a plot precisely equivalent to the one I postulate, where a comic cook is sent away

---

[1] For a frustrated cook complaining, cf. Men. *Epitr.* 434 ff.

because of family troubles directly before a wedding. Neverthe-less secret pregnancies are such a pervasive theme of New Comedy,[1] that it is not difficult to believe that they were sometimes linked in the way I suggest with the theme of the complaining cook.

[1] See Libanius 64. 73 and Legrand, p. 254. A Menandrean example occurs in *Georgus*. The situation of Phaedria in Plaut. *Aul.* could have been used for the theme of the disrupted wedding feast. She is pregnant by Lyconides but is promised to Megadorus. In fact what disrupts the wedding preparations is the loss of Euclio's gold.

EXCURSUS

CGF 244 and *CGF* 289b

In the article mentioned earlier in this chapter Max Treu makes a bold suggestion as regards the part the cook's speech in P. Heidel. 184 had in the Strobilus play (*CGF* 244). His starting-point is the striking similarity between this speech and another cook's speech to be found in *CGF* 289b (from the so-called *Livre d'écolier*). In the latter we have a cook describing his exploits with pride. What is striking is that the achievements he describes correspond almost exactly with the activities Libys, the Heidelberg cook, lists as typical occurrences in comedy. The boasts of the Cairo cook in *CGF* 289b coincide with incidents recounted by Libys in four particulars.

(i) Cairo cook

  6   ἐπόηc' ἐλάττω ταῦτα (the meat) τὸν ἀριθμὸν δ' ἴca

  Libys

  225 f. κρέαιδια | δύ' ἐξ ἑνὸc ποιοῦcι (sc. cooks in comedy).

(ii) Both cooks mention cuts of sausage using identical phraseology to describe them:

  7   χορδῆc τιc ἦν ὀβελίcκοc· ἐξελὼν τόμουc
      ἐκ τοῦ μέcου τρεῖc . . .

  226   χορδῆc τόμουc
  ἐκ τοῦ μέcου[1] κλέπτουcι

(iii) In both descriptions oil is stolen (*CGF* 244. 228, *CGF* 289b. 12).

(iv) In both passages the thieves use sponges to mop up and in this way steal liquids, in the Cairo play, silphium and sauce, in the Heidelberg play, oil. It is this last detail that leads Treu to suppose a very close link between the two passages.[2]

---

[1] Treu's restoration on the strength of ἐκ τοῦ μέcου in the Cairo papyrus. Perhaps Antiphanes fr. 72 is relevant here.

[2] 'Auf diese Idee ist wohl selbst in Hungerzeiten kein Mensch verfallen; sie ist eine ganz und gar originelle Erfindung eines Komödiendichters.'

Treu rejects the idea that the Heidelberg papyrus represents a 'literary polemic' directed against the author of the Cairo play[1] (or a playwright satirizing his own earlier work) in favour of the idea that the two passages emanate from the same play and are spoken by the same cook. This is a somewhat startling conclusion and not one to be accepted lightly.[2]

It is only a devil's advocate who would seek to deny the close connection of these passages. Many of the details in the two speeches can, it is true, be paralleled and Treu himself adduces much helpful illustrative material from Greek comedy. There is a large store of topoi about cooks and it is only to be expected that a cook will steal oil, as is mentioned in both fragments (cf. Men. *Asp.* 228–9). Nevertheless the similarity in choice of topoi and in the order in which they are presented in addition to the striking detail of the use of the sponge,[3] makes it less likely that we are dealing with a mere coincidence.

There is a great deal, however, to be said against Treu's suggestion. First it is scarcely conceivable that a comic poet would repeat almost word for word a narrative of this kind and highly improbable that he would go the lengths implied by Treu's reconstruction of a virtual juxtaposition of the two speeches. So much space devoted to the activity of one cook is unlike anything we know of New Comedy.[4] This cook would as it were have two scenes in a row, a solo (*CGF* 289b) followed by a performance with a 'feed-man' (*CGF* 244).

[1] Treu is wrong to deny to poets of the later Greek comedy any mention of their rivals (op. cit., p. 236). The Araros mentioned in Alexis fr. 179 is certainly the comic poet, son of Aristophanes. It is perfectly possible for this man to have competed against Alexis (mention of Plato as a living contemporary in fr. 180 shows that this is an early play) and ψυχρότερον makes it certain that it is a reference to a literary figure. See also Athenaeus 120 a on Alexis and Timocles.

[2] It is accepted and elaborated on by H. Dohm, *Mageiros* (*Zetemata* 32) (Munich, 1964), p. 92, n. 2.

[3] Treu distinguishes it from the 'Topik' of the other two incidents by calling it a 'Witz'. I am not sure that we should accept such a distinction or Treu's assertion that a 'Witz' is liable to have a short life. Some jokes have a very long life. This can be demonstrated with reference to Old Comedy, since its chronology is better established than that of New and Middle Comedy. The continuing popularity of a particular humorous exploitation of a line from *Telephus* and of a reference to a particular figure of fun like Pauson (Ar. *Eq.* 813 ~ *Plut.* 601, *Plut.* 602 ~ *Ach.* 854) may not be exact analogies for what we have here, but they do show that a dramatist can use the same joke in plays thirty years apart.

[4] It is certain that the Strobilus comedy is from that genre. The typical New Comic cook would have one chance to show off and would return later at the end of a play. Even if a cook appears frequently as in *Epitr.*, the interest is not concentrated on him and his exploits in the way it would be on the cook in the play Treu reconstructs.

Treu misinterprets the tone of the Heidelberg fragment. This is not a cook claiming to be honest in reply to an accusation of theft—and being detected by the audience—for this is the point of having *CGF* 289b precede it.[1] It is the speech of a boastful cook who claims that his thieving activities outdo and are more successful than those of cooks regularly depicted in comedy. His pity for his fellow professionals is not due to a feeling that they are wrongly accused of ill-doing and that comedy brings this kind of shame to them. It is rather the small scale pilfering and lack of success of the comic cook that brings disgrace on his real-life equivalent. This is clear from εἰ τοιαῦτα κλέπτομεν and from the interruption of his interlocutor (231) σὺ δὲ δὴ τί, πρὸς τῆς Ἑστίας;, and his reply ἑνὸς δύο | ἀμέλει.[2] This cook is going to describe how he outdoes such feeble activities as halving pieces of meat and appropriating one of the halves.

The scene makes sense on its own and needs no earlier cook's speech to explain it. It would fit admirably into the pattern exhibited to us by a type of scene which is becoming increasingly familiar, where a cook makes his first appearance in the play and explains his particular skill, sometimes in a monologue, often, as would be the case here, accompanied by someone to prompt him and perhaps be bored to death by him.[3]

We still have to explain the similarities between this scene and the one found in the Cairo papyrus. The first explanation which is scouted by Treu should be taken up again and re-examined. Treu rightly says that serious criticism of the low moral tone of comic cooks is out of the question. No comic poet would polemicize against his competitors in serious disapprobation of the way they treated their stock characters. What comic poet would go on writing who believed his profession was unfair to these stock types? Nor is it credible that a passage like our one could display sincere disapproval of the way a rival handled traditional comic themes. But this brings us nearer to the point of the passage. The poet's motive is not so much polemical as competitive: it arises out of a desire to be one up on his fellow dramatists. The poet is able to

[1] Treu himself recognizes that εἰ τοιαῦτα κλέπτομεν gives the game away (op. cit., p. 237).

[2] The form of the scene is similar to that of Plaut. *Pseud.* 804 ff. where the cook describes how other cooks season their dishes and is asked by Ballio 'what do *you* do?', 'quid tu?' (826), a question which leads to the cook explaining his own methods. σὺ δὲ δὴ τί; will have a similar function here, leading to a speech which outdoes the description of the thieving of comic cooks.

[3] See the *Pseudolus* passage mentioned above. Analogous scenes are to be found in Alexis fr. 173 and Men. *Sam.* 283 ff.

suggest that the treatment of comic cooks by an earlier (and probably recent) competitor[1] was old hat; he, like his cook, is going to outdo his rival.

There are plenty of parallels for the technique here displayed. It is a device which allows the dramatist to 'have it both ways', to tell a hackneyed joke and to complain that it is hackneyed, thereby suggesting that the dramatist is above such things. The classic instance of this is the opening of Aristophanes' *Frogs*. Our passage has the added dimension of play with the illusion.[2]

The poet of New Comedy who, by the nature of the genre, must deal with stock types and stock situations, is always faced with the need to think of something new.[3] The Heidelberg poet has here succeeded admirably in finding something new for a cook to say.

[1] We must reckon with the possibility that only a minority would appreciate how close the correspondence to the earlier play was. The scene is highly amusing and perfectly comprehensible as it stands. Self-parody cannot be excluded.

[2] See above, p. 218.

[3] On the need for καινοτομία in New Comedy see Handley on Men. *Dysc.* 393. A classic statement of the problem is to be found in Hegesippus fr. 1:

> βέλτιστε, πολλοῖς πολλὰ περὶ μαγειρικῆς
> εἰρημέν' ἐστίν. ἢ λέγων φαίνου τι δὴ
> καινὸν παρὰ τοὺς ἔμπροσθεν ἢ μὴ κόπτε με

where the change of speaker after ἐστίν in l. 2 introduced by Kock is unnecessary. The command follows a general statement and βέλτιστε serves as a good-natured reproof to the garrulous cook. Kock's interpretation of l. 29 of this fragment is quite mistaken. According to him τῶν καθημένων are 'adulescentuli qui popinam eius frequentant nunc ipsum cenantes'. Obviously the reference is to the audience (so Fraenkel in the margin of his copy of Meineke which is now in the Ashmolean) who are alleged to have wasted their substance paying for meals the speaker has cooked. There is no strict parallel for οἱ καθήμενοι = οἱ θεαταί, but its meaning is obvious enough. For such exploitation of the audience compare Ar. *Nub.* 1096 ff., *Ran.* 276-7. On the topic of the need to say something new applied to another stock type, the *miles*, see Plaut. *Truc.* 482 ff., a passage in which the audience is addressed directly.

[Some of this discussion requires revision in the light of K. Gaisser, *ZPE* 47 (1982), 31 f.]

INDEXES

I. SUBJECTS DISCUSSED

II. PASSAGES DISCUSSED

(* indicates where textual questions are treated)

III. GREEK WORDS